辅警志愿服务：
美英辅警管理的探索、比较及评估

[美] 罗斯·沃尔夫
[英] 卡罗尔·伯兰德·乔恩思 著

刘君玲 译

中国人民公安大学出版社
·北 京·

图字：01-2021-3889
图书在版编目（CIP）数据

辅警志愿服务：美英辅警管理的探索、比较及评估/（美）罗斯·沃尔夫，（英）卡罗尔·伯兰德·乔恩思著；刘君玲译. —北京：中国人民公安大学出版社，2021.11
书名原文：Volunteer Police，Choosing to Serve：Exploring，Comparing，and Assessing Volunteer Policing in the Unit
ISBN 978-7-5653-4247-9

Ⅰ.①辅… Ⅱ.①罗… ②卡… ③刘… Ⅲ.①警察-管理体制-研究-美国②警察-管理体制-研究-英国 Ⅳ.①D771.235 ②D756.135

中国版本图书馆 CIP 数据核字（2021）第 259854 号

VOLUNTEER POLICE，CHOOSING TO SERVE——Exploring，Comparing，and Assessing Volunteer Policing in the United States and the United Kingdom，1st Edition By Ross，Wolf；Carol Borland，Jones/9780367429591

辅警志愿服务：美英辅警管理的探索、比较及评估

［美］罗斯·沃尔夫
［英］卡罗尔·伯兰德·乔恩思　著
刘君玲　译

出版发行：中国人民公安大学出版社
地　　址：北京市西城区木樨地南里
邮政编码：100038
经　　销：新华书店
印　　刷：涿州市新华印刷有限公司

版　　次：2021 年 11 月第 1 版
印　　次：2021 年 11 月第 1 次
印　　张：17.5
开　　本：787 毫米×1092 毫米　1/16
字　　数：305 千字

书　　号：ISBN 978-7-5653-4247-9
定　　价：68.00 元

网　　址：www.cppsup.com.cn　www.porclub.com.cn
电子邮箱：zbs@cppsup.com　zbs@cppsu.edu.cn

营销中心电话：010-83903991
读者服务部电话（门市）：010-83903257
警官读者俱乐部电话（网购、邮购）：010-83901775
公安业务分社电话：010-83906108

谨以此书献给全世界自愿奉献自己的时间为社区服务的男性和女性辅警们。

此书亦献给众人的榜样——约翰·伯兰德教授。

作者简介

罗斯·沃尔夫博士是美国卫生和公共事务学院的院长助理以及中佛罗里达大学刑事司法系的副教授。他还在奥兰治县（佛罗里达州）县治安官办公室担任局长后备助理。他曾受委派在国际警察局长协会（IACP，International Association of Chiefs of Police）的警察管理委员会工作，以及在（美国）国家治安官协会（NSA，National Sheriffs' Association）的外联委员会和后备执法专门小组工作。2017 年，他被指派到全球家园协会理事会和国家安全专家组工作，并被英国北安普顿大学公共安全、犯罪和司法研究所聘为客座研究员。他发表了 30 多篇学术论文，参编著作若干，并且出版了若干专著。他主要研究警察审讯，警察决策管理和执行管理，辅警，警察使用武力，旅游警务以及国际警务。他除了与全美的警察机构开展合作，还与加勒比海地区、英国、俄罗斯、中国香港地区以及新加坡的警察机构开展合作。他获得奥兰治县县治安官办公室“行政优秀奖”“治安官奖”以及“卓越服务奖”。因为他研究辅警，他还获得美国“每日之光”称号、国家治安官协会“功勋章”奖以及美国总统“终生待命服务”奖。沃尔夫博士是佛罗里达州评议委员会的理事，该职位由佛罗里达州前州长委任。

卡罗尔·伯兰德·乔恩思博士是英国北安普顿大学公共安全、犯罪和司法研究所研究助理。在担任这一职位之前，她在切斯特大学和格洛斯特郡大学做高级讲师。她发表了多篇学术论文，参编著作若干并且出版了若干专著。她主要研究辅警、旅游和犯罪、旅游警务和受害人。卡罗尔参与了一些研究项目，而且目前她正就英国警务中的志愿者角色开展合作研究。她是毛里求斯共和国受害人支持项目的顾问。她还与澳大利亚、加纳、爱尔兰、荷兰和美国的学术机构有合作。

目　　录

中文版序言一

December 3, 2020

This book came about because of a common interest discovered by the authors after being introduced by a mutual friend who also served as a professor in the academy. Each had an interest in volunteer policing, but initially we used this shared academic focus to develop an international exchange program for criminal justice students in each country to complete a short-term study abroad course through the other's academic institution. Students from our own countries (US students under Dr Wolf, and UK students under Dr Borland-Jones) studied under each of our faculties in their home country and then would travel to the country of the other. The students would then be immersed in active learning by doing ride-alongs (where students would participate in a partial or full shift with full-time officers or volunteer police in a patrol car or on foot patrol), visits to police museums, involvement in police lectures and programs along with the host country's university students, and watching police demonstrations and training. Students came away from these study visits with a new, deeper understanding of the similarities of their policing structures, rules, laws, and policies between the two countries, as well as an understanding of our sometimes-significant differences. While initially these exchanges focused mostly on full-time policing, over time these international study experiences developed to focus particularly on volunteer policing as a central topic. We were encouraged when our students began also to focus on this topic, and as a cumulative exercise many developed this theme in their final class projects. These shared experiences as faculty over these study-abroad sessions led the two of us to consider an academic partnership where we would work together on academic articles and manuscripts about how volunteer police are similar, yet different in the UK and the USA. Our plans came at a particularly pertinent time in UK. Police recruitment had routinely taken place under the auspices of the National Policing Improvement Agency (NPIA)[①] and training was undertaken by each police force at their expense. Shortly before the NPIA was closed and its many roles were divided into existing or new organisations overseen by the newly formed College of Policing, a significant shift in training came about as universities and colleges went into partnership with regional police forces and policing degree programmes were established. This meant that the cost of training fell on the students, and as a result, policing courses sprung up around England and Wales as potential police officers were guided to these degrees to learn the basic skills. This applied to both UK volunteer police and UK regular officers.

To explore volunteer policing as a comparison between the UK and the USA, we first had to understand the nature of volunteering in the two countries and review the state of volunteering internationally. Individuals throughout the world volunteer for policing in an assortment of different ways and in a variety of functions for many different purposes. Volunteerism can be formal, where programs are structured and supervised, or informal, where an individual or group may decide to do something without any supervision to help where they believe there is a need. The participation in these roles is most often driven by an intrinsic and inherent human drive to help others, to serve in a position that benefits society, and may also be a consequence of national or community pride. As examples, individuals may volunteer to assist in humanitarian efforts to provide food and shelter during emergencies, provide assistance in hospitals, assist in animal shelters or rescues, help to build houses for others without the means, or to transport the elderly to doctor's visits or for hospital care. Each of these ways of volunteering requires a different level of training, from very little or no training at all other than someone asking for assistance and directing the labour, to extremely complicated volunteer work that requires a significant number of hours of training and also may require repetitive monthly or annual retraining. Examples of these more complicated volunteer positions may include volunteer firefighters and paramedics, volunteer nurses and hospital assistants, and volunteer police. Volunteering in these roles requires not only more training than might be found in other positions but may also introduce liability for improper application of responsibilities.

The focus in this book is on the many ways that individuals, particularly in the U-

---

① Until December 2012.

nited Kingdom and the United States of America, serve their communities in volunteer rolcs within police agencies. These functions are not specific to England, Wales, or the 50 states of the United States of America, however, and can also be found in numerous countries throughout the world. Volunteerism in policing in the many varied countries that utilize citizens in this way has developed in various ways within specific legal systems and rules and is not restricted to any particular custom or tradition. Some examples of the many countries that utilize some form of volunteering can be found in this book, but the examples provided herein are in no way exhaustive.

Our plan in putting together this book was to provide a clear and commonsense explanation of volunteer policing, predominantly in the United Kingdom[①] and the United States of America[②]. Our research however found that, while we were aware of differences in the roles, experiences and backgrounds of the Special Constable (in the United Kingdom) and reserve/auxiliary law enforcement officers (in the United States), once we started to explore volunteering in other countries, the definitions of both volunteering and policing are ever more varied.

Volunteerism can be defined as the act of doing something for someone else, without any reward of money or benefit. Volunteer police are no exception to this definition, and most of these individuals often serve in these roles without any monetary stipend or promise of any type of remuneration or compensation. But like many of the things you will learn from this text, there is no norm or consistent practice throughout the world or even within the countries where we have focused our research. Volunteerism, in some jurisdictions and places around the world, does also allow for some amount of allowance, either based on hourly duties or on a combination of duties, responsibilities, and rank. Volunteers may be provided with hourly or monthly stipends to offset personal costs, but also may be provided with additional types of rewards, including travel benefits, hotel use for overnight police responsibilities, and opportunity to use police or officer's clubs. Volunteering in policing, specifically, and in other types of government-sponsored opportunities, may also provide the volunteer with some amount of prestige or standing in

① United Kingdom comprises England, Wales, Scotland and Northern Ireland. However, while England and Wales follow a unified policing system, Scotland and Northern Ireland enjoy a level of autonomy and are therefore not included in the content of this book.

② In addition, within the United States of America where there are 50 States, there are levels of autonomy within each state, in each county, and at local levels, as well as different levels of policing.

society, either formally or informally. While not a specific focus of this book, individuals who serve in a volunteer policing role may find that they feel important, feel needed, or feel a greater responsibility by participating in volunteer policing.

However, the definition of volunteer police does not include individuals who receive some sort of hourly or weekly pay that would equate to the same amount of money, based on their hourly commitment, as their time as their full-time counterparts. These individuals, although they may be performing the exact same role as volunteer police, fall into a different category called "part-time police" as they work in exchange for earnings.

Framing the Context of Volunteer Policing in the UK and the USA

American policing is based largely on the policing model developed in London in the mid-1800s. So too, is the American model of volunteer policing. More information on this linkage between the two countries (understanding that the USA was once a colony of England) is examined more within this book. But it is important to understand that volunteer policing predates the regular police constabulary in the United Kingdom.

In 1829, Sir Robert Peel, Home Secretary in the English Government introduced the Metropolitan Police Act which was the first formalisation of policing in London. Prior to the adoption of these new laws, 'policing' was a reactive affair carried out by watchmen and part-time constables. These men (women were not considered for the role) were generally unpaid and were called upon on an ad hoc basis. Following the formalisation of the Metropolitan Police Act, the Special Constables Act[①] was passed in 1831 and while currently Specials are generally required to serve a minimum of 16 hours per month, under the 1831 Act Special Constables had to respond to all calls with no minimum or maximum number of hours. The Metropolitan Police Act was expanded in 1835 by the Municipal Corporations Act to spread the new police to provincial towns but it was not until the County and Borough Act of 1856 that required all local authorities to introduce and follow the new police regulations that policing became truly national. Special Constables have been an important feature of policing in times of emergency such as during World War II when regular officers were called up for military service to be replaced by Specials who were employed in reserve occupations, were over the age limit or had certain health issues.

① Formally known as, An Act for Amending the Laws relative to the Appointment of Special Constables, and for the better preservation of the Peace.

When the Olympic Games came to London in 2012, regular officers were sent to areas where sporting events were being held while Specials filled their places in their local forces. While most law enforcement in the U. S. are attached to a local jurisdiction (apart from Federal agents), in the UK, both regulars and Specials are warranted to work in any force in England and Wales since all forces must follow centralised policies. At such times of national importance, as the Olympics were, recruitment of Specials escalates. However, once the event is over, the numbers of volunteer police drop.

In the UK the modern utilization of Specials has had mixed receptions; because police uniforms for both regular and special constables are similar, members of the public often don' t know or realise that it is indeed a volunteer officer who has responded to a call. Their presence in times of extreme and higher risks such as terrorism threats is welcomed by the public and law enforcement. However, in times of economic stress, regulars have been known to refer to these volunteer officers as ' hobby bobbies' (' bobbies' are slang in the UK for police. Robert is the given name of Sir Robert Peel, and ' Bob' is a nickname for Robert) and accused of taking paid overtime from the regular officers. There is a perception that these volunteer police, who, in the UK have the same powers of arrest as their regular counterparts provide "policing on the cheap" and, while it is true that they are not paid, they must attend ongoing training, wear the same police uniform and face similar risks as their full-time counterparts. In exchange for their participation as volunteers, Special Constables are paid only for personal expenses realized as part of their service.

Many in the UK Special Constabulary and in American reserve or auxiliary police decided to volunteer to assess whether they really are interested in becoming full-time, regular officers. In this way the role of volunteer police becomes a way of training future full-time police and as a way for the agency to screen volunteer police for their likeliness to succeed in full-time policing positions. However, many others (who are referred to in the UK as "career specials" because they stay in this role for the length of their policing career) in both UK and USA organizations serve in this policing role because it provides them with an interesting, supportive, community-minded pastime. This interest in volunteering for the intrinsic reward of helping others is like that of other volunteers who give their time and energies to support charities and other emergency services.

As the reader will find later in this text, the literature in the USA suggests that 30%-35% of all public safety organizations utilize volunteer officers. With approximately 18,000 different law enforcement agencies within the United States, that means that more than 5,000 policing agencies use volunteer officers in some capacity. Although estimates vary, the US Department of Justice Bureau of Justice Statistics (BJS) reported that in 2013 there were approximately 29,500 sworn reserve or auxiliary volunteer police officers with full police powers in the USA (Reaves, 2015), and about 29,000 sworn volunteer sheriff's deputies with full police powers (United States Department of Justice, Office of Justice Programs. Bureau of Justice Statistics. Law Enforcement Management and Administrative Statistics [USDOJ/ LEMAS], 2015). The most recent data available for reserve and auxiliary police and sheriff's deputies shows that there are also approximately 9,700 volunteer police and 9,300 volunteer sheriff's deputies (BJS, 2014) who do not have the police power of arrest (called "non-sworn" in the USA). This would put a total estimate of sworn and non-sworn volunteer police and sheriff's deputies at approximately 77,500. As stated above, however, volunteer policing can take many different forms, depending on the agency, state law and the training provided to the volunteer.

In a 2015 study of volunteer law enforcement officers in sheriff's offices throughout the USA, respondents were asked to indicate what motivated them to become volunteer law enforcement officers. Seventy-three percent responded that they wanted to contribute to their community. This was followed by 69% who responded that they "see it as a way to develop as a person," 65% reported "I have an interest in law and policing in general" and 62% who reported "I have skills/knowledge from my daily life that can enhance the policing agency" (Wolf, Holmes and Jones, 2016).

About the authors

Ross Wolf began his policing career as an auxiliary police officer in Florida. The role of an auxiliary in Florida is defined by the limited amount of police training, and also by the fact that an auxiliary officer, by state law, must be under the immediate control of a fully-certified full-time or reserve officer. After attending approximately 300 hours of an auxiliary police academy (as a volunteer with no pay and with no reimbursement for expenses), and after spending the equivalent of six months of forty-hour weeks under the tutelage of a field training officer (again as a volunteer), Ross felt that policing was a career that he would feel better appreciated than in the other work he had been doing. After being selected to become a full-time police officer, Ross left what was a very good paying job and went back through a full police academy of approximately

790 hours to become a full-time police officer. While the role of a full-time police officer did not pay as well as his former full-time career, he felt happy in this role and felt that he was serving his community and society. As a full-time police officer, Ross served as a member of the agency honour guard, as a field-training officer (training new recruits in the first six months in the role) and on a tactical investigative unit as a detective. During this time, he earned several awards including awards of distinction in investigations, in lifesaving, and in administrative excellence. While a detective, and while working in a unit that required on-call status one out of every three weeks, Ross continued to take courses in higher education, and earned his doctorate degree. When Ross was asked to take a position within higher education as a university faculty member, he left full-time status in policing and again became a volunteer police officer by serving as a reserve.

Although initially Ross focused his academic scholarship on police use of force in America, and then on Tourism Oriented Policing, his passion for volunteering in policing led him to expand his research and writing about this topic. While serving as a reserve police officer, Ross was promoted to the rank of Reserve Chief Deputy where he was in command of his agency's reserve personnel. As an advocate for volunteer policing, he received several national-level awards and was elected as President of the Volunteer Law Enforcement Officer Alliance, an international organization promoting the use and proper training for policing volunteers.

Carol Borland Jones had a career in tourism until the company she worked for closed and so, in 1996 she found herself unemployed and a need to find another career. During her time working in the tourism industry she was aware of the many levels of crime taking place to tourists, ranging from simple shoplifting to much more serious robbery, violence, and rape. At the time Carol's husband was a Special Constable in the same area and through discussions she learned that, in order to maintain an air of tranquillity for tourists, most crimes were not reported to the police and so never added to the statistics. In 1997 Carol enrolled for a first degree in criminology at her local university and for her final year research study wrote of her observations relating to crime in tourist areas. Based on that study she was offered a placement to research the topic for a PhD① and in September of that year she moved several hundred miles away from home to

① A PhD in the UK and the USA require the individual to undertake and produce research and findings and the degree is awarded based on a viva voce—an oral defence of the research. Most programs in the USA also require a written dissertation.

begin her new career in research and teaching. Of particular interest was the problem of policing tourist areas, which, in winter were sparsely populated, but in the Spring and Summer months the same number of police officers had to cover the same areas with a rapid arrival of people staying for the short term as tourists.

In those formative years she presented at conferences in South Africa, was advisor to Victim Support, Mauritius and undertook work for the Home Office as well as several regional research studies.

When she took up a new lectureship in another university, she found that this new university was in discussions with their local police force about the development and implementation of police training. A former lecturer at the university where Carol had completed her first degree was recruited as Professor to plan and develop a degree that would provide a rigorous programme in which all students would begin their studies as Special Constables. It was Professor John Borland's incisive curriculum that drew Carol into the significance of volunteering and specifically the Special Constabulary. This two-year study programme allowed potential police officers to study and experience the basic principles of policing in the classroom and on duty with trained tutors① and full-time officers. It was not unusual to see groups of uniformed Special Constables walking around the university campus under the guidance of a tutor or two checking cars and buildings. Within a couple of years, a fully working institute of policing was embedded in the university and continues to this day. Professor Borland's program continued to expand, and upon successful completion of the basic training, students were enabled to take up a full-time post within the constabulary that was partnered with the university or apply for another of the 43 police forces in England and Wales.

What this book is NOT about

Volunteer police are civilians that choose to provide policing services within a structure provided by the police agency or the government. As an example of a similar "policing" role within society, the development and use of private security companies in both the United Kingdom and United States has expanded, and in some cases private security personnel may serve public areas (such as parks, government buildings, etc.). But while such employees wear uniforms, they are only authorized to patrol and only have se-

① Those who were teaching the various modules were all fully trained and warranted officers prior to taking up their new roles.

curity powers within those areas that they are paid to survey, such as shopping malls, housing estates and commercial properties. In the United Kingdom, these security personnel have no formal policing powers, and in the USA, they usually do not have formal policing powers. However, due in large part to the fragmented way the United States has developed governing bodies, such private security personnel may, depending on the jurisdiction and the authorities granted by state law, be authorized with full police powers of arrest. Interestingly, and on the contrary, there are some auxiliary/volunteer law enforcement officers within cities or local jurisdictions in the United States who wear the same or similar uniforms as their full-time police counterparts, but are not granted any police powers, and therefore may be restricted from carrying firearms, or may not be authorized to affect an arrest. Private security officers are not included in this text due to their limited policing use, but this shows again how policing can be so similar throughout the world, while at the same time may be vastly different.

There are also many other ways that volunteers may assist police agencies other than serving in a uniformed "sworn" or "warranted" (having the authority to make arrests and have the power of the police) capacity. Police volunteers may include individuals who serve police as chaplains (non-denominational religious representatives, usually used to provide faith services for victims and for police personnel), who serve as assistants in front desk police station reception or in report writing roles, individuals who serve in youth services volunteer roles that are sponsored by police agencies, and may also include community "citizens on patrol" or "neighbourhood watch" volunteers. While these types of volunteers do provide needed and often complicated tasks, they are not used to supplement police, and are therefore not the focus of this text.

What this book IS about

The first chapter of this book is intended to provide the reader with these definitions in further detail and to give an idea of the extent of their uses in the UK and in the USA and may be a good place to begin to explore similar issues in your own country. While we do provide a definition of volunteering for the purposes of clarity to our readers, your country or your city may have a different definition. In some countries, for example, a volunteer police officer may receive a paycheck, but because they have not received the same level of training as their full-time officers, they fall under a different classification.

Our second chapter refers to cases where reserve/volunteer officers in the U. S. have identified and addressed events where they have either been first on the scene or have joined their regular colleagues in responding to incidents. In spite of the divergent policing practices across the US, where reserve/auxiliary law enforcement officers are utilised, they face the same levels of danger as the full-time officers in a country where guns are widely held by the citizenry and gun crime can be prevalent. In many jurisdictions in the United States, volunteer police are authorized to carry firearms and may be required to carry a gun while on duty, but also while off duty. While on duty as police these American volunteers may also carry pepper spray, electronic control devices (Tasers), batons, and handcuffs. In contrast, guns are strictly regulated in the UK and guns are carried only by specially trained police officers that are called upon in limited cases. UK Special Constables, while they are usually authorized to carry pepper spray, batons, and handcuffs, are not currently permitted to carry guns or Tasers. In the case of the latter, however, during the writing of this translation, there are discussions underway to introduce training for some Specials to carry Tasers.

In the latter part of the twentieth century, volunteer police in the UK were generally used in less confrontational roles. For example, in the 1980s and 1990s Dr Borland-Jones and her family lived in a rural part of Wales with a sparse population and, in the summer months holidaymakers swelled this significantly and during the spring and summer months there were a number of agricultural shows that drew large crowds. At those events Dr Borland-Jones's husband would take time off from his paid employment to serve as a Special Constable and control traffic outside the showground and, when this calmed down he would walk around the grounds checking such issues such as the sale of alcohol in the beer tent (to make sure that it was not going to underage drinkers), making sure that shoplifting was not an issue at the craft stalls, and that people were adhering to the instructions being announced. As the day came to an end, he would return to the road to control traffic and to ensure that vehicles could leave the showground. Throughout the UK Special Constables could also be used to undertake special duties; again in North Wales briefly in the early 1990s these Special Constables were trained to police the seas off the coast with jet skis while in other, rural parts of the UK Special Constables undertook their shifts on horseback using their own horses.

In spite of USA policing principles being founded in the UK's practices, over time they have diversified federally, across states and in counties so that volunteer officers, depending upon their jurisdiction will have different responsibilities and these issues are further explored throughout our book in in the following chapter.

Our chapter on the history of volunteer policing requires little explanation but it is here that we touch upon the Special Constabulary in Northern Ireland and Scotland, the other two countries that, with England and Wales make up the United Kingdom in its entirety.

Following we discuss the evolution of volunteer policing in the USA which illustrates the growth in civilian volunteers across the country fulfilling roles previously undertaken by paid civilians but, since the global economic downturn in 2007, many of those paid posts have disappeared, the gaps being filled by volunteers. This is mirrored in UK policing.

In spite of criticisms from individual, regular officers as well as the Police Federation①, the union representing full-time officers, who may regard Special Constables as "policing on the cheap", over the past decade or so the skills that UK Special Constables utilise in their everyday employment is gradually being recognised as transferable skills that are valued in the police family. While it is not obligatory for those Specials to bring those specialist skills to their policing role, where they are willing to do so means that they alleviate the need for the police to either hire experts with those skills or train their existing staff. Ironically, Special Constables who are in their day jobs highly trained in medicine or are medical doctors, are still required to undertake the UK police's own first-aid course!

The backgrounds of Special Constables and American reserve and auxiliary police are varied and the skills that many bring can provide proficiency to needs and roles of the police agency. This is most noticeable among those who, in their day-to-day employment are highly qualified in valuable skills. In interviews with Senior ranked Special Constables in 2017 and in 2018, and in reports from American volunteer police, it was learned that many volunteer police hold managerial roles in industry, are expert trainers, or serve as paramedics, airline pilots, or other important positions. It was found that these all demonstrated confidence, reasoning, and excellent leadership skills. Sometimes, in spite of them being the most senior volunteer of their force with routine leadership of numerous personnel in the volunteer police role, they still must adhere to the senior regular full-time police officer who holds the portfolio for the volunteers.

① Since this book was written, the Police Federation, which had vociferously shunned membership for Specials, has done a U-turn and is currently encouraging Specials to join.

Why studying Volunteer Police is Important

As discussed earlier in this preface, while there are many reasons why people volunteer to become UK Special Constables or USA reserve or auxiliary police, a great number do so to test their compatibility to the role prior to joining the regular police. Many also join as volunteers to provide service to their communities and do not do so with any intention of ever serving as a full-time officer. Volunteer police in the UK and the USA also share the similarity that the backgrounds and full-time positions of these volunteers are so diverse that their expertise and knowledge of subject matters that may be important to the policing role is similarly varied. These skills that are external to policing, however, may also be an important strength of their service if the police agency can utilize these talents. While UK Special Constables and USA reserve and auxiliary police have routinely worked together with regular officers, regular officers must receive specific training for any specific role within policing. However, it has only relatively recently been recognised and accepted that volunteer police bring with them skills and knowledge from their daytime employment. In some forces, for example the recruitment of individuals who work routinely on cybercrime in banks and other financial services can put that knowledge to good use in their volunteering roles. Similarly, medical personnel may be partnered with an ambulance crew to respond to calls where injuries have been sustained in late-night brawls. That is not to say that, where an individual has such a specialism, they are obliged to perform similar work in their volunteer policing role. Indeed, while some individuals are happy to use their specialist skills in their volunteering role, there are others who see their policing role as a contrast to their usual occupation.

Policing in England and Wales is far more straightforward than in the USA. There are 43 police forces in England and Wales (plus the British Transport Police) and all adhere to centralised policies (although there is some differentiation of utilization even between forces in the UK) while in the USA each of the fifty states has a governor and elected legislative body who oversee law making and governance. This is compounded by the fact that many states allow individual localities to further refine or define the laws of the states to fit the needs of the local citizenry. While there are federal laws that are countrywide in the USA, the variation in laws vary from state to state and the varying levels of law enforcement within each state also add to the complexity of the American fragmented model. It is also important to note about policing in both countries that policing has historically been a male dominated field. The UK has been more successful that the USA at recruiting women into policing. Similarly, the diversity of the UK Special Constabulary is more representative of society in both gender and ethnicity than the regular force in the UK, but in the USA, there has been no such correlation noted.

Although American policing complexity is difficult to comprehend or match, there are also complexities to discuss about the policing model in the UK. While we have focused upon England and Wales thus far in this preface in discussing policing in the UK, the UK also includes Northern Ireland and Scotland. Turbulent political times in Northern Ireland led, in 1970 to the Police Service of Northern Ireland (PSNI) to employ a small force of part time officers. ①Scotland, although a part of the UK, has a legal and criminal justice system that varies from the remainder of the UK. Although it is a member, it has a background in which a policing act was introduced before the 1829 Metropolitan Police Act. Scotland has a large, geographically rural area and Special Constables are commonly used in those locations where populations are low. A similar circumstance exists in the United States. While most of the USA follows British common law (as a former UK colony), each state has developed specific laws within as interpreted and needed by their citizenry. To add to this complexity, the state of Louisiana, which did follow English law in the development of its criminal law, this state's civil law, consisting of contracts and torts, is based on a combination of both French and Spanish law. Louisiana also has developed flexibility for policing agencies in the establishment of reserve or auxiliary programs. While training is required for volunteer police, for example, the many different parishes (counties) within Louisiana have varying standards.

As already indicated, the UK's policing structure is far less complex than that of the USA, even with the existence of three differing countries regarding governance②. Police training in England and Wales currently falls under the policies of The College of Policing and all forces must follow the standards set down by the college. While the methods of training can vary from force to force, but all candidates who successfully

① For further detail relating to the structure of the PSNI see Hazlet A. (1972) The B Specials: A History of the Ulster Special Constabulary, London, Stacey.

② The United Kingdom parliament represents all geographic areas (England, Wales, Scotland and Northern Ireland), but each country has devolved powers. The Northern Ireland Assembly, Scottish Parliament and Welsh Assembly have individual powers with Wales only operating their criminal justice processes in line with the English Parliament.

complete the training, regardless of geographical location, should have achieved the same levels of understanding and practices thus making them fit for duty in any part of England and Wales. The same is not true in the United States, where certification as a police officer in one state is not necessarily accepted in another.

To be able to produce this book, both qualitative and quantitative research was undertaken in England and Wales and those jurisdictions that come under the National Sheriff's Association (NSA) in the USA, along with substantial review of records from scholarly and technical articles about other American volunteer policing. In both cases the research was the largest population ever undertaken of both auxiliary/reserve/volunteer officers in the USA and Special Constables in England and Wales. It is our intention to continue the themes identified in this book with other forces in other countries to enable policing organisations globally to learn and potentially improve processes in their own jurisdictions. While it must be acknowledged that laws, culture, and criminal justice processes vary, the underlying principles of policing, it can be argued, are to maintain law and order through processes individual to different jurisdictions. By drawing on comparisons predominantly between the United States and England and Wales, we hope that this will lay a foundation for you to consider your own practices and policies.

Professor Ross Wolf

and

Dr. Carol Borland Jones

中文版序言一译文[①]

我们两人是经一个同在大学任教的共同朋友介绍认识的。在此之后，我们发现我们之间有共同的研究兴趣，所以合作写作了本书。我们都对辅警管理很感兴趣。起初，因为这一共同的研究关注点，我们在各自国家为刑事司法专业的学生开发了一个国际交换项目，我们各自的学生都要在对方的学术研究机构完成一个短期学习任务。来自我们两国的学生（沃尔夫博士指导的美国学生和乔恩思博士指导的英国学生），在我们每位同事的教导下，完成在自己国家的学习之后，即前往对方国家。然后学生们全身心投入学习：见习巡逻工作（学生加入巡逻部分轮班或全部轮班，与全职警察或者辅警一起驾车巡逻或者步行巡逻），参观警察博物馆，与主办方国家大学生一起参与警察讲座和节目，观看警察演练和训练。学生们参加这些参观学习之后，对英国和美国在警察工作的组织结构、规则、法律以及政策方面的相同之处有了全新的、更深入的理解，对两国警察工作在有些时候存在的明显差异也有了一些认识。尽管最初这些交换学习的侧重点在于全职警察工作，但是随着时间的推移，这些国际学习经历的侧重点变成了辅警管理，辅警管理成为中心主题。在学生也开始关注辅警这一主题的时候，我们备受鼓舞，而且许多学生在期末作业中延伸了这一主题。我们作为同事多年参与这些国外学习活动，这些共同的经历使我们考虑开展学术合作，我们一起撰写学术论文和著作，研究英国和美国辅警有多相似，又有多不同。我们计划著书的时间，恰逢英国处在一个特别时间点。过去，警察招聘工作照例在英国国家警务改进局（NPIA，National Policing Improvement Agency）[②] 的赞助下操作，而且英国每个警察局实施培训并且自行承担培训费用。后来，英国国家警务改进局被裁撤，其许多职责被划归至现存机构或新组建的机构，这些机构处在新成立的警务学院的监

① 此文为原书两位作者为本译著所写的序言的中文译稿。

② 直到 2012 年 12 月。

督之下。在此之前不久，培训就发生了显著变化：大学和学院与地方警察局合作；警务学位培养方案出台。这意味着培训花费由学生承担，结果就是：在英格兰和威尔士，警务课程如雨后春笋般涌现，很多想当警察的人受到引导加入课程学习基本技能。在英国，辅警和正规警察都可以获得这种培训。

从英国和美国对比的角度探讨辅警管理，我们首先需要了解两国志愿行为的本质属性并回顾志愿行为的国际现状。世界上每个志愿从事警务工作的人，参与方式混合多样，发挥着不同的作用，出于众多不同的目的。志愿服务可以是正式的——所有项目均结构清晰且监管到位；也可以是非正式的——个体或群体可以决定做一些事情，不受任何监管地在他们觉得有需要的地方提供帮助。做这些事最常见的动机是，受内在和基本的人性驱动去帮助他人，在一个岗位上提供有益于社会的服务；也可以是为了成为国家或社区的骄傲。例如，个人可以志愿提供人道主义援助，在紧急状态下贡献食物和帐篷，在医院提供帮助，在动物保护站或庇护所提供帮助，帮助没有财力的他人建房造屋，或者将老年人送到医疗诊所或者使其得到医院救治。这些志愿行为的每一种都要求不同水准的培训，从很低水平的培训或者说根本不用培训——只是有人请求帮助和进行务工指导，到一种极其复杂的志愿工作——要求相当时数的培训，并且还要求月度或年度再培训。那些更为复杂的志愿岗位的例子，甚至包括消防志愿者和急救志愿者、护士志愿者和医院护工志愿者以及辅警。与其他岗位相比，这些岗位上的志愿行为不仅要求更多的培训，而且可能要承担不当履行职责导致的法律责任。

本书的研究重点是个人在警察机构内的志愿岗位上为其社区提供服务的诸多途径，尤其关注英国和美国的情况。当然，志愿从事警务工作的人不是在英格兰、威尔士或者美国的50个州才有，全世界许多国家或地区都有他们的身影。许多国家采用警务志愿服务这种方式引导民众，而不同国家在各自的法律体系和规定之内，已经发展出多种多样的方式，而且并没有局限于任何特殊的习俗或者传统。有众多采用某种形式志愿行为的国家或地区，本书描述了其中一些国家或地区作为例子，但是本书给出的例子绝不是毫无遗漏。

我们一起撰写本书，计划对辅警管理——尤其是英国①和美国②辅警管理——进行一个清晰的、常识性的说明。然而，尽管我们清楚（英国的）特别

① 英国包括英格兰、威尔士、苏格兰和北爱尔兰。但是，英格兰和威尔士采用统一的警务体系，而苏格兰和北爱尔兰享有一定的自治权，因而不在本书说明的范围内。

② 在美国50个州内部，每一个州、每一个县以及地方各层级都有其自治权，警务水平亦存在差异。

警员和（美国的）后备警察/辅警在角色、经历和背景方面存在差异，但是我们一开始探讨其他国家或地区的志愿行为，就发现对志愿行为和警务的界定存在更大差异。

志愿服务可以被定义为：为他人做事，没有任何金钱或利益上的回报。辅警符合这一定义，而且这些人中有很多常常从事这份工作，没有得到任何金钱报酬或者得到任何类型的酬劳或者补偿的许诺。但是，就像你能从本文了解到的许多情况一样，在全世界或者甚至在我们研究关注的国家里，现在仍没有行为规范或者统一的操作。在世界上的一些司法管辖区域和地区，志愿服务同样不允许得到什么补贴，不论是根据计时任务还是根据综合任务、职责以及级别。志愿者也可能会获得时薪或者月薪以抵消个人开销，而且可以额外获得一些形式的补偿，包括交通费、通宵履行警察职责发生的住宿费以及有机会在警察或官员俱乐部消费。特别是在警务中的志愿行为，以及在其他类型的由政府资助的领域中的志愿行为，还可以正式或非正式地为志愿者树立一定的威望或者社会地位。那些在志愿性质的警务工作中提供服务的个人，可以发现自己感受到自身很重要、有了被需要的感觉，或者通过参与志愿警务工作体会到更加伟大的责任感。但是这不是本书关注的研究点。

然而，辅警的定义并不包括那些接受某种时薪或者周薪的个人。他们接受这些报酬是按其工作的小时数支付的，这与其全职同事工作同样时间所得金钱的数额相同。这些个人，尽管他们一直在扮演与辅警完全相同的角色，但是他们属于不同的类别，被称为“兼职警察”，因为他们工作是为了挣钱。

英国和美国辅警管理的基本情况

美国警务很大程度上以十九世纪中期在伦敦建立起来的警务模式作为蓝本。美国的辅警管理模式亦是如此。有关两国之间（大家都知道美国曾经是英国的一个殖民地）这种关联性更多的内容，本书进行了不少回顾。但是，大家要知道，英国辅警管理在正规警察力量出现之前就产生了，这一点很重要。

1829 年，罗伯特·比尔爵士，英国政府的国务卿，提出议案《大都会警察法》。《大都会警察法》标志着正式警务在伦敦首次出现。在通过这些新法律之前，“警务”是由守夜人和兼职安全员们从事的反应型工作。这些男人（女人被认为不适合这类工作）通常是没有报酬的而且是临时召集起来的。随着《大都会警察法》的正式出台，《特别警员法案》[①] 在1831年被通过，尽管当今的特别警员一般被要求每月至少工作16个小时，但根据1831年《特别警员法案》，特别警员得处理所有的电话，没有最低或最高工作时数要求。《大都会警察法》在1835年经《自治市行会法案》被扩展，省级城镇出现警察这支新生力量，但是直到1856年的《县和区法案》要求所有地方政府遵照执行新警察法规，警务才真正在英国全境出现。在紧急状况下，特别警员是一个重要的警务现象，如在第二次世界大战期间，当正规警察被招募服兵役时，取代他们的是那些受聘待在后备岗位的特别警员们，这些特别警员不是超龄，就是有某种健康问题。

当2012年伦敦举办奥运会的时候，正规警察被派往比赛场馆，与此同时特别警员在当地警察局填补正规警察的岗位。虽然在美国，大多数执法机构附属于某个地方的司法管辖区域（与联邦部门没有关系），但是在英国，不论是正规警察还是特别警员，都获得许可在英格兰和威尔士的任何警察局工作，因为所有警察局必须遵循中央统一的政策。类似奥运会这样的国家重要时段，招募特别警员数迅速上涨。但是，一旦大型活动结束，数量就降下来。

在英国，民众对当今政府使用特别警员的方式反应不一；因为不论是正规警察还是特别警员，他们的警察制服是相似的，民众常常不知道或者说没有意识到处理电话的人实际上是一名辅警。辅警在类似恐怖威胁这样的极端、高危时刻参与处置工作，受到民众和执法部门的欢迎。然而，在经济紧张时期，众所周知的是，正规警察把这些志愿性质的警察称为“警察业余爱好者（‘hobby bobbies’）”（“bobbies”在英国是称呼警察的俚语。罗伯特·比尔爵士的名字是Robert，而“Bob”是罗伯特的昵称）并且抱怨辅警使正规警察得不到加班费。有一种观点认为：在英国，这些辅警与他们的正规警察同事拥有相同的逮捕权，提供“廉价警务”；尽管事实上他们没有报酬，但是他们必须不断参加培训，身穿与其全职警察同事相同的警察制服并且面对相似的危险。作为他们以志愿身份加入警察工作的交换，特别警员获得的报酬仅仅是他们提供服务时实际产生的个人开销。

英国许多特别警员以及美国后备警察或者协警，决定自愿去评估他们是否真的喜欢成为全职、正规警察。这样，辅警成为培训未来全职警察的一个途径，也成为警察机关审查辅警的一种方式：看辅警是否有意愿在全职警务岗位上取得成功。然而，不论是在英国还是在美国的组织中，其他许多人（他们在英国被称为

① 正式名称是《任命特别警员有关法律修正案》，此法案出台是为了更好地维护治安。

“特别职业人”，他们在其警察职业生涯中一直是辅警身份）在警务岗位上提供服务，因为这使他们的闲暇时间充满乐趣，他们助人为乐而且为社区着想。他们从帮助他人获得内在回报，对志愿行为的这种兴趣，类似于其他志愿者奉献时间和精力支持慈善以及在其他紧急时刻提供服务。

读者在本书后文里会看到，美国文献资料认为，在全部公共安全组织机构里，有30%至35%的机构在使用志愿性质的官员。在美国大约18000个不同的执法机构里，这意味着有超过5000个警察机构在使用志愿性质的警察从事某种工作。尽管估算存在差异，但是美国司法部司法统计局（BJS, Bureau of Justice Statistics）的报告认为：2013年，美国大约有29500名宣誓后备警察或者协警拥有全部警察权力（Reaves, 2015），大约有29000名宣誓志愿性质的县治安官助理拥有全部警察权力（美国司法部，司法项目办公室，司法统计局，执法管理和行政统计［USDOJ/LEMAS］，2015）。关于后备警察和协警以及县治安官助理的最近可得的数据表明：还有大约9700名辅警和9300名志愿性质的县治安官助理（BJS，2014）没有逮捕权（在美国，他们被称为“非宣誓”警察）。这样，宣誓和非宣誓辅警以及县治安官助理的总数约为77500名。但是，根据不同的警察机构、州法律以及辅警接受的培训，辅警管理有许多不同形式，这一点我们在前文说过。

2015年，在一个对全美县治安官办公室里的志愿性质执法官员开展的研究中，答卷人被要求描述他们做志愿性质执法官员的动机是什么。73%的答卷人这样回答：他们希望为自己的社区作些贡献；接下来有69%的答卷人说他们“把它视为发展自己的一种途径”；65%的答卷人说“我通常对法律以及警务感兴趣”；62%的答卷人说“我从日常生活中习得的技能/知识可以助力警察机构”（Wolf, Holmes and Jones, 2016）。

关于作者

罗斯·沃尔夫的警察职业生涯开始于佛罗里达州，他当过协警。佛罗里达州协警角色的特点，一个是协警接受有限的警察培训，还有一个是下面这个事实：根据州法律，协警必须处于获得全部授权的全职警察或者后备警察的直接管控之下。罗斯在一所协警学校参加了大约300个小时的学习（作为一名志愿者，没有报酬也没有报销花费），而且接受了一名实战培训教官相当于6个月的每周40个小时的指导（再次作为志愿者）。此后，罗斯觉得，同其之前一直在做的其他工作相比，警察是令其感觉更适合自己的一个职业。在警察局挑选罗斯成为全职警察之后，罗斯为了成为一名全职警察，他放弃了薪酬不菲的工作，重新回到学校，进入一所培养警察的院校，学习了大约 790 个小时。尽管做一名全职警察，罗斯拿到的薪水不如其之前的全职岗位多，但是他感到做全职警察很幸福，觉得他是在为其社区和社会服务。作为一名全职警察，罗斯曾是警察机构仪仗队里的一员，做过实战培训教官（在新人职业生涯的最初六个月培训新录用人员），还在一个战术调查组做过侦探。在此期间，罗斯荣获几个奖励，包括调查荣誉奖、拯救生命奖以及最佳管理奖。罗斯在做侦探以及在一个部门工作——该部门要求每三周值班一次接听电话——的时候，他继续学习深造，并获得博士学位。当罗斯受到邀请到一个高教机构做大学老师的时候，他离开全职警察岗位，以后备警察的身份提供服务，再次成为一名辅警。

尽管起初罗斯的研究关注点是美国警察对武力的使用，随后又研究旅游导向警务，但是他对警务中志愿行为的兴趣使他拓展了研究范围并撰写了以这方面为主题的文章。在罗斯以后备警察身份提供服务的时候，他被提拔到局长后备助理的职位，在这个职位上，他领导其所在机构的后备警察人员。作为志愿辅助警务的倡导者，他荣获了几个美国国家级奖励，并且当选为志愿性质执法官员联盟主席。志愿性质执法官员联盟是一个国际性组织，旨在促进使用和合理培训警务中的志愿者。

卡罗尔·伯兰德·乔恩思曾从事过旅游业工作，直到她工作的公司倒闭。所以，在 1996 年，她失业了，需要找到一份别的工作。在从事旅游业工作期间，卡罗尔注意到以游客为目标的各种犯罪行为，从一般的小偷小摸到更为严重的抢劫、暴力行为和强奸。当时，卡罗尔的丈夫是她工作区域的一名特别警员。通过讨论，卡罗尔知道了一个事实：为了让游客觉得旅游期间的氛围一直是和平安宁的，大多数犯罪行为没有被报告给警方，因而就从来没有被纳入统计数据。1997 年，卡罗尔在当地的一所大学登记入学，学习犯罪学，这是她的第一个学位。卡罗尔在其毕业论文里写了她对旅游地区犯罪的评述。因为这个研究，她得到一个实习机会，研究旅游犯罪，攻读博士[①]学位。在那一年的 9 月，她离家数百里，开始她全新的研究教学生涯。旅游地区治安维护存在一个特别有意思的问题：冬

① 英国和美国的博士学位要求学位申请者开展研究并形成研究结果。授予博士学位必须经历一次现场答辩——针对所开展研究的口头答辩。在美国，不少博士学位培养方案还要求学位申请者撰写一篇学位论文。

季游客很少，但是春、夏两季那几个月，相同数量的警察得在相同区域迎接蜂拥而至、作为游客短期停留的人们。

在那些求学深造的岁月里，卡罗尔参加过在南非召开的一些会议，做过毛里求斯的被害人援助顾问，为内政部工作，开展了几个区域性学术研究。

当卡罗尔在另一所大学接受了一个新的讲师职位的时候，她发现该所新大学在与该地警察局讨论开发、完善警察培训。在卡罗尔完成第一个学位的那所大学里担任讲师的一个人，受聘担任教授。该教授制订计划并设置一个学位，提供一个严格的培养方案，在此方案里，所有学生将以特别警员的身份开始学习。正是约翰·伯兰德教授开设的精品课程，驱使卡罗尔关注志愿行为，尤其是特别警员。这个为期两年的学习计划，使想当警察的人有机会在课堂上、在一线，与训练有素的辅导员①和全职警察一起，学习并实践警务基本原理。所以，人们常见到一群身穿制服的特别警员，在一位或两位辅导员的带领下，在大学校园里四处走动，检查车辆和建筑物。在几年的时间里，一所运转良好的学院在大学里开花结果，一直持续到现在。卡罗尔教授的计划继续拓展，在即将顺利完成基础培训之际，学生们有能力在与大学有合作关系的警察局里的全职岗位上工作，或者可以向英格兰和威尔士 43 家警察局中的其他警察局提出任职申请。

本书没有探讨的内容

辅警是民众，他们选择在一个由警察机关或政府建立的机构内提供维护治安的服务。作为社会内部一个类似“维护治安”角色的例子，建立和使用私人保安公司在英国和美国已经是普遍做法。在一些情况下，私人保安人员可以在公共区域（如公园、政府大楼等）提供服务。然而，尽管这样的雇员穿着制服，但是他们仅仅被授权从事巡逻工作，在那些他们受雇巡查的区域仅有保安权力，如购物中心、住宅区和商业地产。在英国，这些保安人员没有正式的警察权力；在美国，他们通常没有正式的警察权力。然而，因为美国的分权制在很大程度上塑造了其治理体制，类似的私人保安人员可以——根据司法管辖区域和州法律许可的职权——被授权拥有全部警察逮捕权。相反，一个有意思的现象是：在美国的城市或者地方司法管辖区域内部，存在一些协助/志愿执法官员，他们身穿与其全职警察同事一样或相似的制服，但是没有被授予任何警察权力，因此他们在携

① 辅导员，是指那些讲授各种教学模块的人员，他们全部是训练有素的、获得认证的警察，处在担任新职务之前阶段。

枪方面受到限制，或者没有被授权参与逮捕行动。私人保安官员不在本书讨论范围内，因为他们在警务方面的使用受限，但是这再次表明警务在全世界是如此相似，却又纷繁复杂。

除了以穿着制服的“宣誓”或者“被许可的”（具备逮捕权并拥有警察权）身份提供服务，志愿者还有许多其他方式可以帮助警察机关。警察志愿者可以包括下列个人：在警察局做牧师（非教派宗教代表，通常被用于为被害人和警察职员提供信仰服务）；在派出所前台做接待员或者撰写汇报材料；在警察机关的资助下做青年服务志愿者；以及社区“公民巡逻”或者“邻里守望”志愿者。尽管这些类型的志愿者的确为必要的且通常复杂的任务提供服务，但是他们未被用于补充警力，因而不是本书的关注点。

本书研究的内容

本书第一章旨在为读者更为详尽地解释诸多概念，让读者知晓这些概念在英国和美国的使用情况，从而使读者确定在自己国家讨论相似问题的起点。尽管我们给读者提供了出于慈善目的的志愿行为概念，但是读者所在的国家或者城市可能有不同的定义。例如，在一些国家，志愿性质的警察可以获得薪水，但是因为他们没有得到与其全职警察相同水平的培训，他们属于不同类别。

本书第二章给出了一些例子，这些例子是美国后备警察/辅警确定并处置案事件的情况：他们要么是首批到达现场的人员，要么与其正规警察同事一起处置事件。在美国，后备/协助执法官员被用在警务工作中。尽管美国各地警务实践存在不同，但是在这个国民广泛持枪且涉枪犯罪高发的国家，他们面对的危险级别与正规警察面对的别无二致。在美国许多司法管辖区域，辅警被授权携带枪支而且可能被要求不论在上班时还是在下班时都要带枪。在上班时，美国这些辅警还可以带胡椒喷雾器、电控装备（泰瑟枪）、警棍和手铐。与此相反，在英国，枪支受到严格管控，而且只有受过特别训练的警察在处置个别案件时才可以带枪。英国的特别警员，尽管他们通常得到授权可以携带胡椒喷雾器、警棍和手铐，但是现在没有获得携带手枪或者泰瑟枪的许可。然而，关于特别警员携带泰瑟枪这个问题，在本书翻译过程中，英国正在讨论培训一些特别警员携带泰瑟枪。

在二十世纪的后半期，英国的辅警通常被用在对抗性不大的情境。例如，在二十世纪八十年代和九十年代，伯兰德·乔恩思博士及其家庭住在威尔士人口稀少的村庄里。在夏季，度假的人们享受着这种特别的宁静。在春季和夏季，一些农业展览吸引着大批人群。在这些时候，伯兰德·乔恩思博士的丈夫要从其有偿工作上请假来做特别警员，在展览场地外疏导交通。当不用疏导交通的时候，乔恩思博士的丈夫就在展览场地上巡查存在的问题，如查看在啤酒售卖帐篷中销售啤酒的情况（此举为了确保啤酒没有被卖给未成年人饮用），确保在工艺摊位不存在小偷小摸问题，确保人们听从正在发布的指令。在展览即将结束的时候，乔恩思博士的丈夫会返回路面疏导交通，确保车辆离开展览场地。在整个英国，特别警员还可以被用于履行特别职责；同样在北威尔士，在二十世纪九十年代初期，这些特别警员受训驾驶摩托艇维护海岸附近海域的治安秩序，与此同时，在英国其他乡村地区，特别警员骑着自己的马儿轮班工作。

尽管美国警务原则根基于英国的实践，但是随着时间的推移，他们在联邦政府中、在各州和县中都实现了多元化。所以，根据辅警所处的司法管辖区域，辅警承担不同的职责，而且这些问题在本书余下章节中有更深入的探讨。

本书有关辅警管理历史的章节几乎不需要解释，但是正是在这一章，我们会论及英国其他两个地区——北爱尔兰和苏格兰——特别警员的情况，这两个地区与英格兰和威尔士构成了整个英国。

接下来我们讨论了美国辅警管理的演变，描述了全美公民志愿者的成长历史，他们填补了之前由受雇公民履行的职责。但是，自从全球经济在2007年下滑，许多这样的有偿岗位都消失不见了，是志愿者填补了这些不足。英国警务也是同样的情况。

尽管对辅警的质疑来自个人、正规警察以及代表全职警察的工会①——警察联合会，他们可能把特别警员视为“廉价警务”，但是在过去的十几年里，英国特别警员在其每日工作中使用的技能，逐渐被认可为可转移使用的技能，这些技能在警界很有价值。尽管将那些专业技能用在警务角色当中，不是那些特别警员必须做的事，而特别警员愿意这样做则意味着他们缓解了对警方的需求：要么雇用具备那些技能的专家，要么培训其现有的职员。具有讽刺意味的是，那些在其日常工作中受过高等医学训练的特别警员，或者身为医生的特别警员，仍然被要求学习英国警方自开的急救课程！

特别警员的背景以及美国后备警察和协警的背景各不相同，而且许多辅警具

---

① 自从本书成文以来，过去吵吵嚷嚷特意回避特别警员加入的警察联合会，如今态度已经来了一个一百八十度的大转弯，现在正鼓励特别警员加入。

备的技能能够令警察机关满足自身需求、发挥自身作用。在那些掌握很高技能从事每日工作的人当中，这一点是最明显的。从 2017 年和 2018 年与具备高等衔级的特别警员的访谈中，以及从来自美国辅警的报告中，我们知道：许多在工厂从事管理工作的辅警都是专业培训师、辅警们或者是急救人员、飞机驾驶员，或者是从事其他重要岗位上的工作。我们发现，这些辅警全部表现出自信、推理能力和极佳的领导技能。有的时候，尽管他们在其队伍里是最高等级的辅警，日常管理不少人员履行辅警职责，但是他们仍然必须听从高级正规、全职警察的领导，这些正规、全职警察为辅警们保管档案。

研究辅警的重要性

正如我们在本序言前面讨论过的，尽管人们志愿成为英国特别警员或者美国后备警察或者协警的原因有很多，但是很多人这样做是为了在他们成为正规警察之前，试试自己是否能够从事这份工作。还有许多人做辅警是为了给自己的社区提供服务，他们这样做不带有任何以全职警察身份工作的意图。英国和美国辅警还具备相似之处：这些辅警的背景和全职工作十分多样，以至于他们具备的有可能对警务工作十分重要的专业和知识，同样多种多样。当然，如果警察机关能够使用这些警务之外的技能，这些技能也可能是它们服务的一个重要优势。在英国特别警员和美国后备警察与协警日常与正规警察一起工作的时候，正规警察必须接受特殊培训，以备警务工作的不时之需。然而，直到最近，辅警从白天工作中带来的技能和知识才被警察局认可和接受。例如，那些日常在银行以及其他金融机构对抗网络犯罪的人员，受聘到一些警察局，可以在辅警岗位上很好地使用他们的知识。同样，警察局可以将医护人员和救护车工作人员搭档，接听求助电话，前往处置在深夜斗殴中受伤的人员。这并不是说只要辅警具备这样的专业技能，他们就有责任在辅警岗位上从事相似的工作。实际上，尽管一些人喜欢在辅警岗位上运用他们的专业技能，但是还有一些人在其警察角色中不做其平常职业做的事情，形成反差。

英格兰和威尔士的警务比美国的警务更为简单。英格兰和威尔士有 43 家警察局（加上英国交通警察总队），而且全部都遵守中央统一政策（尽管在英国甚至不同警察局之间都存在一些政策运用上的差异），然而在美国的 50 个州中，每一个州都有州长和经选举产生的立法机构，立法机构监管立法和治理。令这种情况雪上加霜的是：许多州允许地方进一步精炼或定义州法律，从而满足地方民众的需要。尽管美国有适用全国的联邦法律，但是在法律上，从州到州纷繁复杂，每一个州内部执法水平的差异同样为美国分权制模式的复杂性添砖加瓦。同样重要的是，人们要注意英美两国警务存在的同一现象：自古以来警务都是一个男性占主导的领域。英国比美国更进步一些，因为英国招聘女性入警。同样，与英国的正规警察局相比，英国特别警员队中的多样性更能反映社会的性别和种族。但是，在美国，我们还没有发现这种相关性。

尽管美国警务的复杂性令人费解，但是在讨论英国警务模式的时候，我们同样遇到复杂性问题。迄今我们在本序言中讨论英国警务的时候，我们关注的是英格兰和威尔士的警务情况，但是英国还包括北爱尔兰和苏格兰。北爱尔兰政治动荡时期促使北爱尔兰警察局（PSNI，the Police Service of Northern Ireland）在1970年雇用一支小规模的兼职警察。① 尽管苏格兰是英国的一个组成部分，但是其法律和刑事司法体系与英国其他地方都不一样。尽管苏格兰是英国大家庭中的一员，但是在苏格兰警务历史发展中，它有一部关于维护治安的法律在1829年《大都会警察法》出台之前就已经存在了。苏格兰是一个地域广阔、地理位置偏僻的地区，其特别警员一般被用在人口数量较低的区域。美国也存在类似情况。尽管大多数美国地区（作为英国前殖民地）遵行英国的普通法，但是每一个州在各自的州内出台了自己的法律，解释权在民众，满足民众所需。加重这种复杂性的情况是，路易斯安那州的确遵照英国法律制定自己的刑法，但是该州的民法、规范合同和侵权行为，是法国和西班牙法律的结合物。路易斯安那州还允许警察机关在开发后备警察或协警项目时保持灵活性。例如，警察局要求辅警接受培训，然而在路易斯安那州，许多不同教区（县）有不同的培训标准。

我们已经指出，英国警务架构的复杂性远不及美国的，即便英国存在三种不同政府模式。② 英格兰和威尔士的警察培训目前遵照警务大学的政策规定，所有警察局必须按照警务大学设定的标准实施培训。尽管在培训方法上局与局之间存在不同，但是所有候选人，只要成功完成培训，不管你在什么地理位置，都应该具备了同一水准的理解力和操作能力，从而使这些候选人能够适应英格兰和威尔士任何地方的警察工作。而美国不是这种情况。在美国，你在一个州获得的警察

---

① 有关北爱尔兰警察局机构的具体情况，参阅 Hazlet A.（1972）The B Specials：A History of the Ulster Special Constabulary，London，Stacey。

② 英国议会统领全部地理区域（英格兰、威尔士、苏格兰和北爱尔兰），但是英国议会将权力下放到每个地区。北爱尔兰大会、苏格兰议会和威尔士大会手握各自的权力，威尔士只在运行其刑事司法程序方面与英格兰议会协调一致。

资格证书不一定被别的州承认。

为了使本书能够出版，本书作者在英格兰和威尔士以及那些在美国的全国县治安官协会指导下的司法管辖区域，开展了定性研究和定量研究。同时，本书作者还广泛搜集了有关美国辅警管理的学术和技术论文。本书作者开展的研究，不论是在美国有关协警/后备警察或者说辅警的研究，还是在英格兰和威尔士有关特别警员的研究，都是迄今涉及人数最多的研究。我们希望能够与其他国家和地区的警察局，将本书关注的问题继续研究下去，使全球的警察机构能够学习并完善所在司法管辖区域的执法程序。当然，必须指出的一点是：尽管法律、文化和刑事司法程序各不相同，但是可以说，警务的基本原则是通过不同司法管辖区域的不同程序来维护法律和秩序。通过主要比较美国以及英格兰和威尔士的辅警情况，我们希望读者可以在此基础上思考自身的实践和政策。

罗斯·沃尔夫　教授

和

卡罗尔·伯兰德·乔恩思　博士

2020 年 12 月 3 日

中文版序言二

创新辅警管理，推进平安建设

安全是人的基本需求。在公共治理现代化进程中，如何高质量地开发辅警人力资源、最大限度地发挥其警察助手作用，这是各国政府，特别是各国警察机构面临的共同挑战。

新时代平安中国建设，离不开公安机关辅警管理的制度创新。制度创新需要立足中国国情、坚定制度自信，也需要关注和借鉴国外有益实践经验和研究成果。

由美国学者沃尔夫教授、英国学者乔恩思博士合作撰写的《辅警志愿服务：美英辅警管理的探索、比较及评估》一书立足全球视野，理论和实践相结合，探讨了辅警管理创新问题。该书具有以下主要特色：

一是选题前沿。尽管法律地位、职责和权力不尽相同，但各个国家和地区的辅警都是志愿参与警务的社会力量。辅警队伍建设是公共治理现代化和人力资源管理创新的产物，它契合了警察机构减少成本、利用社会人力资源、建设警民伙伴关系的需要，也是公众服务公共安全、锻炼职业能力的有效途径。与辅警队伍和管理实践的快速发展相比，辅警研究尚显滞后。《辅警志愿服务：美英辅警管理的探索、比较及评估》结合英、美等国家和地区的最新实践，比较深入地探讨了辅警的概念与效应、历史发展与当今职责、主要职权、培训与开发、发展趋势等基本问题，是迄今为数不多的、以全球视角系统论述辅警问题的学术著作之一。

二是方法多元。该书在梳理大量研究文献、对辅警的内涵和要素进行理论分析的基础上，回顾辅警的起源和演进，比较分析了多个国家和地区，特别是英美两国的辅警人力资源开发实践，并就辅警的最初动机、基本职责等问题，对美国部分县警察局辅警以及英国的英格兰和威尔士部分辅警进行了问卷调查。定性研究与定量研究相结合、规范分析与实证研究相结合、宏观研究与微观研究相结合，这大大增强了该书的逻辑性和论证力。

三是观点独特。作者总结了最新实践和研究成果，提出了一些有价值的见解。例如，辅警是指“个人直接为一个政府部门工作，并经授权拥有预防、侦查和处罚犯罪活动以及维护公共秩序的合法权力，其从事上述工作未受到强制要求亦未因此获得可观的报酬”，这一定义体现了辅警所具有的公共性、专业性、志愿性、合法性和工作危险性等基本特征；再如，辅警群体具有多样化的专业背景和工作经历，有利于警察机构解决医疗、网络、财务等技术人才不足的问题；又如，警察机构需要根据辅警职能和岗位特征，对辅警的权力行使、选拔、培训和使用，实施分级分类的标准化管理。此外，该书还对警察管理体制对辅警管理的影响、辅警管理的国际比较等内容进行了深入思考。

尽管该书主要立足英美等国家和地区的实践，有些提法仍需商榷，辅警素质标准有待深入研究，但是，它提出了一个前沿课题和一些创新观点，方法科学，案例典型，数据鲜活，论证严密，参考文献比较权威、丰富。翻译此书，对于提升我国公安辅警管理的人本化、科学化和法治化水平，进而促进公安工作现代化和平安中国建设，对于拓宽公安学、人力资源管理理论研究视野，都具有积极的意义。

应译者之邀，谨以此为序。

萧鸣政博士
北京大学政府管理学院教授、博士生导师
北京大学人力资源管理与开发研究中心主任
中央“马工程”人力资源管理首席专家
中国人才研究会副会长

2021 年 1 月

专家推荐

《辅警志愿服务：美英辅警管理的探索、比较及评估》将美国和英国辅警进行了深入对比，探讨了特别警员、协警和后备警察共同的过往和相似的——有时也存在差异的——演变历程。本书讨论了辅警的历史，当前的职权、职能和培训，还考察了全球兼职警察、协警和特别警员发挥的作用。本书对英国和美国辅警进行了开创性对比研究，而且讨论了英国和美国辅警的未来发展。

本书作者为执法领域的教育者、领导者和管理者，并且为那些获得辅警服务的社区，提供了一个令人印象深刻且富有价值的资料。当今时代，全球执法部门在资源有限的情况下面临着多种挑战，而且所有层级的执法专职人员和教育者，应该知道那些有价值的社区资源——辅警的历史、作用、影响、配置、未来发展及其最佳实践。

——加利福尼亚州奥兰多县巴伦西亚学院公共安全系执行主任杰夫瑞·W.戈尔茨博士

本书是迄今有关辅警的最全面的研究！我坚信，在当前“社区警务”发展中，没有比充满活力的后备警察项目更好的例子了。我把后备警察称为“公民警察”。本书探讨辅警的积极和消极方面，是每位对当前执法趋势感兴趣的人的必读著作。

——得克萨斯州达拉斯城警察局后备警察处处长助理史蒂芬·布罗迪

本书在过去甚少被研究的警务领域——后备警察或者协警，提出引人入胜、发人深省的见解。既往研究倾向研究单独一国的情况，没有从国际视角进行研究。结果，人们显然忽略了从其他国家学习实践和经验的机会。通过比较和对比美国各地以及美国和英国之间使用后备警察的不同方法，本书作者给读者提供了独特机会来思考警务怎样从后备警察获得尽可能多的好处。

——伦敦城警察局特别警员队指挥官杨·米勒（荣获大英帝国勋章员佐勋章）

辅警为警务作出了巨大贡献，但这些贡献常常很少获得认可。这本著作很重要，它从国际视角探讨了这些贡献，明确了英国和美国辅警扮演的角色以及他们对警务的影响，讨论了辅警的未来发展。

——北安普顿大学公共安全、犯罪和司法研究所主任、辅警中心主任以及警察咨询委员会主任伊恩·布里顿

本书导读

■ 刘君玲

翻译本书的原因

比较研究是研究与判断物与物之间和人与人之间的相似性或相异程度，即根据一定的标准，对两个或两个以上有联系的事物进行考察，寻找其异同，探求普遍规律与特殊规律的方法。

比较研究的基础，是被比较的客体有可比性。本书作者在第一章第一句话就指出“比较研究存在概念界定问题”。如果没有概念界定，直接将不同地域的有关情况拿来作比较，很容易出现各说各话的情况，导致无法比较。概念界定的重要性毋庸置疑，因为可以“借此让一地的读者与另一地的读者有一个‘平等的基础’（p. 1①）”。

所以，本书不同于别书的方面，同时也是我们选择本书的一个原因，那就是本书的辅警比较研究以及概念界定。

Volunteer police 的翻译

谈到 volunteer police 的翻译问题，首先要看本书作者怎样界定 volunteer police。而为了界定 volunteer police，作者先界定了 volunteer 和 police。

我们先看中外理解最一致的 police 的翻译。

本书作者对 police 的界定：

An individual who works directly for a government entity and who is authorized with lawful powers of the prevention, investigation, and prosecution of criminal activity and

① 注：“本书导读”中的页码均为原书页码，请查边页码。

the preservation of public order.

汉语翻译：个人直接为政府部门工作且经合法授权拥有预防、侦查和处罚犯罪活动以及维护公共秩序的权力。

所以，将 police 翻译成“警察”，这个没有什么疑问。

下面要谈谈对 volunteer 的翻译。

本书作者借鉴英美学者对 volunteer 的定义，特别参考联合国对志愿行为、志愿服务以及志愿活动的定义“为普通大众的利益自愿从事的（undertaken of free will），且金钱奖励不是主要激励因素的各种活动”，把 volunteer 界定为：

An individual who provides time for a recognized organization or governmental service without significant remuneration for his or her services or imposed requirement.

汉语翻译：个人为一个官方承认的组织或者政府部门奉献时间，没有因他或她提供服务获得可观的报酬，或者没有受到强制要求。

本书作者对 volunteer 不能获得任何报酬的观点提出质疑。本书作者的观点从其对 volunteer 的界定能够看出来：“without significant remuneration for his or her services”意味着有少许报酬，即 volunteer 不是完全无偿性质的。因为“美国和英国的警察部门都可以给参与警务工作的志愿者们提供某一特权；这可以包括报销交通费、报销装备费、一份肉食补贴，或者时间津贴（p. 3）”。

我们提醒读者要注意的是，本书作者在定义里还强调了 volunteer 的“without …imposed requirement”的一面，即志愿者这个概念本身就含有的“a choice freely made by each individual（每一个人自愿作出的选择）”，也就是说志愿者都是自愿者。本书作者用了一页多的篇幅分析志愿者的自愿性质。其总体意思就是，受强制要求、非自愿参与的“志愿者”不是真正的志愿者。

所以，把 volunteer 翻译成志愿者，是顺乎传统翻译的选择。这个定义与中国民众对“志愿者”的理解也是一致的。

为什么我们没有把 volunteer 翻译成“自愿者”，而是仍然翻译成“志愿者”呢？因为，“志愿者”本身就含有自愿之意，只是我们平常只注重其有没有获得报酬这一面而已。所以，我们在此提醒读者，本书作者强调“志愿者”的自愿性。

然而，把 volunteer 和 police 连在一起构成 volunteer police，却不能简单累加翻译成“志愿警察”。

这一点本书作者在 volunteer police 部分开篇即明确指出，“但是至关重要的是，我们要意识到，将两个术语结合起来制造出来的新术语，甚至更难界定清楚，因为要跨越不同文化、语言、联合体、国家和地方司法管辖区域（p. 7）”。

大家看看本书作者对 volunteer police 的定义：

An individual who works directly for a government entity and is authorized with lawful powers for the prevention, investigation, and prosecution of criminal activity and the preservation of public order, and who provides this service without an imposed requirement and without significant remuneration for his or her service.

汉语翻译：个人直接为一个政府部门工作，并经授权拥有预防、侦查和处罚犯罪活动以及维护公共秩序的合法权力，其从事上述工作未受到强制要求亦未因此获得可观的报酬。

从这个 volunteer police 的定义能看出，如果把它翻译成“志愿警察”，这个中文词语没有把英文概念的意思体现出来。因为在我国，“志愿警察”（或称为“义警”）是指出于奉献、友爱、互助和社会责任，经过登记，自愿、无偿地以自己的时间、技能等资源开展社会治安防范和公益服务活动的人员，是一支覆盖各行各业，自愿参与社会群防群治的公安志愿者队伍。例如，治安联防、治安志愿者、护村队、护校队等社会群防群治力量。所以，我国民众对“志愿警察”（或称为“义警”）的理解是属于志愿者性质的，因为他们没有报酬、不穿制服、不具备任何警察职权、自愿为警察机关提供帮助。

那么，英美有没有类似我国的“志愿警察”（或称为“义警”）呢？本书作者在界定 volunteer police 的部分，讲到在美国有一个概念是 volunteers in police service（VIPS），汉语翻译为“警察局里的志愿者”即简称为“警局志愿者”。

美国这个“警局志愿者”与我国的“志愿警察”（或称为“义警”）能等同吗？本书作者这样描述美国的“警局志愿者”：“警局志愿者是志愿者的一种，受到国际警察局长协会（IACP，the International Association of Chiefs of Police）的追踪，而且获得（美国）司法协助局和司法部的资助。警局志愿者项目将志愿者用在各种岗位以帮助警察机构。警局志愿者包括后备警察（reserve officers）和协警（auxiliary officers），还包括从事接待和文件处理的志愿者，以及参与包括邻里守望、公民巡逻和儿童平安 ID 计划在内的很多计划的志愿者（pp. 8-9）”。所以，我国的“志愿警察”（或称为“义警”）类似于美国“警局志愿者”里的“参与包括邻里守望、公民巡逻和儿童平安 ID 计划在内的很多计划的志愿者”。而且，本书作者明确表示：“volunteer police 不能与术语‘警局志愿者’相混淆（p. 8）”，因为本书作者认为下面这些都是 volunteer police 的例子：美国纽约市警察局的协警、[①] 加利福尼亚州洛杉矶市的后备警察（p. 9）；英国英格兰和威尔士的特别警员（SCs，special constables）、支援警察志愿者（PSVs，police support volunteers）。[②]

结合前文本书作者对美国的“警局志愿者”分类，我们明白：在美国，“警局志愿者”是一个包含了 volunteer police 的大概念。

说到这里，应该怎样翻译 volunteer police 呢？从 volunteer police 的定义，我们能看出这与我国的警务辅助人员或简称“辅警”相似。

我国国务院办公厅于 2016 年发布的《关于规范公安机关警务辅助人员管理工作的意见》中规定，警务辅助人员是根据社会治安形势发展和公安工作实际需要，面向社会招聘，为公安机关日常运转和警务活动提供辅助支持的非人民警察身份人员，统称“辅警”。

按照职责分工，警务辅助人员分为文职辅警和勤务辅警，文职辅警负责协助公安机关非执法岗位人民警察从事行政管理、技术支持、警务保障等工作；勤务辅警负责协助公安机关执法岗位人民警察开展执法执勤和其他勤务活动。

警务辅助人员有薪酬，全职在岗工作。警务辅助人员要按规定配发统一的工作证件，统一着装，持证上岗，其工作证件、服装式样和标识由公安部统一确定。根据工作需要，警务辅助人员可配备必要的执勤及安全区防护装备，但不得配备或使用武器。

警务辅助人员协助人民警察依法履行职责的行为受法律保护，履行职责行为后果由所在公安机关承担。

鉴于本书作者对“志愿者”的定义强调其“自愿”性质，所以 volunteer police 定义里有“without an imposed requirement”。特别是本书作者在讨论“志愿者”的“自愿”性质这一点时，举了军人的例子——“美国和英国的军队全部都是由‘志愿者们’组成的。这意味着没有人是被迫参军的，即如果他们不想参军，那么他们就可以不参军（pp. 2-3）”，令我们想到我国公安机关在招聘辅警时，采取公开招聘择优录取，申请人是自愿报名。

综上所述，根据本书作者对 volunteer police 的界定以及我国辅警的概念和我

① 尽管本书作者在第一次提到纽约市警察局的协警时说他们“受到严格的职权限制，使其不太像警察，倒更像公民志愿者（p. 7）”，但是根据本书第 8 章中有关纽约市警察局协警的描述，我们知道，纽约市警察局协警履行的职责与我国的“勤务辅警”的职责相似（pp. 127 128）。

② 从本书作者对英国的“支援警察志愿者”的描述（参见第 3 章注释 4），英国的“支援警察志愿者”相当于我国辅警中的文职辅警。

国公安机关管理使用辅警的制度和做法，我们将 volunteer police 翻译成“辅警”。

当然，这样翻译不是说我国的辅警与英美两国的辅警是一样的。首先是因为英美两国内部就没有一个统一式样的辅警。这也是本书作者多次指出的现实情况。例如，英国英格兰和威尔士地区与英国其他地区使用辅警的方式存在不同；美国东北部地区与美国其他地区使用辅警的方式也完全不同，在美国甚至在一个司法管辖区域都存在不同。其次是因为我国国情和英美两国各有不同，管理制度也不同，所以，我国辅警与英美辅警存在差异是完全正常的现象。

分章导读

第一章　引论：界定辅警

首先，本书作者依次界定了 volunteer、police 和 volunteer police。参见“本书导读”前文。

然后，本书作者考察了在美国和英国的英格兰和威尔士“现在有多少辅警?”在第一章注释 2 里，本书作者指出美国的辅警数据存在来源不明以及可能被严重高估的情况。

第二章　辅警的作用

本书作者开篇列举了 4 个辅警积极英勇执法的例子、4 个导致辅警死亡的事件、2 个辅警及时发现警情的例子以及在 2012 年伦敦奥运会期间英国正规警察和特别警员通力合作的例子，说明辅警不为大众所知、默默无闻地为维护治安发挥着作用。本书作者还举了一名后备警察因为身份曝光被枪杀的例子，说明辅警和正规警察一样容易成为暴力目标。

本书作者在论述了上文这些英国和美国辅警可以给警察在社区里的工作带来积极影响之后，列举了 2 个例子说明辅警给警察在社区里的工作带来的消极影响。

然后，本书作者指出，在美国，有关辅警的资料数据没有保留，因为美国警察系统各自为政，对辅警的组织管理少有研究。对后备警察或协警的定义和培训，美国都缺少统一性。英国的情况不同于美国。在英格兰和威尔士，所有的警察局被要求执行中央的政策，当然个别警察局的措施会有差异。

接下来，本书作者先后以下列标题为引领——“警察的角色”“为警方提供志愿服务”“为什么做辅警”“谁做辅警”“为什么一个警察机构愿意实施志愿者项目”“一个警察机构不愿意实施志愿者项目的原因可能是什么”，回答读者关心的一系列问题。

第三章　英国、美国辅警的使用和配置

本书作者开篇指出对志愿服务有浓厚兴趣的联合国在《2015 年世界志愿主义状况报告》中，没有提到全世界任何以警察身份工作的志愿者。这可以说明联合国没有把以警察身份工作的志愿者看作志愿者。

接着，本书作者论述了“英国警务中志愿者职责的扩展”“志愿者为公众利益服务”“英国的 43 个司法区域，一个整体力量”“美国警务中的志愿者”“认可辅警和辅警专业化”五部分内容。从中，我们知道：

（1）本书成书期间，恰逢英国、美国以及全球大多数国家的经济衰退不断恶化的时候，而且在一些国家，经济衰退为该国社会及其社区中出现志愿者角色提供了基础。

（2）在英国，执法部门使用志愿者情况的增长，导致有人批评这是“廉价警务”；正规警察抵触特别警员，因为特别警员让正规警察失去加班工作的机会，从而失去加班费这个额外收入。

（3）在美国，因为各州之间各自为政，整个美国境内警务演变各不相同，辅警的演变亦是如此。例如，纽约市警察局的协警与佛罗里达州的协警就完全不同。

（4）美国警察工会现在很少接纳辅警项目或者辅警。正规警察对辅警价值的看法各种各样，既有积极看法，也有消极看法。

（5）随着资源减少以及对个人特殊专业领域的要求持续升高，英美许多警察机构依赖志愿者来帮助自己降低成本。英国特别警员的专业被日益用在像打击网络犯罪和医疗卫生服务领域。美国执法机构使用志愿者做被害人辩护律师、翻译人员以及其他专业岗位的工作。

第四章　辅警的历史发展

本书作者首先考察了英国特别警员的历史。英国特别警员在全职、“正式”警察之前几百年就出现了。本书作者回顾了英国从太兴制（tithing）的全民维护治安到 1829 年《大都会警察法》以及其后的法律建立起全职、有偿、职业警察的历程。然后，本书作者讲道：根据《特别警员法案：1831 年》，特别警员正式创建。

《特别警员法案：1831年》允许在不安定时期挑选辅警，而且授权他们拥有全部逮捕权。这个法案还授予这些没有薪金的辅警于特殊时期在相邻县工作的职权。警察局还给特别警员配发了履职所需的必要物品和武器。这个法案使治安法官有能力给付出劳动的特别警员发放合理的津贴——这个规定到现在还有效——发放用餐补助和其他报酬以换取志愿者履职。最后，这个法案有一个有趣的规定，要求那些被确定做特别警员的人，必须履职，如果拒绝就要被罚款5英镑（在当时这是相当可观的一笔钱）。因为第一次世界大战，政府被迫修订了《特别警员法案：1831年》。修订后的法案包括准予发放津贴，用以补偿时间损失费、补偿医药费以及被杀害特别警员家属的抚恤金，而且如果被任命的特别警员想辞职，就给他补偿金以便他辞职。1949年，女性特别警员首次出现。

接下来，本书作者继续对英国"北爱尔兰的特别警员""苏格兰使用特别警员的情况"进行了描述。读者注意：北爱尔兰的特别警员队实际上由三个单独部分组成——"A""B""C"特别警员队；苏格兰特别警员每年可以获得1000英镑的酬金，但这不应被视为报酬，而且英格兰和威尔士现在也在实施这个"赏金"制度。

然后，本书作者依次描述了"美国辅警的演变""2001年9月11日恐怖袭击以来美国的志愿精神""警务角色文职化"。

其中，在"美国辅警的演变"部分，本书作者首先描述了美国从北美殖民地时期到二十世纪警务，即民众自我警务的发展简史，然后点明美国许多现代辅警组织历史可以追溯至二十世纪四十年代和五十年代的国民防卫组织。在美国，随着犯罪和暴力增长、国内秩序动荡不安以及遏制犯罪巡逻的增多，许多司法管辖区域转而使用志愿者以提高人力水平，而且许多政府扩展使用志愿者，经常在警方的支持下使用国民防卫部门。但是，美国东北部明显是一个例外。在美国东北部，这些使用辅警的倡议受到强大的警察工会和警察协会的阻挠。

值得注意的是，在"警务角色文职化"中，本书作者告诉我们：警察组织已经成功地将一些宣誓警察岗位变成文职岗位，包括接待人员、沟通人员、饮酒驾车（DUI，driving under the influence）或者证据技术员、人力资源人员、研究和制订计划人员以及其他可以更有效率地用不那么昂贵的雇员来从事的岗位。例如，犯罪现场勘查岗位，过去只有那些有警察工作经验和警察权的人才能做；但是，现在许多警务机构用不那么贵的（因为薪水，但是很大程度上还因为福利降低了）受过训练的文职人员来做。

第五章 辅警的当代角色与作用

在美国和英国，在现代警界开启有偿、全职、正规执法职业生涯，对一个人的理念和心理都有要求，因为要有奉献精神、吃苦耐劳的毅力以及身处监督调查的承受力。但是，成为志愿性质的执法官员则把这些要求提升到了一个新的高度。英国特别警员除了要承受工作带来的挑战，还要经受来自正规警察的非难，因为尽管志愿者们自愿贡献自己的精力和时间，正规警察对辅警的看法常常是一成不变的东拉西扯和贬低轻蔑。然而，这种情况不只出现在英国的特别警员身上；美国辅警要经常面对的全职正规警察，把辅警看作“周末斗士”或者“想当警察之人”。在美国的一些地方，辅警遭到全职警察和主管们的蔑视，这些人抱怨：对日日维护治安的“真”警察来说，辅警是个累赘。

本书作者告诉我们，在英美两国，不论是学界、警界还是普通民众，都知道罗伯特·比尔的“警务中的公民”原则。另外，英国警界改变以往避免使用辅警从警务工作之外所获专业技能的做法，开始在侦查贩卖人口、武器和毒品、网络犯罪（互联网诈骗、勒索软件攻击以及剥削儿童）以及经济犯罪等侦查工作中运用辅警的专长。

接着，本书作者阐述了“对辅警的领导、管理和认可”“后备警察、协警和特别警员中的名人”（共 11 位名人）两部分内容。其中，在“对辅警的领导、管理和认可”部分，本书作者指出，因为辅警贡献自己的时间，获得有限的奖励或者没有正式奖励，警察机构必须思考能够满足个人需求、动力以及技能的方法；这可以包括一个内部管理组织，包括一个等级架构。英美警察机构都对辅警实行类似正规警察的衔级管理。本书作者也指出，关于正规警察和辅警之间的级别高低问题存在很大争议。英美的规定是正规警察级别比辅警的级别高，二者的等级制度是分离的。

第六章 辅警培训

尽管本章标题是“辅警培训”，但是本书作者在这一章描述了“正规警察培训”“辅警培训”两部分内容，每部分都分别阐述英国和美国有关培训的情况。本书作者这样安排内容，是为了将英美辅警培训与正规警察培训进行对比，使读者更好地理解辅警培训。本书作者在本章开篇点明：“要给美国的培训标出界线是相当困难的，因为不单是州与州之间，甚至是州内的地方司法管辖区域之间都不一样，这使人们很难理解培训需求以及辅警的角色。但是，在英格兰和威尔士，正如警务学院所界定的，对正规警察的培训和对特别警员的培训都采纳更加同质化的结构。”

另外，在“辅警培训”部分，本书作者增加了一部分内容，即“专业培训”。警察机构还可以允许辅警参加专业部门工作（如自行车巡逻），或者允许辅警携带特种装备，需要附加专业技能培训（例如，自行车技术培训、枪支使用培训）。

第七章　美国、英国辅警比较

本章是一篇将美国、英国辅警个体情况和看法进行比较的研究报告。根据分别在美国和英国警察机构开展的辅警问卷调查搜集到的数据，本书作者撰写了这篇研究报告。研究报告框架如下：

样本和数据

调查工具

结果

人口统计样本

美国（附：表 7.1 美国样本的人口统计信息）

英格兰和威尔士（附：表 7.2 英国样本的人口统计信息）

“执法职责和服务动机”

美国（附：表 7.3　美国：你当辅警的动机是什么
表 7.4　美国辅警的职能和执法职责）

英格兰和威尔士（附：表 7.5　英国辅警的职能和执法职责
表 7.6　英国：回顾当初你决定成为一名辅警的时候，你最希望从这一经历收获什么）

报酬

思考和局限

本书作者告诉读者，总体而言，学界对美国和英国辅警执法研究不太重视。2013 年和 2016 年，本书作者参与了为研究美国、英国辅警个体情况以及看法开展的问卷调查。本书作者坦诚介绍了问卷调查前后过程，从问卷设计到问卷发放和回收，此间经历让读者感受到问卷调查操作起来遇到的诸多困难。本书作者指出，“尽管如此，回收的调查问卷有足够的数据来提供有用的资料性信息”。本书作者也指出问卷调查存在的局限：“因为两个问卷调查都依赖自我报告的数据，局限性包括归因（把积极的措施归因于自己的机构）以及夸张（表现出比实际可能更有意义的结果）。”

第八章　全球辅警

本书作者开篇再次提醒读者，在使用辅警方面，全世界政府和警务机构既有相似性也有差异性，而且再次指出各地定义“志愿者”存在差异。本书作者列出定义“志愿者”涉及的三个疑问，提醒读者给“志愿者”下定义不是一件简单的事情。

然后，本书作者依次向读者描述了下列国家或地区的辅警：

“英国特别警员”

“伦敦城的特别警察队”

“奥兰治县（佛罗里达州）县治安官办公室的后备警察”

“纽约市警察局的协警”

“加利福尼亚州后备警察”

“以色列国民卫队”

“爱尔兰共和国辅警后备处”

“匈牙利国民卫队”

“百慕大后备警察”

“俄罗斯哥萨克人”

“多伦多协警”

“哈密尔顿警察局协警”

“中国香港辅警队”

“新加坡志愿特别警员队”

“泰国普吉岛旅游辅警”

“马来西亚警察志愿后备队”

“南非后备警察队”

在本章最后的“结论”部分，本书作者还简单介绍了韩国辅警、（英属）开曼群岛的皇家警察局后备辅助人员和特别警员、荷兰辅警、巴哈马皇家警察局后备队、百慕大后备警察以及西澳大利亚辅警部门。

第九章　辅警的未来发展

本章的论述框架如下：

美国辅警的未来

　　地方控制和国家控制

选拔

培训

使用前全职职员做辅警

关于辅警项目以及参与者的年度数据

英国辅警的未来

英国警务的现状

特别警员的看法以及对特别警员的看法

网络犯罪

有关辅警的其他问题

下班后和晚间角色

新技术以及装备开销

结论

其中，在关于美国辅警未来的“地方控制和国家控制”部分，本书作者指出，鉴于美国警察体制的高度分散性这一“现实造成的障碍存在一个大家都熟知的问题：全美对待辅警身份宣誓警察的方式有太多不同，以至于无法制定一项在所有司法管辖区域、在所有州以及对所有当选的县治安官都适用的单一政策建议”。本书作者告诉我们，本书作者之一的沃尔夫和其他两位学者在2015年提出建议，“现在需要标准化，至少应根据辅警的职能确定他们的称谓”。三位学者将辅警分为5个级别：级别1、级别2、级别3、级别4、级别5。确立一个全国分类体系的作用是，这“将会使地方警察和县治安官办公室对其希望辅警能够去做的事情可以保持地方控制，而且将会为讨论那些在各种‘级别’上提供服务的人员的职权时，创造一个全国通用的术语”。

第一章　引论：界定辅警

P1

1999年，莫比指出比较研究存在概念界定问题。本书虽然不像贝利研究日本那样需要翻译（Bayley，1976；参见 Mawby，1999），但是的确需要解释术语，借此让一地的读者与另一地的读者有一个“平等的基础”。所以，尽管从表面上看，在世界范围内每一个司法区域的辅警看起来都能自圆其说，但是界定术语的工作表明，各地有不同定义，而且辅警作为一个概念千差万别。虽然本书从头至尾都存在解释诸多术语的必要，但是“辅警”是核心术语，需要在一开始就对其加以界定。为了介绍“志愿者”“警察”和“辅警”这些术语的概念，每一部分都以引用文献开头，被引用的文献都是以往各界试图给这些术语进行的界定。

志愿者

志愿行为（英格兰和威尔士）

我们给志愿行为下的定义是：任何需要花费时间、没有报酬去做一些以造福环境或者某一人（个体或群体），而不是以近亲属为目标的活动。这一概念的关键之处在于，志愿行为必须是每一个人自愿作出的选择。

（National Council for Voluntary Organisations，n. d.）

（一）个人致力于花费时间、没有报酬（交通费和其他被审定的计划外开销除外）去做一些以造福第三方，而不是以近亲属为目标的活动。

（Legislation. gov. uk，n. d.）

P2

志愿行为（美国）

众多关于志愿行为的定义不包括可能对志愿者家庭或者朋友有益的活动，尽管不清楚志愿者的工作与为陌生人所做的同样工作有何区别。

（Carson，2000，p. 68）

（一位）妇女通过当地的剧院教儿童们表演，可能被视为志愿者；相反，一位妇女自己为邻居儿童们组织垒球比赛，就调查而言，她可能不被算作志愿者。

（Boraas，2003，p. 11）

做志愿者就是选择为满足需要而行动，具有社会责任感而且不考虑金钱上的回报，其所做超越个人基本义务。

（Ellis & Noyes，1990，p. 4）

志愿行为（联合国）

志愿行为、志愿服务以及志愿活动这些术语指的是……为普通大众的利益自愿从事的，且金钱奖励不是主要激励因素的各种活动。

（United Nations Volunteers，2015，p. xxiii）

心理学家们很难理解为什么有些人为某些费力的事情自愿奉献自己的时间，而其他人不这样做。2015 年，全球有超过 10 亿人自愿为他们的社区提供服务（United Nations Volunteers，2015），然而，究竟是什么激发他们这样做一直令人费解（Stukas，Snyder & Clary，1999；参见 Krebs & Miller，1985）。[①] 因为对不同的文化、社区和人们来说，“志愿者”这一术语已经被用于指代不同的事物，而且在不同的学术研究中，该术语的使用方法各异，所以很难决定一个人的付出怎样可以被视为或不可以被视为志愿服务（Stukas et al.，1999）。一个人按要求参加志愿服务可以被视为志愿者吗？例如，如果一所学校或大学要求学生为社区提供志愿服务，以便学生获得一些毕业所需的学分，那么这是真正的志愿服务吗？

定义中另一个令人困惑的方面是，许多人把志愿服务等同于没有任何报酬的工作。如果有人自愿参加一项通常是必需的工作，那么这还是志愿服务吗？例如，美国和英国的军队全部都是由“志愿者”组成的。这意味着没有人是被迫参军的，即如果他们不想参军，那么他们就可以不参军。然而，美国军事人员履职是有报酬的（很多人可能会说他们的工资不够多）。世界上其他一些国家要求他们的公民在达到某一年龄时，提供某些社会服务，如与军队、警察一起工作或者参与紧急状态应对工作。一旦公民完成这一义务，公民可以在同一服务领域继续做兼职志愿者并为贡献的时间得到报酬。这是志愿服务吗？美国和英国的警察部门都可以给参与警务工作的志愿者们提供某一特权，这可以是报销交通费、报销装备费、一份肉食补贴，或者时间津贴。如果这笔资金的额度远低于付给提供相同服务的全职雇员可能获得的报酬，那么这还是志愿服务吗，或者他们收取任何报酬这一事实否定了其付出的志愿性质？

最后，正如在上面引文中提到的，志愿服务有可能发生在它不是一个有组织活动的组成部分的时候。例如，公民可以自己决定黄昏时分在居民区里走动并向警察报告任何可疑活动。尽管个人在居民区走动以及用电话或通过互联网向警方反映问题花费的时间，可以被认为是他们用于志愿服务的时间，但它不是官方行为。这不是警务志愿者的例子。然而，一个人参加邻里守望组织，采取相同的举动，可能被认为是警务志愿者。

联合国报告说，全世界关于志愿服务的术语、类别以及定义，已经使项目评估变得困难，亦使对志愿服务对各国政府和民间组织的影响的评估变得困难（United Nations Volunteers，2015）。通过采用埃利斯和诺叶思（Ellis& Noyes，1990）给志愿服务下的定义，志愿者的行为具有“社会责任感”且超越“个人基本义务”（Ellis & Noyes，1990，p. 4）。从本书目标考虑，我们采用下面这个定义界定术语“志愿者”。我们将讨论全世界范围内警务中其他类型的志愿服务，而在我们偏离这个定义的地方，我们会明确指出。

志愿者：个人为一个官方承认的组织或者政府部门奉献时间，没有因他或她提供服务而获得可观的报酬，或者没有受到强制要求。

不过，术语“志愿者”不应与术语“业余爱好者”混淆。一名业余爱好者可能不是一个受过训练的人，或者可能不是一个技艺高超的人，或者可能不是一个像非业余爱好者那样的专业人员。虽然一些参与警务工作的志愿者们可能没有获得与他们的全职同事相同的培训，但他们中许多人与那些在这些岗位上全职服务的同事一样，受过良好的培训，得到认可，并且获得高度评价（Carson，2000）。

警务

警务（英格兰和威尔士）

在整个英格兰和威尔士，警方基本上不被视为狭义上个人安全的提供者，而是犯罪和平安的责任人。警方不是社会平安和秩序“守护者”的象征，而是社区价值和非正式社会控制的责任人。

（Jackson & Bradford，2009，p. 2）

对“什么是警务?”这一问题的简单回答是：警务即警察所做之事。

（Waddington，1999，p. 1）

警务（美国）

通过改革，我们的警务系统必须要明确的不仅仅是警方的角色与责任，还有社区的角色与责任……社区参与警务系统的程度以及每个社区成员通过协助警方以及与警方合作所承担的个人责任程度，极大地影响着这个系统的成效。

（Davis，2016）

警察必须做的决定有政治方面的、社会方面的以及心理方面的，而且受美国社会性质的影响非常大。

（Remington，1965，p. 361）

上述对警务的描述，每一个都是由相关领域的知名学者和专家们给出的，呈现出非常不同的解释，但是又都是合理的。自从学界开始研究警务，就很难界定这个概念。对一些人来说，警务是积极对社会使用法律、给民众提供秩序、强调制定可接受的行为规范和标准的一种社会作用（Row，2014）；对另外一些人来说，警务是政府的延伸，试图干预他们的生活并且剥夺他们的自由。

对（良好和公平）警务的广泛理解仍然存在于美国宪法关于警察权力的信条之中。其中，美国最高法院明确认为警务包括治理任务。

（Walker，2011，p. 578）

不论一个人怎样看待警务，该术语在历史上直到晚近时期才与特定政府机构产生关联。希腊文 *polis* 和拉丁文 *politia* 共同指代国家，然而，到 18 世纪初，*la police* 和 *die Polizei* 被用于解释内部行政、监控以及保护领土（Rowe，2014）。在我们进一步深入本研究之前，我们或许得指出，“警务”这个词语的现代词意，不仅在不同国家里词意不同，而且在同一个国家内词意也不同。

P5

克劳福德的警务定义（Crawford，2003；参见 Reiner，2000）明确指出，“警务”行为实施的方式既是正式的，也是非正式的；例如，过路人通常通过自然监视实施非正式警务，其方式与警察局成员在日常巡逻中的方式大致相同。然而，就“警方”而言，这样的监视就是正式的，但是二者都是“警务”的例子。

保安和商店里负责抓小偷的雇员在英国和美国都是在实施“警务”，这些人没有普通公民权以外的逮捕权，但是那些身着制服现身的人能起到威慑作用，而且商店负责抓小偷的雇员还通过监控实施警务。戴维斯（Davis，2016）认为不能把警方从他们服务的社区分离开来，他还说这就“好比把病患与卫生保健系统分离开来，或者说好比把学生与教育系统分离开来”。社区参与警务系统的程度，是本书的基础，极大地影响着警方工作的效果（Davis，2016）。

警务，经常被视为政府的一个职能，同样能够被私人实体实施。尽管一个私人保安的作用可能很容易与一个公共警察的作用区别开来，但是在美国的一些司法管辖区域，二者之间的区别不那么容易被确定。美国的一些州允许某些私人实体雇用个人做私人警察；他们受私人资助，但是获得公开认证，拥有宣誓/正当执法权（MacDonald，Klick& Grunwald，2015）。私人警察力量已经成为美国历史的一部分，这从 19 世纪初期就开始了，当时的居民愿意付费给个人或者组织，去巡逻他们的居民区并保护个体经济（Stringham，2015）。例如，当今的弗吉尼亚州法律允许公民私人向法院请愿获得下列职权：携带枪支、佩戴徽章以及实施逮捕，只需接受有限的训练。这些弗吉尼亚州的治安特别保护员（SCOP，Special Conservators of the Peace）在商业区和居民区巡逻，受到松散管理，而且可以在法律上被自行认定为“警察”（Jouvenal，2015）。

人们可以在下列情形中发现警务商业化的一种不同类型，即“通过签订正式的合同协议以及从自愿付钱的消费者那里……警方收钱提供服务，依法采取行动”（Mulone，2011，p. 166）。美国的私人组织能够与警务机构签订提供私人安保服务的合同。这些私人组织处在两个“保护伞”的保护之下：法律和提供给政府警察的职权。不过，这种类型的警务被视为一种实践，在美国是合法、合理的，所以可以被认为是警务一般定义的一部分。警务的这种私有化产生了诸多问题，超出了本书的范围，但是的确可能会对辅警有影响。正如本书稍后将讨论的，辅警在某些司法管辖区域参与这种类型的“下班后工作”或者“晚间或周末第二份职业”。穆龙（Mulone，2011）对这种类型的警务提出诸多重要问题。警察组织应该采纳什么样的规定和政策去保障提供的服务合乎伦理？在这种私人警务类型中的警察的活动与通常警察工作怎样加以区别？这种私人警务类型会不会导致私人警察数量上升，“其目的仅为富人而已”（Mulone，2011，p. 178）？

为了澄清这一点，下面这个定义就是本书采用的术语“警察”的定义。我们将讨论全世界范围内其他类型的警务，而在我们偏离这个定义的地方，我们会明确指出。

警察：个人直接为政府部门工作且经合法授权拥有预防、侦查和处罚犯罪活动以及维护公共秩序的权力。

因为在美国，作为执法官员的“警察”和“县治安官”，二者之间存在差异，术语“警察”可能仍会引起歧义。本书中术语“警察”将同样包括县治安官办公室的职责，尽管不是所有美国的县治安官办公室的基本职责都是执法职能。这个定义同样能够包括英国警察部门，基于他们在自己政府的警察组织中扮演的角色。尽管术语“执法官员”可能看上去更笼统，因而是一个更合适的术语，但是英格兰和威尔士的警察通常不认为他们的基本职能是执法。

虽然许多围绕全职警察的组织和文化问题对辅警来说同样存在，但是这些问题可能有很大不同。在过去几十年里，学界一直在研究警务中的一个问题，即警察的合法性问题。对这一问题的开创性研究是从泰勒开始的（Tyler，1990）。感觉受到警方不公正对待的人们，更有可能质疑程序的公正性、刑事司法程序和职业的合法性，因而更不可能遵从规章、法律和条例（Tyler，1990；参见 Tankebe，Reisig& Wang，2016）。警察应该执法，但是要在其职权范围内执法，警用资源的分配应该是合理的，而且应该被公平分发。泰勒（Tyler，1990）发
P7 现：公民在偶遇警察时关注的是尊重、礼貌和尊严；常见的警察与公民之间的偶遇，即便时间短暂，同样能够建立或者挑战社区和个人对警方的看法，进而是对警察合法性的看法（参见 Tankebe et al.，2016；Reisig，Bratton& Gertz，2007）。社区内一名警察或者一个警察机构的合法性程度，能够影响社区与警方协作的程度，即便警方已经掌握了已知的包括个体低自制力在内的犯罪活动预测因素（Tankebe et al.，2016）。

合法性对警务的作用至关重要（Mulone，2016），而且迄今众多公民分不清全职警察和辅警。对辅警来说，关键是要在使用他们的社区内保证他们的合法性。美国和英国在过去十年中，共同经历了一个崭新的警务合法性时期，而且警察非常清楚当今技术世界的新变化。质疑警察行为的问题不仅出现在全职警察身上，任何人假借政府职权所做的可疑举动，都经常给职业中其他每一个人招致严厉批评。对警务的看法能够影响到公民对警方的态度，影响到警察组织的效率。“我希望，通过激发公民的信任，以更公平的领导方式来塑造公平警务”（Van Craen，2016，p. 8）。如果说辅警是警察组织和公民社会之间的桥梁，一个潜在的结果就是：对辅警组织、警察局和政府来说，警察的合法性之感更强。

辅警

界定“志愿者”和“警察”为本书打下了坚实的基础。但是至关重要的是，我们要意识到将两个术语结合起来制造出来的新术语，甚至更难界定清楚，因为要跨越不同文化、语言、联合体、国家和地方司法管辖区域。尽管一些志愿者们可以被明确地称为“辅警”，如英格兰和威尔士的特别警员（SCs，special constables），或者加利福尼亚州、得克萨斯州或者佛罗里达州的后备警察，但是在这些司法管辖区域和其他任何地方都存在没有全部警察权力的志愿者。本书将在后面讨论纽约市警察局（NYPD，New York City Police Department）的协警。不过，纽约市警察局的协警受到严格的职权限制，使其不太像警察，倒更像公民志愿者。同样的情况出现在英国的支援警察志愿者（PSVs，police support volunteers）身上。支援警察志愿者是一种志愿服务类型，最近在英国全国范围内呈现人数扩大的情况。这些志愿者协助警方，但是没有警察权。反过来，有一些个人可能被视为拥有全部警察职权，但是不符合上面给出的志愿者的定义：个人可以当警察去提供少于全职警察的服务，但是因为提供服务获得了可观的报酬。

鉴于整个美国和英国在警务中使用志愿者的情况已经普遍存在，明确界定与志愿者发挥作用有关的关键术语已经变得日益困难。界定英国的“特别警员”很容易，尽管在过去十年内他们的职责已经扩展了。一名特别警员，或者说“特勤”，是英国某一警察局的一名志愿性质的成员，他或她拥有逮捕和侦查犯罪活动的职权。特别警员没有因为提供服务获得报酬，但他们可以报销差旅费和饭费。历史上，特别警员只在其警察局的司法管辖区域里拥有执法权，由警察局局长授权。然而，随着2012年英国女王伊丽莎白二世登基六十周年庆、2012年伦敦奥运会以及2010年和2011年伦敦骚乱的发生，特别警员的权力得到了扩展，扩展范围包括英格兰和威尔士全境。

正如我们将在本书中进一步讨论的，术语“协警”和“后备警察”经常被互换使用，而且每一个定义都可以包含拥有全部或者部分警察权力的、可以或者不可以履行警察职能的官员。格林伯格（Greenberg，2005）选择将美国的“协警”和“后备警察”两个定义合并，提出“辅警”这个概念。格林伯格（Greenberg，2005）这样界定辅警：

一个常设机构（或者一个在战时动员期间建立的机构）的成员，或由政府行为授权或由社会行为授权，目的是以公开的方式履行一个或多个警务功能（超出监控或沟通工作的功能），获得极低的薪水或者没有薪水。

这个定义可以适应不同司法管辖区域使用警察志愿者的各种可能方式，而且还考虑到一些志愿者实际上可能接受一些各种名义的经济支持，作为他们参与警务工作的交换。这个定义不包括试图与警察产生关联的有组织团体，所以，类似于“护卫天使”或“妈妈反对醉酒驾车（MADD，Mothers Against Drunk Driving）”这样的团体不可能被视为辅警，即便他们声称或者表现出具有警务功能或者与警察有关的功能。但是，辅警不能与术语“警察局里的志愿者（VIPS，Volunteers in Police Service）”（简称“警局志愿者”）相混淆。警局志愿者是志愿者的一种，受到国际警察局长协会（IACP，the International Association of Chiefs of Police）的追踪，而且获得司法协助局和司法部的资助。警局志愿者项目将志愿者安排在各种岗位以帮助警察机构。警局志愿者包括后备警察和协警，还包括从事接待和文件处理的志愿者，以及参与包括邻里守望、公民巡逻和儿童平安 ID 计划在内的很多计划的志愿者（Godshall，2009）。这些志愿者在警察机构内工作，全都做着各种必要的但又常常吃力不讨好的工作，可是根据上述格林伯格的定义，他们不一定是“辅警”。

P9

然而，即便是术语“辅警”，对警察机构内部履行类似职责的、众多相似种类的职员，也不能面面俱到。“警察探险家”是一个童子军小组，可以履行辅助的执法功能，如搜集停车场信息、仪仗队信息，实施小规模交通指挥或者场地安保工作，因此看上去符合上文给出的辅警定义。“警察探险家”经常配发与警服类似的制服（不过通常有一些明显的区别），而且对一个不经意的观察者来说，他们看上去是十分年轻的警员（“警察探险家”成员的最大年龄为 21 岁）。警察实习生，通常是大学学生，他们在一个警察机构里做“志愿者”，看上去也符合上文给出的辅警定义。众多警察实习生没有因付出时间获得任何报酬，但他们经常参与侦查、撰写报告以及其他似乎使他们符合格林伯格定义的任务。从本书目标考虑，下面这个定义就是给术语“辅警”的界定。我们将讨论全世界范围内警务中其他类型的辅警，而在我们偏离这个定义的地方，我们会明确指出。

辅警：个人直接为一个政府部门工作，并经授权拥有预防、侦查和处罚犯罪活动以及维护公共秩序的合法权力，其从事上述工作未受到强制要求亦未因此获得可观的报酬。

全美警察机构设置辅警部门成员的权力、职权、工作职责以及职能的方法各式各样。纽约市警察局的协警部门使用辅警的一种方式，可以作为例子。纽约市警察局的协警部门有大约 4500 名辅警；本书已经提到这个部门，并将在本书第八章对其进行深入探讨。纽约市警察局的协警没有逮捕权，被安排在街面用于震慑犯罪，实施小规模交通控制，而且被用作公共关系资源，而不是警察权力的补充。然而，在使用辅警方面与纽约市警察局使用协警方法截然相反的城市是加利福尼亚州的洛杉矶市。洛杉矶市使用的志愿后备警察大约有 650 名，他们已经确定了培训要求而且和全职警察有同样的职责和职能，包括逮捕权。整个美国，这里那里的机构都在使用自己的后备警察或协警（Dobrin & Wolf，2016；Wolf， P10
Albrecht& Dobrin，2015）。

在英格兰和威尔士，警察局里的志愿服务是由一些没有工资的个人来做的，而特别警员拥有与他们的正规警察同事一样的权力，而且根据每个警察局所在的地域，特别警员可以承担广泛的职责（目前不包括需要配枪的岗位）。英国警察机构会使用志愿性质的特别警员，在整个英格兰、威尔士和苏格兰的警察局里，志愿性质的特别警员以不配枪、获得认证的警察身份提供服务。虽然他们被授予了相同的权力，像他们的全职同事一样维护法律，但是他们明显缺乏基本训练。特别警员经常以团队形式工作，不是与其他特别警员一起工作，就是与全职警察一起工作，但是他们还可以被批准单独巡逻（Wolf，Pepper& Dobrin，2016；Seth，2006）。

现在有多少辅警？

尽管许多美国警察机构和组织使用志愿者、后备警察和协警，但是美国辅警部门的精确数字以及辅警的人数仍然未知（Berg& Doerner，1988；Kakalik & Wildhorn，1971）。然而，最近多布林和沃尔夫（Dobrin& Wolf，2016）使用美国司法部提供的数据，得出的数字是：拥有宣誓警察权的后备警察或协警以及县治安官助理大约有 58500 名；拥有有限权力的后备警察和协警以及县治安官助理 P11
大约有 19000 名。二者合计，共有超过 77500 名公民志愿者在美国以辅警身份工作，即在 404000 名全职执法官员中，大约占比 20%（Dobrin& Wolf，2016）。[2]在美国辅警中，一些人拥有执法权，本书将在后文讨论这个问题，而另一些人没有执法权。沃尔夫、霍尔摩斯和乔恩思（Wolf，Holmes& Jones，2016）报告说，在一个关于美国县治安官办公室后备警察的研究中，答卷人指出，他们被指派的任务大多数与指派给全职执法警察的任务是一样的。

在英格兰和威尔士，大约有 17000 名特别警员，即在 125000 名全职警察中，大约有 14%的特别警员。因为英国的警察通常没有配枪，仅有某些经过特别训练的正规警察可以配枪，所以特别警员目前未获允许或者未经授权成为配枪人员。

本书将要考察英国和美国辅警的历史和职能，但同时将采用来自其他地方的案例研究来展示全世界的不同之处和相似之处。这些地方包括前英国殖民地，如新加坡，还有英对中国香港进行殖民统治时期的辅警制度，而且不是所有这些地方都完全符合我们在上文给出的定义。本书也将讨论这些地方使用辅警以及它们与美国和英国使用辅警的相似之处和不同之处。另外，本书还将考察志愿者在那些基本被视为政府服务的职能中发挥的作用。本书也将考察辅警在社区导向警
P12 务、旅游导向警务、情报导向警务以及问题导向警务中发挥的作用。

注释

①克莱瑞等人（Clary et al.，1998）开发了一个测量工具来收集人们当志愿者的功能动机的数据，这个测量工具名为志愿者功能量表（VFI，the Volunteer Function Inventory）。志愿者功能量表是一个有着 30 个题目的调查，用以收集个人选择志愿服务的功能动机。测量维度被分为六个动机要素：自我保护、价值表达、职业发展、社会交往、学习理解以及自我提升。该测量工具已经被用于分析对比那些被要求提供“志愿服务”之人的动机和那些没有受此要求之人的动机。克莱瑞等人的发现表明，许多履行志愿者职责的人这样做是为了实现多种动机（Stukas et al.，1999）。

②有意思的是，这里由多布林和沃尔夫（Dobrin & Wolf，2016）报告的美国宣誓辅警的人数与赫德隆德和布尔科（Hedlund & Burke，2006）计算的数字有巨大差异。赫德隆德和布尔科报告说美国可能有多达 400000 名后备警察，但是他俩的数据来源于后备警察协会，而这个组织现在已经不存在了，没有办法判定这个数字是怎么来的。德姆普瑟和福斯特（Dempsey & Forst，2007）在自己的著作里使用了赫德隆德和布尔科的数据，这有可能是一个被严重高估的数据。

参考文献

Bayley，D. H.（1976）（贝利）. Forces of Order：Policing Modern Japan（《秩序之师：维护现代日本治安》）. Berkeley，CA：University of California Press（伯

克利，加利福尼亚州：加利福尼亚大学出版社）.

Berg, B. L., & Doerner, W. G. （1988）（伯格和多尔奈尔）. Volunteer police officers：An unexamined personnel dimension in law enforcement（《辅警：未经审查的执法人员》）. *American Journal of Police*（《美国警察》）, 7（1）, 81—89.

Boraas, S. （2003）（包拉斯）. Volunteerism in the United States（《美国志愿服务》）. *Monthly Labor Review*（《劳动评论月刊》）, 126（8）, 3—11.

Carson, E. （2000）（卡尔森）. On defining and measuring volunteering in the United States and abroad（《美国及他国志愿行为界定和评价研究》）. *Law and Contemporary Problems*（《法律与当代问题》）, 62（4）, 67—71.

Clary, E. G., Snyder, M, Ridge, R. D., Copeland, J., Stukas, A. A., Haugen, J., Meine, P. （1998）（克莱瑞、斯尼德尔、瑞德格、科佩兰德、司徒卡思、海于根和梅纳）. Understanding and assessing the motivations of volunteers：A functional approach（《理解、评估志愿者的动机：一个有用的方法》）. *Journal of Personality and Social Psychology*（《人格与社会心理学》）, 74（6）, 1516—1530.

Crawford, A. （2003）（克劳福德）. The pattern of policing in the UK：Policing beyond the police（《英国警务模式：警方之外的警务》）, in T. Newburn（Ed.）（牛博恩主编）, *Handbook of Policing*（《警务手册》）, pp. 136—168. Cullompton, UK：Willan Publishing（卡伦顿，英国：威兰出版社）.

Davis, R. L. （2016）（戴维斯）. Police reform vs. policing reform（《警察改革和警务改革》）. *Community Policing Dispatch*（《社区警务调度》）, 9（8）. 2017年8月12日检索网址 https：//cops. usdoij. gov/html/dispatch/08-2016/police_reform. asp.

Dempsey, J. S., Forst, L. S. （2007）（德姆普瑟和福斯特）. *Police*, 2nd Edition（《警察》第二版）. Boston：Cengage（波士顿：圣智出版公司）.

Dobrin, A., & Wolf, R. （2016）（多布林和沃尔夫）. What we know and what we don't know about volunteer policing in the United States（《我们知道的以及我们不知道的美国辅警管理》）. *International Journal of police Science and Management*（《警察科学与管理国际期刊》）, 18（3）220—227.

Ellis, S. J., & Noyes, K. H. （1990）（埃利斯和诺叶思）. *By the people：A history of Americans as volunteers*（《民治：美国志愿者历史》）. San Francisco：

P13

Jossey-Bass（旧金山：巴斯出版社）.

Godshall, S. L. （2009）（高德沙尔）. Engaging volunteers in your law enforcement agency：The Volunteers in Police Service（VIPS）program（《在你的执法机构做志愿者：警察局里的志愿者项目》）. *Sheriff*（*September/October*）（《县治安官》九月/十月）, 48—52.

Greenberg, M. A. （2005）（格林伯格）. *Citizens defending America*：*From colonial times to the age of terrorism*（《保卫美国的公民：从殖民地时代到恐怖主义年代》）. Pittsburgh：University of Pittsburgh Press（匹兹堡：匹兹堡大学出版社）.

Hedlund, K. , & Burke, T. W. （2006）（赫德隆德和布尔科）. Reserve officers：A valuable resource（《后备警察：一个宝贵的资源》）. *FBI Law Enforcement Bulletin*（《美国联邦调查局执法公报》）, 75（12）, 11—15.

Jackson, J. , & Bradford, B. （2009）（杰克逊和布拉德福德）. Crime, policing and social order：On the expressive nature of public confidence in policing（《犯罪、警务与社会秩序：论警务公信力的表现性》）. *British Journal of Sociology*（《英国社会学》）, 60（3）493—521.

Jouvenal, J. （2015, February 28）（乔维纳尔，2015 年 2 月 28 日）. Private police carry guns and make arrests, and their ranks are swelling（《私人警察携带手枪并实施逮捕，而且他们的队伍在不断壮大》）. *The Washington Post*（《华盛顿邮报》）. 2017 年 8 月 12 日检索网址 www. washingtonpost. com/local/crime/private-police-carry-guns-and-makearrests-and-their-ranks-are-swelling/2015/02/28/29f6e02e - 8f79 - 11e4 - a900 - 9960214d4cd7 _ story. html？ utm _ term =. 8d9853f5e911.

Kakalik, J. S. , & Wildhorn, S. （1971）（卡卡力克和维尔德霍恩）. *Special-purpose public police*（《特种公共警察》）. Santa Monica, CA：Rand Corporation（圣莫妮卡，加利福尼亚州：兰德公司）.

Krebs, D. L. , Miller, D. T. （1985）（克雷博斯和米勒）. Altruism and aggression（《利他主义和挑衅》）. In G. Lindzey & E. Aronson（Eds.）（林德泽和阿龙森主编）, *Handbook of social psychology*, Volume 2, 3rd Edition（《社会心理学手册》第二卷，第三版）, pp. 1—71. New York：Random House（纽约：兰登书屋集团公司）.

Legislation. gov. uk（n. d.）（日期不详）. The Police Act 1997（Criminal Records）Regulations 2002（《1997 年〈警察法案〉〈犯罪记录〉2002 款》）. 2017 年 8 月 12 日检索网址 www. legislation. gov. uk/uksi/2002/233/regulation/2/made.

MacDonald, J. M., Klick, J., & Grunwald, B. (2015)（马克唐纳、克里克和格伦沃德）. The effect of private police on crime: Evidence from a geographic regression discontinuity design（《私人警察对犯罪的影响：来自地理回归不连续性设计的证据》）. *Journal of the Royal Statistical Society*（《英国皇家社会统计学》）, 179 (3), 831—846.

Mawby, R. L. (1999)（莫比）. *Policing across the world: Issues for the twenty-first century*（《世界警务：二十一世纪面临的问题》）. Abingdon, UK: Routledge（阿宾登，英国：劳特利奇出版公司）.

Mulone, M. (2011)（穆龙）. When private and public policing merge: Thoughts on commercial policing（《当私人警务与公共警务融合的时候：对商业警务的思考》）. *Social Justice*（《社会正义》）, 38 (1/2), 165—183.

Mulone, M. (2016)（穆龙）. The politics of private policing: No force and no legitimacy（《私人警务中的政治：无武力无合法性》）. In M. Deflem (Ed.)（德富勒姆主编）, *The politics of policing: Between force and legitimacy*（《警务中的政治：在武力与合法性之间》）, pp. 277—294. Bingley, UK: Emerald Group Publishing（宾利，英国：翡翠集团出版公司）.

National Council for Voluntary Organisations（n. d.）（志愿组织全国委员会〈日期不详〉）. Volunteering（“志愿行为”）. NCVO（志愿组织全国委员会）. 2017 年 8 月 12 日检索网址 www. ncvo. org. uk/policy-and-research/volunteering-policy.

Reiner, R. (2000)（雷纳尔）. The Politics of the Police, 3rd Edition（《警察中的政治》，第三版）. Oxford: Oxford University Press（牛津：牛津大学出版社）.

Reisig, M. D., Bratton, J., & Gertz, M. (2007)（雷思国、布莱顿和戈尔茨）. The construct validity and refinement of process-based policing measures（《过程型警务措施的结构效度与精细化研究》）. *Criminal Justice and Behavior*（《刑事司法与行为》）, 34 (8), 1005—1028.

Remington, E. J. (1965)（雷明顿）. The role of police in a democratic society

（《民主社会的警察角色》）. *Journal of Criminal Law and Criminology*（《刑法与犯罪学》），56（3），361—365.

Rowe, M. （2014）（罗维）. *Introduction to policing*, *2nd Edition*（《警务概论》第二版）. London：Sage（伦敦：赛格公司）.

Seth, R. （2006）（赛斯）. The specials（《特别警员》）. *Trowbridge*, UK：Cromwell Press（特洛布里奇，英国：克伦威尔出版社）.

Stringham, E. （2015）（斯特灵海姆）. San Francisco's private police force（《旧金山的私人警察力量》）. *Reason*（《探因》），47（4），48—54.

Stukas, A. A., Snyder, M., & Clary, E. G. （1999）（司徒卡思，斯尼德尔和克莱瑞）. The effects of "mandatory volunteerism" on intentions to volunteer（《强制性志愿服务"对志愿服务意图的影响》）. *Psychological Science*（《心理科学》），10（1），59—64.

Tankebe, J., Reisig, M. D., & Wang X. （2016）（唐克柏、雷思国和王）. A multidimensional model of police legitimacy：A cross-cultural assessment（《警察合法性的多维模型：跨文化评估》）. *Law and Human Behavior*（《法律与人类行为》），40（1），11—22.

Tyler, T. R. （1990）（泰勒）. *Why people obey the law*（《人们为什遵守法律》）. New Haven, CT：Yale University Press（纽黑文，康涅狄格州：耶鲁大学出版社）.

United Nations Volunteers（2015）（联合国志愿者）. 2015 *state of the world's volunteerism report*：*Transforming governance*（《2015 年世界志愿服务现状报告：转变治理》）. Washington, DC：United Nations Volunteers（华盛顿特区：联合国志愿者）. 2017 年 8 月 12 日检索网址 www. unv. org/sites/default/files/2015%20State% 20of% 20the% 20 World% 27s% 20Volunteerism% 20Report% 20%20Transforming%20Governance. pdf.

Van Craen, M. （2016）（冯·克莱恩）. Fair policing from the inside out（《由内而外的公正治安》）. In M. Deflem（Ed.）（德富勒姆主编）, *The politics of policing*：*Between force and legitimacy*（《警务中的政治：在武力与合法性之间》）, pp. 3-20. Bingley, UK：Emerald Group Publishing（宾利，英国：翡翠集团出版公司）.

Waddington, P. A. J. （1999）（沃丁顿）. *Policing citizens*（《护卫民众》）.

Abingdon，UK：Routledge（阿宾登，英国：劳特利奇出版公司）.

Walker，A.（2011）（沃克）. Racial profiling-separate and unequal keeping the minorities in line：The role of law enforcement in America（《种族成见论——分裂及不公正对待少数族裔：美国执法作用》）. *St. Thomas Law review*（《圣托马斯法律评论》），23（4），576—619.

Wolf，R.，Albrecht，J.，& Dobrin，A.（2015）（沃尔夫、阿尔布雷希特和多布林）. Reserve policing in the United States：Citizens volunteering for public service（《美国后备警察管理：公民志愿参与公共服务》）. *The Police Chief*（《警察局长》），82（10），38—47.

Wolf，R.，Holmes，S. T.，& Jones，C.（2016）（沃尔夫、赫尔摩斯和乔恩思）. Utilization and satisfaction of volunteer law enforcement officers in the office of the American sheriff：An exploratory nationwide study（《美国县治安官办公室志愿性质执法官员的使用及其满意度：一项全国性研究》）. *Police Practice and Research：An International Journal*（《警察实践与研究：国际期刊》），17（5），448—462.

Wolf，R.，Pepper，I. K.，& Dobrin，A.（2017）（沃尔夫、帕珀和多布林）. An exploratory international comparison of professional confidence in volunteer policing（《辅警职业自信心的国际比较研究》）. *The Police Journal：Theory，Practice and Principles*（《警察学报：理论、实践与原则》），90（2），91106.

P15

第二章　辅警的作用

2011 年 3 月 20 日，佛罗里达农业与机械大学（FAMU，Florida Agricultural and Mechanical University）行进乐队指挥罗伯特·钱皮恩被发现失去意识，当时他在乐队的大客车上，该车停在奥兰多旅游区一个繁忙的旅馆外面。该案迅速成为美国全国性新闻，媒体报道了一个年轻生命被欺凌仪式[1]终结的悲剧以及行进乐队根深蒂固的欺凌文化。然而，新闻里永远不会报道的事实是，第一个作出反应到达事发现场的穿着制服的执法官员们——那些对钱皮恩先生做口对口人工呼吸和心肺复苏术以努力挽救其生命，然后对事发现场展开初步调查以及受调度员指派应对紧急呼叫的执法官员们——县治安官办公室非全职的、无报酬的雇员。尽管他们驾驶着喷有县治安官办公室标识的轿车，穿着与县治安官办公室的全职助理相同的制服，佩戴徽章并携带随身武器，是宣誓执法官员，但是他们实际上是志愿性质的后备警察助理。这两名志愿者都是从奥兰治县县治安官办公室（OCSO，Orange County Sheriff's Office）全职岗位退休的人员，当时正以后备警察的身份工作。在离开县治安官办公室全职岗位后，后备警察队队长提姆·伍德就到奥兰多县一所私立大学的私营机构做安全主管，然后又在一个可以说是美国最大的会议中心做安全主管。后备警察助理石提武·布莱克顿在县治安官办公室工作很长时间后退休，当时正在享受退休时光，以顾问身份工作。两个人在那晚都穿着制服，在一场足球比赛后，作为志愿者在旅游区内工作。而佛罗里达农业与机械大学行进乐队在该足球比赛上进行了表演。[2]

2012 年 1 月初，上百名加利福尼亚州的执法官员在搜寻一名在洛杉矶市好莱坞西区制造系列纵火案的嫌疑人。后备警察助理塞尔文·拉雷扎里，一名全职比佛利山地产律师，自愿在一个八小时的志愿轮班结束后继续加班加点工作，并注
P16 意到一辆厢式货车司机与监控视频里纵火犯影像匹配。拉雷扎里当时刚刚完成他的实战培训项目，这使他获得单独一人巡逻的许可。那天他工作时，恰好是他第

四个单独巡逻轮班。他叫停该车并且在交通站对之进行调查，之后司机被逮捕并被指控至少一项罪名——在有人居住的房屋纵火。该司机名叫哈里·布卡尔特，他最终被指控在不到一个星期的时间里纵火超过 53 次，造成超过 300 万美元的损失（Johnson，Bonner& Hanser，2017）。洛杉矶县的县治安官李·巴卡向新闻记者们发表评论：后备警察助理拉雷扎里逮捕了加利福尼亚州历史上最恶劣的系列纵火案嫌疑人。与本章描述的第一个案例相比，本次事件让公众知道了辅警为使我们的社区更加安全发挥的重要作用。拉雷扎里荣获了几个地方级、州级和国家级荣誉，还在美国电视脱口秀节目《艾伦秀》上做嘉宾。在《艾伦秀》上，拉雷扎里的调查技巧受到公众高度赞扬。

2014 年 9 月，在俄克拉荷马州俄克拉荷马县做县治安官后备警察助理的马克·沃甘，下班后枪击了一名嫌疑人，该嫌疑人因提前离职在工作场所制造暴力事件。从 2010 年开始，后备警察沃甘就在俄克拉荷马县治安官办公室的巡逻处以后备警察的身份工作。他还在该机构的特警队做狙击手，并且是枪械训练队的队员。他的全职工作是沃甘食品公司的首席运营官，该公司是他在 1988 年成立的。本案嫌疑人在与沃甘工厂的一名同事发生争吵后已经停职了，因为据说他声称不喜欢白人。嫌疑人开车到工厂，驾车撞到一辆停着的车上，后进入管理办公室，在管理办公室里，他割掉了一名女性职员的头并且攻击了另一名职员，显然其试图把她的头也割掉。面对这种紧急情况，后备警察沃甘离开他位于工厂的办公室，从车里拿上他的枪和背心，背心上印有证明他身份的文字“县治安官”。随后，他面对嫌疑人，当时该人手里还有一把刀而且正在攻击第二位女职员。嫌疑人突然跑向沃甘，沃甘开了三枪，击中了嫌疑人。嫌疑人被到达现场的警察逮捕，并在 2016 年年底被判杀人罪。但是，案件法官不接受被告的辩护，质疑被告精神上的行为能力。在该事件调查期间，嫌疑人被发现明显痴迷极端宗教主义。后备警察助理沃甘的英雄行为被俄克拉荷马县县治安官办公室认可，他获得了荣誉奖（Liu，2014）。在一份对公众发表的关于该事件的声明中，俄克拉荷马县县治安官约翰·维特塞尔说：“俄克拉荷马州县县治安官办公室有能力为俄克拉荷马县的公民们提供执法服务和保护，其中后备警察助理们发挥了十分重要的作用。后备警察助理是这样的公民——他们参加严格的执法训练并且自愿用自己的时间为大家服务。马克·沃甘的例子正说明这些男士和女士们对我们的公民来说是多么的重要。”

2016 年 6 月 12 日，一名独行枪手进入佛罗里达州奥兰多的脉动夜总会，制造了自2001年9月11日以来美国死亡人数最多的恐怖袭击，杀死49人、伤53人。在进入夜总会的时候，该枪手枪击了一名警察，该警察正在附近执行特别任务。该警察开枪还击枪手并随后发出“发生枪击/警察需要帮助”的无线电呼叫。马上，有超过100名在该区域工作的执法官员，从奥兰多警察局、佛罗里达州高速公路巡逻队、中佛罗里达大学警察局到奥兰治县和塞米诺尔县县治安官办公室以及其他机构，对这次可怕事件做出应对，与此同时，那个活跃的枪手仍然在夜总会里面。在对该事件作出应对的执法官员里面，有三名奥兰治县县治安官办公室的后备警察助理，他们本来正在准备结束他们的志愿轮班工作，因为他们一直以后备警察班组在奥兰治县东部地区执行巡逻特别任务。这些志愿者是首批到达事件现场的警察中的几位，另外还有计算机软件专业人员后备警察中尉詹姆斯·蒙哥马利，企业主管后备警察中士杰苏斯·杰·洛萨瑞奥以及已退休的执法官员后备警察中士罗伯特·耐特。这些无报酬、志愿者、公民警察，和现场其他全职警察一起动员起来，进入仍然不安全的夜总会中救出伤员——当时嫌疑人手持强力突击步枪和半自动手枪，而且还在夜总会里面。执法人员努力帮助受伤人员和被困人员，即便在嫌疑人声称他有炸弹的时候也没有停止。[③]后备警察中士耐特关于本次事件的报告由县治安官办公室发布并被广泛报道，该报告描述了这些志愿者们的英勇举动，他们多次进入夜总会帮助受伤人员撤离，然后在“成堆”的有可怕伤口的尸体中搜寻幸存者。这些辅警因为他们的勇敢被奥兰治县县治安官办公室授予最高荣誉——勇气勋章。后备警察中士罗伯特·耐特和奥兰治县县治安官办公室的两名全职助理被授予（美国）全国县治安官协会国家勇气勋章，以奖励他们的英雄壮举。

正如这些例子所展示的，做一名后备警察是有危险的。事实上，已经有导致辅警死亡的事件发生。一名阿肯色州约翰逊县后备警察助理于2015年3月15日被杀，被杀前他正与一名入室盗窃嫌疑人对峙。后备警察助理索尼·史密斯和其他助理们正在搜查嫌疑人并与该嫌疑人遭遇，然后该嫌疑人就向史密斯开枪了。史密斯本能够开枪回击，但是射中他的子弹刺穿了他的肺，后来在医院里他被宣告死亡。这名后备警察助理是一个5岁孩子的父亲，而且在约翰逊县县治安官办公室工作过11年，具有丰富的工作经验。嫌疑人72岁，被判一级和二级谋杀罪，被判处有期徒刑28年（Rains，2016）。

2007年3月14日，两名纽约市警察局的协警被杀，当时二人穿着看上去与纽约市警察局正规警察非常相似的制服，[④]在纽约市格林威治村开始追捕抢劫杀人案嫌疑人。该事件开始于该嫌疑人——一名前美国海军陆战队成员，“莫名其妙”开枪射击餐馆里的一名员工，把他杀死。两名正规警察听到枪响就开始追捕嫌疑人，此人随后碰上两位协警。纽约市警察局的协警都未配枪，当嫌疑人转身向两位协警开枪时，两人试图躲在停着的车辆后面。两名协警，时年28岁的尼克拉斯·佩克亚罗和时年19岁的叶甫盖尼·马沙力克，均当场死亡。嫌疑人被赶到现场的纽约市警察局的警察击毙（Hope，2007）。[⑤]马沙力克在事件发生前大约18个月加入纽约市警察局协警部门。他是一位从车臣到纽约的移民，他和他的家人为了逃离发生在车臣的残酷战争而来到纽约。他还是纽约大学的一名学生，打算去法学院学习，将来想成为一名检察官。佩克亚罗已经做了大约四年的协警，事发当时他是一家书店的售货员，同时他在曼哈顿的帝国学院学习（Wilson，2007）。

即便是在做一些被认为是“常规”的工作，如指挥交通，做一名辅警还是可能陷入死亡境地。这样的一个例子发生在2005年5月14日。华盛顿特区大都会警察局后备警察约瑟夫·波泽尔当时正在乔治镇的一个十字路口指挥交通，他被一辆机动车撞到了，他因伤而亡。另一个类似的例子发生在拉姆西县（明尼苏达州）县治安官办公室后备警察助理马克·威尔肯身上。2009年10月25日，他正在一年一度的万圣节鬼屋指挥交通，被一辆机动车撞击而亡（Officer Down Memorial Page，n. d.）。

在英格兰和威尔士，与上文类似的事件很少发生，而且通常发生在帮派和毒品活动比较猖獗的地方。政府不允许公民持有手枪。其他枪支许可仅仅在对申请人进行了广泛背景调查并且考察储存枪支的地方的资产状况之后才会被签发。尽管因为日益增长的恐怖主义压力，现在配枪警察更常见了，但是这并不意味着是英国每日警务的常态。辅警（特别警员）目前还没有获得配备泰瑟枪（Tasers）或者枪支的许可，但是正规、全职警察可以在众多勤务中使用这些武器。

1992年6月7日（星期日），在北约克郡塔德卡斯特，警察桑迪·科利和特别警员格莱恩·古德曼在他们的警车里执行常规巡逻任务。他们注意到一辆停在镇上一家啤酒厂附近的轿车。该轿车飞驰而去，科利和古德曼驾车紧追不舍，随后二人被波尔·马基枪击。波尔·马基是一名众所周知的爱尔兰共和军恐怖分子。马基向古德曼胸部开了两枪，古德曼被打死。马基随后向科利开了四枪，科利受伤但活了下来。古德曼先生时年37岁，他平常的工作是一名卡车司机。古德曼先生已婚，有一个十一个月大的儿子。他是自1942年以来第一个在上班期

P19

间被杀害的特别警员。古德曼先生加入特别警员队伍仅仅在几个月前，他当特别警员是为申请成为正规警察做准备（Kirby，1993）。

2016年，特别警员乔治·布朗在成功抓获一名男子后，获得大都会警察总监颁发的荣誉。该男子携带一把武士刀而且试图杀人。2017年1月，一个头脑灵活的特别警员在注意到一辆机动车横停在一座大门前的时候，发现情况可疑。司机步行离开，被该名辅警抓住。司机被逮捕后，在机动车货柜里发现了一大堆被盗的园艺设备。这件事发生在英格兰西南部偏远的萨默赛特郡的一个小村庄里。这样的地区是被视为没有什么犯罪问题的地方，所以警务人员稀少；经常仅有特别警员在工作，使这样的地方得到一定程度的护卫。

为应对各种潜在事故而进行适当培训，其重要性不言而喻，而且正规警察和辅警二者在一起工作的能力尤为重要。下面就是正规警察和辅警团队合作的例子。2013年12月，恶劣天气和潮水汹涌导致英国埃塞克斯郡东部海岸发生洪水，从而使志愿性质的埃塞克斯警察局特别警员队被召集起来。在仅仅一个24小时的时间段内，特别警员们回应的要求服务的电话就超过150个，同时一些警察工作轮班超过了18个小时。埃塞克斯警察局特别警员队队长评论：辅警们辛苦工作；正规警察和辅警团队“适应需求高峰期”，有能力应对这种类型的灾害（Deller，2013）。

2012年伦敦奥运会提出的勤务方案要求很多警察执勤，这就出现了对额外警务人员的需求。起初的设想是这些有警察职权且穿着警察制服的特别警员们，可以被派去帮助护卫在伦敦的以及其他天气炎热地方的比赛，一些特别警员们都很期待这次机会。但是最后，计划改变，全职警察被调用，特别警员顶替被调用警察的岗位。尽管如此，伦敦大都会警察局报告说在2012年伦敦奥运会期间，有史以来最多有5677名特别警员提供警务服务。在接下来的四年里，这个数字下降了43%，到2016年中，人数降到3253名（Davenport，2016）。在2015年3月，在英格兰和威尔士全境一共有16101名特别警员（Home Officer，2015）。

这些事件作为事例证明了对后备警察、协警和特别警员来说“超越”意味着什么。公众经常不能辨别由辅警作出的举动，因为他们认不出来这个人是一名辅警还是一名“下班”警察，因为这个人穿着与警服类似的制服，履行着类似警察的职业责任。许多人可能甚至不知道英国或者美国警务工作中有辅警存在。不幸的是，这也意味着，就像正规警察仅仅因为是警察就成为暴力目标，辅警也容易成为暴力目标。2016年2月，四名帮派成员被判有罪，因为他们四人杀死了

45 岁的弗吉尼亚州韦恩斯伯勒的后备警察队队长凯文·奎克。后备警察队队长奎克被杀于 2014 年 2 月，当时他被攻击并被迫说出自己的个人银行账户信息，帮派成员从他的账户里转走了 400 美元。当他们发现奎克的身份是一名警察的时候，他们开枪射中奎克的头部并把他的尸体藏起来。四天后奎克的尸体才被发现。带头攻击奎克的人因绑架罪和谋杀罪被判处终身监禁外加 132 年监禁，两名共犯被判处终身监禁外加 82 年监禁，还有一名共犯被判处终身监禁外加 10 年监禁（Bryan & Burns，2016）。

不幸的是，还有一些事例使辅警被“放在显微镜下”审视，因为有的辅警做了让人非难的事。像任何全职警察容易出现的问题一样，辅警中有一些人作出错误决定、作出错事或者犯下彻头彻尾的罪行。存在这样一起事件吸引了全世界媒体的注意，那就是俄克拉荷马州塔尔萨的一名后备警察助理，在 2015 年 4 月，开枪打死了一名毒贩，这名毒贩被怀疑携带了武器。当时这位后备警察助理显然是用左轮手枪射击的那个毒贩，而他还以为自己手里拿的是泰瑟枪。新闻媒体关注的事实是，后备警察助理罗伯特·贝茨是一位辅警，所以新闻媒体质疑罗伯特·贝茨是否应该在后备警察助理这个岗位上、身处如此危险的情境之中而且佩带枪支。因为这位后备助理经济富裕并曾向其提供志愿服务的县治安官办公室捐赠钱款，所以媒体（和公民自由联盟）质疑这位后备警察助理是不是用钱“买”下了后备警察助理这个职位。这位后备警察助理被指控犯了杀人罪，导致媒体和公众使用这个例子来指责美国的辅警（Campoy & Elinson，2015）。陪审团发现这位前志愿后备警察助理触犯了二级杀人罪，并建议判处这位后备警察助理有期徒刑 4 年（Ellis，Lett& Sidner，2016）。审理此案的法官同意陪审团的意见并判处这位后备警察助理有期徒刑 4 年，即便贝茨的辩护律师提供判例数据，以证明缓刑是对二级杀人罪的标准量刑（Pickard & Jones，2016）。

2016 年年初，在英国，特别警员安德鲁·布莱德斯被迫辞职并且有了犯罪记录，因为之前他使用自己驾驶的巡逻车作为障碍物逼停了一位骑自行车的人，该人当时正骑着自行车冲向布莱德斯的警察同事。“警界高层声称布莱德斯没有接受过这种驾驶技巧训练，布莱德斯昨天被宣判犯有危险驾驶罪”（Mansfield，2016）。

这些例子都是重要的实例，说明不论是在英国还是在美国，辅警可以给社区里的警务带来积极影响，也可以带来消极影响。

不幸的是，对辅警的角色，学术文献资料和公众的了解都不多。因为美国警察系统各自为政，即便是在职后备警察的人数都很难估算；没有一个单独的实体来负责保留辅警的档案资料，而且没有两个州有相似的数据（Dobrin & Wolf，2016；Berg & Doerner，1988）。在美国，使用后备警察、协警和其他类型辅警的警务机构，在组织自己的员工方面没有独立的最佳实践，而且对后备警察的组织架构也只有很少的研究（Dobrin & Wolf，2016）。对后备警察或者协警的定义，美国缺少统一性，此外，对这些人员的培训也不一致。本书将会用更长的篇幅讨论这两个问题。

与美国情况相反的是，在英格兰和威尔士，所有的警察局都被要求执行中央的政策，当然个别警察局的措施会有差异。然而在美国，所有的全职执法警察或者说正规执法警察均武装了枪支，而且在许多司法管辖区域，后备警察和协警同样武装了枪支。但是，英格兰和威尔士的警察日常不携带枪支。英国所有的警察局根据每个警察局的行动计划决策，经过挑选的全职职员携带枪支作为特别反应小组的成员。所以，警察局给全职警察配发防刺背心、喷雾剂、手铐，而且越来越多地配发泰瑟枪，全职警察也可以被指派到特别小组从而可以携带枪支。特别警员携带相似的装备，但是警察局既没有给特别警员配发泰瑟枪，也没有配发枪支。

警察的角色

随着首支现代警察队伍于1829年在伦敦建立，罗伯特·比尔爵士关注犯罪预防并建立了一个组织，但其性质是民用的而不是军用的。为完善大都会内部和周边的警察组织机构而颁布的法案，也就是众所周知的《大都会警察法》，强调执法部门在预防犯罪方面的作用。这反映出来的观念是：预防犯罪要好于接听求助电话。大都会警察们，昵称"bobbies"——这个称谓后来变得家喻户晓，以纪念他们的创始人——仿效军队的样式建设组织机构，即采用衔级架构，并且部署地点位置靠近居民，从而使民众容易找到他们，并使警察部门能根据时间和地域分配警力。这样的组织成为许多其他警察组织的样板。这里的其他警察组织是指现在或者过去是大英帝国的一部分，包括美国的警察组织。尽管英国警务以及其他国家警务遵循英国的模式，可能在某些方面有所不同，但是这些组织关注的核心是：如果没有警察所护卫社区的自愿参与，警察是不可能成功的。所以警方致力于鼓励社区资源主动参与警务工作，对犯罪活动保持警惕，并且分担各种警务职能。这一做法在一些地方、在不同的时间要比在其他地方更成功。

美国和英国的现代警务都是在“比尔原则”的基础上建立起来的，但是已经演变出了截然不同的模式。当英国殖民者在十七世纪早期首次到达美洲并创建他们自己的“警务”机构的时候，他们借鉴了当时的英国模式。郡最高司法长官、治安员以及更夫都被采纳以适应美洲的特殊需要。然而，这些都是效率低下、腐败常发的组织，因为其允许政治干预。甚至在罗伯特·比尔爵士在伦敦实行了英国警务模式以后，由于城市化、工业化、移民以及种族间发生的骚乱，美国警察机构还在与腐败和低效作斗争。根据伦敦模式建立警察机构的美国城市遇到来自民众的怀疑，很大程度上是因为民众担心警方可能会被政治派别控制——这种担忧大多数都成为现实（Arch bold，2013）。

在美国警务的“政治时期”（1830—1920），美国警察被选择的依据是他们与政治的联系或者他们对当权政党的贡献。在美国警务这个早期时代，警察局浸淫在地方政治中，政治势力干预警方的职能和行动，包括晋升。但是在英国，对每日常规警务的这种同样的政治影响没有出现过，而且伦敦警察总监们根本不受外部政治的影响，这在很大程度上使他们免受腐败之害，而腐败在当时的美国一直存在。

这种差异一直延续到现在，美国许多地方警务机构采用选举或者政治委派的方式产生警务机构主管。而英国模式仅在最近才开始采用类似于任命和选举产生的警察和犯罪总监（PCCs，police and crime commissioners）。警察和犯罪总监这一职位设置于2012年。在地方负责和社区警务时代，警察和犯罪总监的作用被认为优于以前的警察职权。政策交流智库为美国类型的警察总监设置了基调。美国类型的警察总监将由地方选举产生并且要在他们的管辖范围内承担预算的责任，还要承担追究高级官员的责任（Bullock，2014）。根据警察和犯罪总监协会（APCC，the Association of Police and Crime Commissioners）的解释，“警察和犯罪总监的角色是做人民的发言人并追究警方的责任。他们对全部警务负责”（Association of Police and Crime Commissioners，n. d.）。推行警察和犯罪总监这个职位的工作获得的支持不多，通常是因为全体选民对这个职位缺乏了解，结果是提交有效投票表的选民总计仅有15.1%，许多选民浪费了自己的选票。2012年11月15日，当选举进行时，在41个合法的警察区域，选民投票率在11.6%至19.8%之间徘徊（Electoral Commission，2013）。许多候选人以政治派别成员的身份拉选票：在2012年，成功当选者中有27.5%的当选者宣称自己是“独立候选人”，但是在最近的选举中，即2016年的选举，这一数字下降到7.5%。尽管当选者与政治派别的从属关系很明显，但是警察和犯罪总监被要求公平履职。

在英国经济处于衰退状态的时候，警察和犯罪总监选举开始实施。许多候选人作出承诺，呼吁增加更多的特别警员以填补全职警察人数减少出现的岗位空缺。这个问题被许多媒体推波助澜（如苏塞克斯郡、柴郡以及亨伯赛德郡）。

沃克和卡茨（Walker & Katz，2013）解释说，伦敦警方从建立之日起就日益专职化，而美国警察则受到种族和宗教紧张关系、分配的不稳定性以及非职业行为的羁绊。“区别是，伦敦大都会警察总监不受政治干预的影响，有能力保持职员的高标准。结果就是，伦敦警察们最终赢得了公众的尊重”（Walker & Katz，2013，p. 32）。当然，这种尊重在不同时期都受到质疑，但是英国警方努力维持罗伯特·比尔爵士的首要理念：让民众护卫民众。警方以及刑事司法系统自身，在许多不同层级严重依赖公众，而且“毫不夸张地说，该系统有赖于公众的参与及合作”（Gill & Mawby，1990，p. 5）。

在使用可用的武器装备方面，英国和美国警务模式之间存在更深层次的差异。美国警察在警察历史早期就开始携枪，这是美国日益严重的暴力以及美国对枪支的态度导致的结果。枪支在美国是一个存在争议但又被大众接受的事物，主要根源是美国宪法的《权利法案》。由于英国君主之前采取的军事行动，该法案有条款要求保持一支武装军事力量。这已经渗透进了现代美国社会，而且使现在美国许多州存在非常自由的枪支法律。英国警察没有回应相似文化的必要，所以得以反对这一变化。现代武装反应团队在当今英国警务中仍然存在，但是在比较美国和英国警察的时候，这种突出的文化差异导致两国警察在应对暴力活动方面采取明显不同的方式。这种差异还存在于两国辅警采用的培训和装备上。在美国，后备警察或者协警可能会受到枪支培训以及使用致命武力的培训，也可能不会，而英国的特别警员没有这方面的培训。美国辅警只有在他们接受了枪支培训并被授权在工作时可以携枪的时候，才会认为自己与带薪的全职警察地位相等。那些没有接受这种培训的美国辅警可能觉得自己好像是“二等的”，或者觉得自己做着与全职同事们不一样的工作。

为警方提供志愿服务

在美国和英国的警务历史中，志愿履行警务责任的精神有着辉煌的历史。志愿者为美国警方提供支持的方式有正式的，也有非正式的，如志愿队、搜救队、沟通队以及由政府支持的协警或者后备警察职能。在美洲英国殖民时期，地方志愿者是首批治安员，他们是更夫，在夜晚上岗警戒。后来许多主要城市改为带薪夜晚警戒制度，或者多种多样的市镇长官、治安官以及治安法官（Greenberg，1984）。然而，志愿精神在警务中一直延续着，我们如今可以在下面这些警务中发现志愿精神：邻里守望项目、受害者辩护律师、语言翻译、青年探索者或者警官学员项目、公民巡逻以及后备警察和协警项目。

实施无补偿警务的时间可以追溯到至少1000年前。格林伯格（Greenberg，2005）将美国辅警的历史划分为五个时期。格林伯格把这五个时期命名为：（1）非专业执法时期，包括控奴巡逻以及治安员和更夫制度；（2）守望者时期，包括使用民众组成的搜捕人犯小队以及私家侦探；（3）告密者时期，包括来自反酒馆联盟的个人和保护美国联盟的个人；（4）变革时期，包括为特殊目的建立的后备警察的演变；（5）同化时期，包括民防人员和其他辅警成为许多警察机构社区警务的一部分。本书第四章将更细致地考察辅警的历史以及正规警察的历史。

在美国现代警务中，对“协警”或“后备警察”这样称谓的含义没有什么标准界定。1971年，兰德公司发布了一份报告，报告内容是关于美国特殊目的警察的。而且该报告有一部分讨论了后备警察问题。“后备警察力量，通常由志愿者组成，在正规公共警察机构的指导和管控之下执勤，在发生内乱或自然灾害事件的时候，作为一支应急后备人力资源使用”（Kakalik & Wildhorn，1971，p. 4）。美国后备警察和协警现在仍然作为后备职员，被用于对警察有大量需求的特殊情况。后备警察经常被用作“正规”警察的补充，他们可以在两人巡逻的时候被用作辅助人员，或者在对执法职员需求量大的时候在岗工作。然而，要理解后备警察作为执法官员真正做的事情还是令人困惑，原因是各州使用后备警察的方式各种各样。

在美国许多州，一名协警拥有有限的职权或者没有职权，且是作为来自公众的支持提供服务，而不是作为一名执法人员。在其他州，一名协警可以使用武器，有逮捕权，履行与全职警察相同的职责、发挥相同的作用，但是其仅仅是一名志愿者。一些机构还可能使用协警从事那些不是每日必须做的工作，如骑马巡逻或者在骚乱控制队或者水下搜救队工作（Kakalik & Wildhorn，1971）。尽管一些机构可能限制协警的职责，给他们分派特定的而且经常是更为普通的任务，另一些机构可能给协警提供警务培训，外加特定培训（Greenberg，1984）。

总的来说，美国人受到鼓励去当志愿者，而且美国政策制定者们已经发起倡议促进志愿精神。两任美国总统乔治·H. W. 布什和巴拉克·奥巴马已经实施了诸多项目，并认可志愿服务的重要性（Nesbit & Brudney，2010）。2001 年 9 月 11 日的恐怖事件对美国志愿者的使用还是有积极影响的；县级政府以及人口众多的城市出现对志愿服务产生兴趣的公民人数增长的现象，特别是那些已经有一些公共志愿者的社区（Gazley & Brudney，2005）。2011 年，6430 万名美国人在所有类型的公民管理岗位做志愿者，志愿服务大约 79 亿个小时，估算价值超过 1710 亿美元（Corporation for National and Community Service，2012）。公民在警察工作中提供志愿服务的好处与地方政府和社区里的公民都有关系（Ren，Zhao，Lovrich& Gaffney，2006）。汉塞尔、博纳和约翰逊（Hanser，Bonner& Johnson，2017）认为，“在警察机构中使用志愿者在美国已经是一个被完全接受的观念”（Hanser，Bonner& Johnson，2017，p. 25），但是在美国，实际上在超过 18000 个执法机构中仅有少数几个执法机构实施正式志愿者项目。最近的文献资料显示，在美国所有的公共安全组织中，仅有 30%的公共安全组织有志愿者部门或者组织（Brudney & Kellough，2000）。

英国同样出现了在警务中扩展使用志愿者的情况。英国让志愿者参与诸多警务项目，如“警察与社区团结起来”（PACT，Police and Communities Together）、邻里守望（Neighborhood Watch）以及特别警员队（special constabulary），结果就如女王陛下警察监察局（Her Majesty's Inspectorate for Constabulary）指出的：“在英国警务中，志愿者发挥着至关重要的作用”（Gravelle & Rogers，2009）。然而，在英国，特别警员的职能首次被正式确定于 1662 年，最初是为了执行法律（Pepper，2012）。1831 年，特别警员的职能变得与英国警察的一致，包括护卫和平（Pepper，2012）。术语“特别（special）”可能同样制造混淆，就像许多不同警察机构试图使用这个词语描述其他警察职能或者部门，如英国警察部门的特殊分支机构——政治保安处（Special Branch）、特别反应队（special response）以及特别巡逻队（Special Patrol Groups）（Gill & Mawby，1990）。最近，相对较新的机构——国家犯罪局也招聘特别警员，该局特别警员的角色更多地属于专家型人才，而且他们的权力在某种程度上不同于“一般的”辅警（National Crime Agency，n. d.）。该术语还可能与那些以“特殊警察（special police）”身份工作或者与私人警察部门一起工作的人产生混淆。现代特别警员是志愿者，他们在主管警察的指挥下工作，而且发挥与一个警察局正式授权的成员同样的作用（Gill & Mawby，1990）。在英国特别警员辅警中，有超过 30%的特别警员是女性，10%的特别警员来自少数族裔群体。特别警员在这些方面的比率要高于英国正式警察的比率（Strickland & Lalic，2010）。

众多特别警员每周数小时在他们当地的警察局做志愿者。他们接受培训，领用一套警察制服（有时制服上有特殊标识，表明他们的志愿者身份），拥有全部警察权力，而且负责履行与全职正规警察一样的职责，包括步行巡逻、机动车社区巡逻以及交通管理（Strickland & Lalic，2012）。

P27

为什么做辅警？

综观美国和英国，个人决定在警务项目中提供志愿服务的原因多种多样。在美英两国，一些人当辅警的原因是他们看到培训和经历是申请警务全职岗位的必要条件（Pepper，2014；Wolf，Holmes& Jones，2016）。实际上，一些美国警务机构已经提出议案，要求向他们组织提出申请的新人要有在执法机构当辅警的经历，这是个人被考虑担任全职警察职位的前提（Scoville，2014）。其他警务机构现在的规定是：只要辅警成为全职警察，就允许把辅警预备做警察的时间计入晋升所需时间（Police Department Disciplinary Bulletin，2006）。众多警务机构要求在任何附加要求参加的培训之外，辅警要参加“在岗”培训项目或者类似项目。“在岗”培训项目是一种实战培训（或者陪同指导巡逻）项目。这种由警察机构准备的“局内”培训，使警察机构作为未来的雇主有机会更好地了解要雇用的特定人选在上岗前可能具有的才能以及可能存在的任何潜在缺陷。警察机构可以通过下列方面考察新任辅警的能力：解决问题，主动性、听从指挥、学习新技术、运用良好的判断力、正直、悲悯和尊重以及有效沟通。

美国志愿性质的执法官员的另一个组成部分，是那些已经从全职警务岗位上退休的警察，以及那些希望与同业、社区和他们曾经一起工作多年的同事保持联系的人（Ferranto，2011；Hunter，2012）。这似乎是美国警务的与众不同之处，在其他使用辅警的国家很少见到。这一群体的成员决定留下做辅警，可能是因为不愿放弃他们的警察权力；或者他们留下可能是为了个人有收获，或者可能是为了用他们的培训和专长获得兼职岗位或者私人安保岗位。这些辅警中有一些人在执法部门从事短时间全职工作后成为志愿者，因为各种原因他们已经转换到别的职业或者在寻找别的机会。另一些人可能当了很长时间的警察，甚至可能在退休并成为志愿者之前，在同一警察机构内或者其他警察机构里担任过高级职务。这使警察机构有机会保留某些管理经验，因为随着高级领导退休，这些经验通常可能会消失，而且这也使警察机构有机会使用那些已经退休或者转换岗位之人的专长、人脉、培训以及能力，一般应正在实施的项目、特殊任务和调查所需。

P28 志愿性质的执法官员的最后一个组成部分，他们是那些从来没有担任过全职执法职务而且没有计划这样做的人。相反，他们把志愿参与警务工作看作为社区提供服务的一种途径，符合他们的兴趣。他们把奉献自己的时间看作为社会福祉作出贡献的一种方式，这种方式令人振奋而且是值得做的。志愿性质的执法官员报告说他们享受帮助公民、学习新事物以及与他人互动带来的兴奋感，把这些作为经历的一部分（Berg & Doerner，1988）。在美国和英国警务中，这一类型辅警有许多共性。

虽然上文把以辅警身份工作的人群类型分成若干组别，但是并没有回答“为什么”这个问题。尽管当我们回顾这些人参加辅警工作的原因时，可能最容易理解的是为什么那些希望申请全职岗位的人可能做辅警，但是其他类型的原因就不能自圆其说了。为什么一个已经在一个职业中工作了 20 或 30 年的人，一个现在能够领取退休津贴的人，愿意以辅警身份在同一个机构继续工作呢？为什么一个对成为被全职雇用的警察不感兴趣的人，选择接受当一名辅警所需的严格训练、投入时间、接受评审和再教育，而不是去别的不那么危险、与社区联系不太紧密的岗位工作呢？毋庸置疑，辅警不是唯一以这一身份工作的个体；志愿性质的消防员同样为了社会将自己的生命和健康置于危险境地。

帕珀和沃尔夫（Pepper & Wolf，2015）研究了两个使用辅警的机构，一个来自美国，一个来自英国。在本次研究中，美国的被调查人填写问卷说他们做辅警是因为受到各种原因的鼓动，但是 25% 的原因是：他们“曾经是正规警察并希望与同事保持联系”，或者“曾经是正规警察并希望让自己的知识以及/或者专长发挥作用”（Pepper & Wolf，2015，p. 217）。英国的被调查人则没有一个说他们之前曾经担任过任何正规全职警察职务。帕珀（Pepper，2014）追踪过 20 名新任特别警员，从他们在英国警察局开始当特别警员时就开始追踪。在本次研究中，有一半的被调查人说他们之前申请过正规警察职务，或者在其他有报酬的警务职位申请过全职岗位。帕珀还报告辅警的动机包括希望回馈社区或者在社区内与众不同。

与犯罪有关的因素，如惧怕犯罪、社会无序以及公民对警察服务水平与合法
P29 性的看法，可能会影响公民参与社区警务的决定。另外，研究已经表明，参与犯罪预防的公民倾向对警方有更积极的态度，而且也更支持社区警务哲学（Randol

& Gaffney，2014）。

谁做辅警？

美国警务中的执法辅警通常是白人男性，接受过专科学校教育，几乎有一半的人年龄超过 40 岁。与其他类型的志愿者相比，他们在执法部门工作之外，更有可能担任全职职务（Hilal & Olsen，2010），这意味着他们在辅警角色之外，通常要投入时间、满足其他工作要求。美国警察后备人员比其他类型的志愿者更愿意承担全职工作，而且更愿意为多个组织提供服务（Hilal & Olsen，2010；参见 Wolf et al.，2016）。志愿性质的执法官员说他们做辅警，是因为他们希望为他们的社区作贡献，他们希望得到“个人发展”，他们一般情况下对法律和警务感兴趣，或者他们希望用以前掌握的技能和知识去提升自己社区的警务工作（Wolf et al.，2016；Dobrin & Wolf，2016）。

关于那些志愿加入英格兰和威尔士的特别警员队的人，他们的原因同样是多种多样的。历史上，英格兰和威尔士的警方已经招聘和培训了他们自己的人员，每一个警察局都在自己的区域内开展招聘工作，以满足自己对全职警察或辅警的需求。但是，在过去十年，许多警察局通过大学实施他们的培训工作，这有利于抵消学生的培训开销。 P30

最近的研究（Britton，2016）表明，许多原因导致特别警员加入警队做辅警。被调查人被要求从一个列表里排列出他们的前三个选择。位列第一的选择是：“我对在警察部门工作感兴趣，而且希望对其有更多了解并且/或者习得技能和经验，为将来申请一个带薪警务岗位打下基础”（41.0%）。位列第二的选择是：“我希望为我们当地社区做点事，在让我们当地社区更加安全这件事上，希望我能发挥重要作用”（31.2%）（Britton，2016，p. 17）。

根据政府的统计，2016 年 3 月，在所有警务群体中，特别警员是种族多样性最高的群体，11.6%的特别警员声称他们不是白人，而正规警察中仅有 5.9%不是白人。当时，人口中有 14%不是白人（Hargreaves，Linehan，Husband& McKee，2017）。

为什么一个警察机构愿意实施志愿者项目？

正如本书通篇将证实的，志愿者持续为提供者和单个或多个接受者——不论他们是个人还是社区——带来广泛的好处。志愿者项目还能够被用于在公共组织和社区之间建立合作。除了这些立竿见影的好处，参与志愿者项目还可以让公民产生与自己的政府紧密相连之感。志愿活动经常有助于提升政府和非营利实体提供的服务（Fredericksen & Levin，2004），并且弥合各个政府组织在服务范围覆盖方面存在的间隙（Nesbit & Brudney，2010）。对犯罪的惧怕经常被认定是公众形成对犯罪和混乱看法的影响因素（Lee，2007），而刑事司法机构内部的志愿者项目，能够通过让公众身临其境，在一定程度上减少这种惧怕的感觉，并且增强公众对当地警察以及其他公共部门的积极认识。美国辅警可以提升公民对问题、指令以及政府行为的理解，因为各种背景和各样经历被带入警察机构内，并且被用于社区内（Ren et al.，2006）。然而，在英格兰和威尔士，志愿者具有的专家级别的技能只在最近才开始被志愿者所服务的警察局使用。

当然，对一个使用辅警的部门来说，志愿者项目还为警方有其他好处。除了提高对当地社区的参与度以及增强公众对警方的信心，辅警还使警务职能有了更大的透明度（Gravelle & Rogers，2009）。例如，通过允许志愿者进入组织，志愿
P31 者自由参与警方制定战术、收集情报以及作出决策的过程，各个警察局正在开放自己，使透明度更高，社区参与度更高。这很有意义，因为与此形成鲜明对比的是，不论是历史上还是已经被看到的，警察局在勤务方面蒙着神秘“面纱”。警务志愿者项目还为警方提供了获取廉价（不是必须“免费”）的或者潜在高技能劳动力的可能性。警方使用志愿者可以减少或者消除人力资源的财务压力（有一些地方“付钱”给他们的志愿者，要么用补贴的方式，要么发薪抵消费用），但在这样一个部门对人员进行管理还是会产生费用的，包括招聘、培训以及业务费用。业务费用的例子包括制服和装备、医疗保险或工伤补偿保险、责任保险以及全职职员为管理或组织志愿者所需的费用（Wolf et al.，2016；Brudney，2000）。

尽管许多辅警参加步行巡逻或者车巡，美国警察机构还可以使用辅警参与其他工作任务，包括公共档案调查、在大型活动中提高公众见警率、交通管控、背景调查、撰写报告、案件侦查、汽车事故调查、执行停车法规，或者加入警察机构内部专家组（Arwood，Hilal，Karsky& Norman，2005）。在英格兰和威尔士，工作任务同样多种多样，尽管与美国的那些工作任务有细微差别。

美国警察机构还得益于其志愿者从其他公共部门或者私营部门获得的工作经验。为使特别反应队在执法中采取医疗措施，许多美国警察机构开始使用训练有素的或者获得认证的急救医疗技师（EMTs，emergency medical technicians）或者医师。警察机构内部的犯罪侦查部门已经在侦查白领犯罪时开始使用有注册会计

师证的辅警。培训部门已经使用有经验的教育工作者担任警察机构的培训教员，而且这个做法现在已经扩展到网上教育，因为许多警察机构开始把短期培训课程设置为在线模式，由有教育经验的辅警提供在线支持。退休的或者前全职人员还会因为他们的知识和阅历被警察机构使用。这包括使用前犯罪侦查员、实战培训教官、背景调查员、招聘人员或者犯罪现场勘查员，让他们履行在工作中曾经履行过的同样职责，或者去培训来承担这些职责的新人。最后，警察机构可以决定为需要专业知识的业务工作建立一支稳定的后备力量，包括在下列这些工作领域 P32
提供高级培训：摩托车巡逻或者骑马巡逻、搜救队或潜水队、拆弹队、航空队或者其他类似的需要很高专业知识的岗位（Wolf et al.，2016）。

在英格兰和威尔士，让警察局认识到具备专业技能的特别警员（实际上还有支援警察志愿者）的好处通常要慢得多。整个英国的警察局关注的是作为特别警员能够给个人带来的好处，而不是反过来。但是，随着专业领域的专家受聘做特别警员和支援警察志愿者（后者的警察权力很少），这种情况在逐渐改变。的确，我们看到许多例子，警察局寻找特别警员和志愿者们并将他们用在需要专家而且警察培训费用很高的地方。另外，从 2010 年开始，大多数警察局管辖范围的警务数量已经下降，导致后备人员需求量降低（Allen & Uberoi，2016）。而在美国，当辅警的机会很多，而且能够给单个警察局和紧缩的预算节省可观的资金。

在过去几十年中，警务机构日益意识到犯罪控制没有社区的支持是不会有效果的。社区以及组成社区的公民必须被纳入犯罪预防工作之中，并在犯罪预防的工作中扮演坚定角色（Randol & Gaffney，2014）。格拉维勒和罗格斯（Gravelle & Rogers，2000）考察了英格兰和威尔士内部在警察局使用公民警察志愿者带来的好处，尤其是在经济下滑的时候。他们报告了三个突出的好处：使用志愿者在经济上的好处，社区凝聚力的增强以及公众对警方信任的提升。除了提高对当地社区的参与度以及增强公众对警方的信心，辅警还使警务职能有了更大的透明度（Gravelle & Rogers，2009；Dobrin，2016）。

正如前文提到的，还有很多活动需要增加人力资源，去帮助警方应付计划好的对人力资源有大量需求的时刻，包括阅兵、体育赛事、政治事件；还要去应付天气紧急状况和自然灾害或者人为灾害（Greenberg，1984；Dobrin，2016）。对一个警察机构来说，应具备准备后备人力资源的能力，这种能力是无价的。备好一支现成可用的训练有素的全职人力资源是不好操作的，而且在经济上也是不可行的，而受过训练并且获得认证的辅警就在手边，提供了随时待命的后备力量。辅警还可以被视为全职岗位的潜在申请者。“志愿者项目可以被视为一个特别项目，依托这个项目，警察局或许可以招聘潜在的全职警察”（Dobrin，2016，p. 720）。

在需要将人力资源从一地调配到另一地的时候，辅警能够帮助减轻全职人员的工作负担。在正规全职人员需要应对高风险或更危险的事件时，拥有全部警察
P33 权力的志愿者能够“填充”巡逻区并处理求助电话。另外，在没有必要用全职部门或者用全职人力资源的时候，受过特别训练的志愿者能够作为一个机构的待命人员（Dobrin，2016）。这样的例子包括特勤组、技术潜水队、船舶操作员、医生或者自行车巡逻组。必要时，调查组很有用，包括那些侦查网络犯罪的专家、技术类专家或者金融犯罪组。从规模更小的警察机构（如我们在美国能看到的那些众多小型警察机构）可以发现，在警卫队或者骑警队使用辅警的性价比很高，不用花钱努力维持全职警察做这些工作。

菲利普和特莱尔-奥尔（Phillips & Terrell-Orr，2013）报告说，警察监管者们，甚至是那些所持态度可能被看作反映了激进执法之人，没有表现出反对在警务中使用志愿者。菲利普和特莱尔-奥尔的研究报告说，许多警察监管者对公民参与警务工作给予了很高的评价，尤其在维护秩序的时候。与人们期望相反的是，警察监管者没有把志愿者看作警务世界的局外人，他们也不会把志愿者看作给警察机构招致更多麻烦的人，相比较而言，志愿者发挥的作用更大。

从多年在英格兰和威尔士开展的田野调查访谈中，研究者们发现，尽管许多高级警官对特别警员的随时可用性给予了很高评价，但还是有些高级警官对特别警员们不屑一顾，甚至一些支持特别警员的高级警官，亦未能认识到特别警员给警察局带来的诸多好处。

P34

一个警察机构不愿意实施志愿者项目的原因可能是什么？

警察机构在组建辅警部门时可能会有迟疑，原因是担忧职权、工作职责以及辅警部门的成员所能发挥的作用。尽管在一些司法管辖区域（如在英国）这些已经有明确规定了，但是在美国，实际情况不是这样。诚如我们在本书第一章讨论过的，纽约市4500名协警没有逮捕权，而且他们被看作摆在街面上对犯罪的一种视觉威慑，而不是执法官员，但是洛杉矶市使用的大约60名志愿性质的后备警察倒是有逮捕权。综观美国和英国，辅警在特殊岗位上的职责差异很大，但

是可以包括办公室任务、公共档案调查、公共事件、交通管控、背景调查、巡逻职责、撰写报告、案件侦查、汽车事故调查或者参与警察机构内部的专家组。当今许多警察机构还尝试使用有全职工作或经验的辅警与警方一起工作。这包括急诊医疗技师或者医生在特殊应对团队里发挥医疗救助作用，或者警方在侦查白领犯罪时开始使用注册会计师，或者使用教育工作者做警察机构的培训教员。

还是有意见认为完全不需要后备警察或者协警。这些意见包括这样一个事实，即为具有如此危险和潜在诉讼风险的岗位招聘志愿者是件很困难的事情。意见还包括：入职培训和后续培训的潜在开销会很高；给警察机构带来潜在的责任风险（Kakalik & Wildbhon，1971）；来自全职（或“正规”）警察的反对；以及公众对“周末卫士”潜在的不信任和不尊重（Phillips & Terrell-Orr，2013；National Advisory Commission on Criminal Justice Standards and Goals，1973）。

赵、吉布森、洛韦利奇和盖福内（Zhao，Gibson，Lovrich& Gaffney，2002）报告说，那些参与犯罪预防工作的公民比那些没有参与的公民，表现出更高水准的社会凝聚力，但是，兰道尔和盖福内（Randol & Gaffney，2014）报告说，“警察从业人员应该考虑到，最困难的事是鼓励收入比较低的、对警方没有良好态度的公民以及平常不参与志愿服务的公民参加”（Randol & Gaffney，2014，p. 244）辅警活动。

注释

①佛罗里达州法令 1006. 63 这样定义“欺凌（hazing）”：“任何举动或者情境，不顾后果或者故意威胁到一名学生的精神或身体健康或者安全，所为目的包括但不局限于，通过特别仪式加入或者准许进入或者隶属于在高等教育机构的批准下开展活动的任何组织。”

②与美国的现象相反，在英国特别警员队里，正式警察离开警察局后继续当 P35
志愿者的可能性要小得多。对这个问题本书后文将做进一步探讨。

③仍然在脉动俱乐部内的、被扣为人质的顾客们警告紧急勤务队员，嫌疑人声称有炸弹。紧急勤务队员们使用炸弹探测警犬队，包括一支来自中佛罗里达大学警察局的团队，对该区域以及嫌疑人的轿车做了地毯式探测，嫌疑人的轿车当时被发现停在附近的停车场里。特警队成员击毙了枪手，当时他们打破了洗手间的墙壁，因为枪手在洗手间里劫持人质。

④纽约市警察局协警穿着的制服与纽约市警察的制服很相像。协警制服的衬

衫袖子袖标上，在“纽约市警察局”字样的上面有一个“横杠”，上面是“协警”字样；而且协警徽章是星形，不是警察徽章的盾形。纽约市警察局的协警未获授权携带枪支执勤，但是被要求完成一个“协警基础培训课程”，该课程确定协警的地位是“未受枪支培训的治安员”，并且协警必须完成一个协警实战培训项目。

⑤起初美国司法部拒绝把因公死亡抚恤金发给2007年阵亡的纽约市警察局协警佩克亚罗和马沙力克的家庭，但是2008年美国司法部改变了决定。纽约市警察局协警米尔顿·克拉克被杀于1993年12月，当时他朝着枪响的方向跑去，而他那时已经下班了。在美国司法部改变对佩克亚罗和马沙力克被杀抚恤金的决定后，克拉克的家庭最终在2010年获得因公死亡抚恤金。

参考文献

Allen, G., & Uberoi, E.（2016）（艾伦和乌贝罗伊）. *Police service strength*（《警察队伍》）, Briefing Paper 00634（简报00634）. London：House of Commons Library（伦敦：公共图书馆）. 2017年1月13日检索网址 http：//researchbriefings. files. parliament. uk/documents/SN00634/SN00634pdf.

Archbold, C.（2013）（阿奇博尔德）. *Policing：A text/reader*（《警务：经典论文集锦》）. Thousand Oaks, CA：Sage（千橡城，加利福尼亚州：赛格出版公司）.

Arwood, D. E., Hilal, S. M., Karsky, J., & Norman, J. M.（2005）（阿尔伍德、希拉尔、卡斯凯和诺曼）. Police officers：Structural embeddedness of self-role merger and volunteering（“警察：自我角色整合者与志愿服务的结构嵌入性”）. *Great Plains Sociologists*（《大平原地区社会学家》）, 17（2）, 36—60.

Association of Police and Crime Commissioners（n. d.）（警察和犯罪总监协会〈日期不详〉）. Role of the PCC（警察和犯罪总监协会的角色）. APCC（警察和犯罪总监协会）. 2015年12月4日检索网址 www. apccspolice. uk/role-of-the-pcc.

Berg, B. L., & Doerner, W. G.（1988）（伯格和多尔奈尔）. Volunteer police officers：An unexamined personnel dimension in law enforcement（“辅警：未经审查的执法人员”）. *American Journal of Police*（《美国警察》）, 7（1）, 281—289.

Britton, I.（2016）（布里顿）. *National survey of special constables and police support volunteers：Initial findings report*（《对特别警员和支援警察志愿者的全国

性调查：初步调查报告》）. Northampton, UK: University of Northampton, Institute for Public Safety, Crime and Justice（北安普顿，英国：北安普顿大学，公共安全、犯罪和司法研究所）.

Brudney, J. L. （2000）（布鲁德尼）. The effective use of volunteers: Best practices for the public sector（“有效使用志愿者：公共部门的最佳实践”）. *Law Enforcement and Contemporary Problems*（《执法与现实问题》）, 4（11）, 219—255.

Brudney, J. L. , & Kellough, J. E. （2000）（布鲁德尼和克拉夫）. Volunteers in state government: Involvement, management, and benefits（“州政府里的志愿者：参与、管理和待遇”）. *Nonprofit and Voluntary Sector Quarterly*（《非营利性志愿部门季刊》）, 29（1）, 111—130.

Bryan, A. , & Burns, J. （2016, September 19）（伯颜和布恩斯〈2016 年 9 月 19 日〉）. Gang members sentenced to life in prison for Cpt（“帮派成员因 Cpt 被判无期徒刑”）. Kevin Quick's murder（“谋杀凯文·奎克的凶手”）. WTVR News（WTVR 新闻）. 2016 年 9 月 22 日检索网址 wtvr. com/2016/09/19/gang-members-sentenced-to-life-in-prison-for-cpt-kevin-quicks-murder.

Bullock, K. （2014）（布洛克）. *Citizens, community and crime control*（《公民、社区和犯罪控制》）. Basingstoke, UK: Palgrave Macmillan（贝辛斯托克，英国：麦克米伦出版公司）.

Campoy, A. , & Elinson, Z. （2015, April 15）（卡姆坡伊和埃林森〈2015 年 4 月 15 日〉）. Volunteer deputy in Tulsa shooting turns himself in（“塔尔萨枪击案志愿助理自首”）. *The Wall Street Journal*（《华尔街日报》）, A3.

Corporation for National and Community Service（2012）（国家和社区服务协会）. Volunteering and civic life in America 2012（“2012 年美国志愿行为与公民生活”）. CNCS（国家和社区服务协会）. 2013 年 5 月 16 日检索网址 www. volunteeringinamerica gov.

Davenport, J. （2016, March 3）（达文波特〈2016 年 3 月 3 日〉）. Huge fall in number of special constables puts “immense strain” on Met（“特别警员人数大幅下降给大都会警察局带来‘巨大压力’”）. *Evening Standard*（《标准晚报》）. 2016 年 8 月 1 日检索网址 www. standard. co. uk/news/crime/huge-fall-in-number-of-special-constablesputs-immense-strain-on-met-a3194641. html.

Deller, J. (2013, December 10)(德莱尔〈2013 年 12 月 10 日〉). Special constables mobilised in force to assist with the policing response to the recent tidal surges on the East Coast(特别警员动员力量，协助警方应对最近的洪涝灾害). Association of Special Constabulary Chief Officers(特别警员队队长协会). 2014 年 6 月 10 日检索网址 www. ascco. org. uk/index. php/news/63-essex-specials-answer-call-to-action.

Dobrin, A. (2016)(多布林). Volunteer police: History, benefits, costs and current descriptions(“辅警：历史、待遇、花费与现状”). *Security Journal*(《安全报》), 30 (3), 717—733.

Dobrin, A., & Wolf, R. (2016)(多布林和沃尔夫). What is known and not known about volunteer policing in the United States(“我们知道的以及我们不知道的美国辅警管理”). *International Journal of Police Science and Management*(《警察科学与管理国际期刊》), 18 (3), 220—227.

Electoral Commission (2013)(选举委员会). *Police and crime commissioner elections in England and Wales: Report on the administration of the elections held on*15 *November* 2012(《英格兰和威尔士警察和犯罪总监选举：关于 2012 年 11 月 15 日选举的管理报告》). London: Electoral Commission(伦敦：选举委员会).

Ellis, R., Lett, C., & Sidner, S. (2016, April 28)(埃利斯、莱特和希德奈〈2016 年 4 月 28 日〉). Ex-Oklahoma deputy Robert Bates guilty of killing unarmed suspect(“前俄克拉荷马助理罗伯特·贝茨杀害手无寸铁的嫌疑人”). CNN News(CNN 新闻). 2016 年 8 月 1 日检索网址 www. cnn. com/2016/04/27/us/tulsa-deputy-manslaughter-trial.

Ferranto, D. (2011)(费兰托). Not “just a reserve.”(“不‘仅仅是一名后备警察’”). *Sheriff*(《县治安官》), 63 (3), 36.

Fredericksen, P. J., Levin, D. (2004)(弗雷德里克森和勒文). Accountability and the use of volunteer officers in public safety organizations(“追责与公共安全组织使用辅警”). *Public Performance and management*(《公共绩效与管理》), 27 (4), 118—143.

Gazley, B., & Brudney, J. L. (2005)(盖兹雷和布鲁德尼). Volunteer involvement in local government after September 11: The continuing question of capacity(“9/11 之后志愿者加入地方政府：一直存在的能力问题”). *Public Adminis-*

tration Review（《公共管理评论》），65（2），131—142.

Gill，M. L.，& Mawby，R. I.（1990）（吉尔和莫比）. *A special constable：A study of the police reserve*（《特别警员：关于警方后备人员的研究》）. Aldershot，UK：Avebury Publishing（奥尔德肖特，英国：阿维伯里出版社）.

Gravelle，J.，& Rogers，C.（2009）（格拉维勒和罗格斯）. Your country needs you！The economic viability of volunteers in the police（"你的国家需要你！警方志愿者的经济生存能力"）. *Safer Communities*（《更安全社区》），8（3），34—38.

Gravelle，J.，& Rogers，C.（2010）（格拉维勒和罗格斯）. The economy of policing：The impact of the volunteer（"警务经济：志愿者的影响"）. *Policing：A Journal of Policy and Practice*（《警务：政策与实践期刊》），41（1），56—63.

Greenberg，M. A.（1984）（格林伯格）. *Auxiliary police：The citizen's approach to public safety*（《协警：公民为公共安全作贡献的方法》）. Westport，CT：Greenwood Press（韦斯特波特，康涅狄格州：格林伍德出版社）.

Greenberg，M. A.（2005）（格林伯格）. *Citizens defending America：From colonial times to the age of terrorism*（《保卫美国的公民：从殖民地时代到恐怖主义年代》）. Pittsburgh：University of Pittsburgh Press（匹兹堡：匹兹堡大学出版社）.

Hanser，R. D.，Bonner，M.，& Johnson，M. S.（2017）（汉塞尔、邦奈尔和约翰逊）. Volunteers in policing in the United States（"美国警务中的志愿者"）. In J. Albrecht（Ed.）（阿尔布雷希特主编），*Police reserves and volunteers：Enhancing organizational effectiveness and public trust*（《警察后备人员和志愿者：提升组织的有效性和公信力》），pp. 7—28. Boca Raton，FL：CRC Press（博卡-拉顿，佛罗里达州：CRC 出版社）.

Hargreaves，J.，Linehan，C.，Husband，H.，& McKee，C.（2017）（哈格瑞阿维斯、兰汉、哈兹本德和麦基）. *Police workforce，England and Wales，30 September* 2016（《警察队伍，英格兰和威尔士，2016 年 9 月 30 日》），Statistical Bulletin 02/17（统计公报 02/17）. London：Office for National Statistics（伦敦：全国统计办公室）. 2017 年 5 月 22 日检索网址 www. gov. uk/government/uploads/system/uploads/attachment_data/file/586508/policeworkforce-sep16-hosb0217. pdf.

Hilal，S. M.，& Olsen，D. P.（2010）（希拉尔和奥尔森）. Police reserve of-

P37

ficers：Essential in today's economy and an opportunity to increase diversity in the law enforcement profession（“后备警察：在当前经济中地位至关重要且是增强执法职场多元化的一个机会”）. *The Police Chief*（《警察局长》），77（10），92—94.

Home Office（2015）（英国内政部）. National statistics：Police workforce，England and Wales，31 March 2015（“全国统计：警察队伍，英格兰和威尔士，2015 年 3 月 31 日”）. 2016 年 9 月 18 日检索网址 www. gov. uk/government/publications/police - workforce - england - and - wales - 31 - march - 2015/policeworkforce-england-and-wales-31-march-2015.

Hope，B.（2007，March 15）（侯坡〈2007 年 3 月 15 日〉）. Two auxiliary police officers killed in Greenwich Village（“两名协警被杀于格林威治村”）. *The New York Sun*（《纽约太阳报》）. 2016 年 9 月 22 日检索网址 www. nysm. com/new-york/two-auxiliary-police-officers-killed-in-greenwich/50486.

Hunter，G.（2012，June 23）（亨特〈2012 年 6 月 23 日〉）. Detroit police chief signs order to beef up reserves（“底特律警察局长签署命令增加后备警察”）. *The Detroit News*（《底特律新闻》），A1.

Johnson，M. S.，Bonner，M.，& Hanser，R. D.（2017）（约翰逊、邦奈尔和汉塞尔）. “Doing more with less”：The professional model of the Los Angeles Police Department（“‘少花钱多办事’：洛杉矶警察局的职业模式”）. In J. Albrecht（Ed.）（阿尔布雷希特主编），*Police reserves and volunteers：Enhancing organizational effectiveness and public trust*（《警察后备人员和志愿者：提升组织的有效性和公信力》），pp. 101—112. Boca Raton，FL：CRC Press（博卡-拉顿，佛罗里达州：CRC 出版社）.

Kakalik，J. S.，& Wildhorn，S.（1971）（卡卡力克和维尔德霍恩）. *Special-purpose public police*（《特种公共警察》）. Santa Monica，CA：Rand Corporation（圣莫妮卡，加利福尼亚州：兰德公司）.

Kirby，T.（1993，March 29）（基尔比〈1993 年 3 月 29 日〉）. Veteran IRA gunman convicted of murder：Two Irishmen guilty of Yorkshire police shootings（“爱尔兰共和军老兵持枪实施谋杀：两名爱尔兰人犯有枪击约克郡警察罪”）. *The Independent*（《独立报》）. 2017 年 3 月 22 日检索网址 www. independent. co. uk/news/uk/veteran-ira-gunmanconvicted-of-murder-two-irishmen-guilty-of-yorkshire-police-shootings1500766. html.

Lee, M. (2007)(李). *Inventing fear of crime: Criminology and the politics of anxiety*(《制造对犯罪的恐惧：犯罪学与焦虑的政治》). Cullompton, UK: Willan Publishing(卡伦顿，英国：威兰出版社).

Liu, X. X. (2014, December 9)(刘〈2014年12月9日〉). Reserve Deputy Mark Vaughan honored with award of valor(“后备助理马克·沃甘获得荣誉奖”). News9. com. 2016年2月10日检索网址 www. news9. com/story/27584381/reserve-deputy-mark-vaughan-honored-with-award-of-valor.

Mansfield, K. (2016, February 11)(曼斯菲尔德〈2016年2月11日〉). Special constable CONVICTED after helping save colleague from motorbike thugs(“在帮助挽救同事免于遭受助力自行车暴徒伤害后，特别警员被宣判有罪”). *Daily Express*(《每日快报》). 2018年1月10日检索网址 www. express. co. uk/news/uk/643159/special-constable-convicted-dangerous-driving-save-colleagues-motorbike-thugs.

National Advisory Commission on Criminal Justice Standards and Goals (1973)(刑事司法标准和目标国家咨询委员会). *Police: A report*(《一份关于警察的报告》). Washington, DC: US Government Printing Office(华盛顿特区：美国政府印刷办公室).

National Crime Agency (n. d.)(国家犯罪局〈日期不详〉). NCA specials(国家犯罪局特别警员). 2016年12月30日检索网址 www. nationalcrimeagency. gov. uk/careers/specials.

Nesbit, R., & Brudney, J. L. (2010)(奈斯比特和布鲁德尼). At your service? Volunteering and national service in 2020(“听候吩咐？2020年的志愿行为和国家服务”). *Public Administration Review*(《公共管理评论》), 70(Supplement S1)(增刊S1), S107—S113.

Officer Down Memorial Page (n. d.)(牺牲官员纪念版〈日期不详〉). Officer Down Memorial Page(牺牲官员纪念版). 2013年4月16日检索网址 www. odmp. org.

Pepper, I. K. (2012)(帕珀). Research study: “Special” or not(“调查研究：是不是‘特别警员’”). Unpublished research(未出版研究成果). Teesside University, School of Social Sciences and Law, Middlesbrough, UK(提赛德大学，社会科学与法律学院，米德尔斯伯勒，英国).

P38

Pepper, I. K. (2014)(帕珀). Do part-time volunteer police officers aspire to be regular police officers?(“兼职辅警渴望成为正规警察吗?”)*Police Journal: Theory, Practice and Principles*(《警察学报：理论、实践与原则》), 87 (2), 105—113.

Pepper, I. K., & Wolf, R. (2015)(帕珀和沃尔夫). Volunteering to serve: An international comparison of volunteer police officers in a UK north east police force and a US Florida sheriff's office(“志愿提供服务：将英国东北部一家警察局和美国佛罗里达州的一个县治安官办公室的辅警进行国际对比”). *The Police Journal: Theory, Practice and Principles*(《警察学报：理论、实践与原则》), 88 (3), 209—219.

Phillips, S. W., & Terrell-Orr, A. (2013)(菲利普和特莱尔-奥尔). Attitudes of police supervisors: Do volunteers fit into policing?(“警察监督者的态度：志愿者适合警务工作吗?”)*Policing: An International Journal of Police Strategies and Management*(《警务：关于警察战略与管理的国际期刊》), 36 (4), 683—701.

Pickard, A., & Jones, C. (2016, June 1)(皮卡德和乔恩思〈2016 年 6 月 1 日〉). Former reserve deputy Robert Bates sentenced to four years in prison for death of Eric Harris(“前后备助理罗伯特·贝茨因埃里克·哈里斯之死被判四年有期徒刑”). *The Tulsa World*(《塔尔萨世界》). 2016 年 12 月 27 日 www.tulsaworld.com/homepagelatest/former-ve-deputy-robert-bates-sentenced-to-four-years-in/article_ec042b6d11d2-See1-95d9-cf9eSee78aba.html.

Police Department Disciplinary Bulletin (2006)(警察局纪律通报). City allows police reserve time to count toward promotion(“本市允许将后备警察时间计入晋升所需时间”). *Police Department Disciplinary Bulletin*(《警察局纪律通报》), 17 (7), 8.

Rains, B. (2016, May 27)(瑞恩思〈2016 年 5 月 27 日〉). Kauffeld sentenced for murder of Johnson County deputy: Jury recommends sentence of 28 years, judge agrees(“考菲尔德因杀害约翰逊县助理被判刑：陪审团建议判他 28 年有期徒刑，法官同意”). 40/29 News on Demand(40/29 新闻点播). 2016 年 12 月 28 日 www.4029tv.com/article/kauffeld-sentenced-for-murder-of-johnson-county-deputy/4959435.

Randol, B. M., & Gaffney, M. J. (2014)(兰道尔和加夫尼). Are block watch volunteers different than volunteers in community-oriented policing programs? Findings from a mature COPS setting(“街区守望志愿者与社区导向警务项目中的志愿者存在不同吗? 来自成熟警察环境的研究发现”). *Police Practice and Research: An International Journal*(《警察实践与研究: 国际期刊》), 15 (3), 234—248.

Ren, L., Zhao, J., Lovrich, N. P., & Gaffney, M. J. (2006)(任、赵、洛夫里奇和加夫尼). Participation community crime prevention: Who volunteers for police work? (“参加社区犯罪预防: 谁志愿做警察工作?”) *Policing: An International Journal of Police Strategies and Management*(《警务: 关于警察战略与管理的国际期刊》), 29 (3), 464—481.

Scoville, D. (2014)(斯科维勒). Reserve officers: For love of the job(“后备警察: 因为热爱工作”). *Police*, 38 (March)(《警察》, 38 (三月)), 34—41.

Strickland, P., Lalic, M. (2010, June 9)(斯特里克兰和拉利克〈2010年6月9日〉). Special constables, Standard Note SN/HA/1154(“特别警员, 标准注释 SN/HA/1154”). London: House of Commons Library(伦敦: 公共图书馆).

Walker, S., & Katz, C. M. (2013)(沃克和卡茨). *The police in America: An introduction*(《美国警察: 概述》). New York: McGraw-Hill(纽约: 麦克劳-希尔出版公司).

Wilson, M. (2007, March 16)(威尔逊〈2007年3月16日〉). Lives intersect violently on busy city street(“在繁忙的城市街道上数人暴力交火”). *The New York Times*(《纽约时报》). 2016年12月28日 www.nytimes.com/2007/03/16/myregion/16cops.html.

Wolf, R., Holmes, S. T., & Jones, C. (2016)(沃尔夫、赫尔摩斯和乔恩思). Utilization and satisfaction of volunteer law enforcement officers in the office of the American sheriff: An exploratory nationwide study(“美国县治安官办公室志愿性质执法官员的使用及其满意度: 一项全国性研究”). *Police Practice and Research: An International Journal*(《警察实践与研究: 国际期刊》), 17 (5), 448—462.

Zhao, J., Gibson, C., Lovrich, N. P., & Gaffney, M. J. (2002)(赵、吉布

森、洛夫里奇和加夫尼). Participation in community crime prevention：Are volunteers more or less fearful of crime than other citizens?（“参与社区犯罪预防：与其他公民相比，志愿者或多或少惧怕犯罪吗?”）*Journal of Crime and Justice*（《犯罪与司法》），25（1），41—61.

第三章　英国、美国辅警的使用和配置

P39

联合国对志愿服务有浓厚的兴趣，其把志愿服务视为那些住在被边缘化地区或者社会经济水平较低区域的人们，获得他们改善自己生活所需的服务、资源以及机会的一种方法。在其《2015 年世界志愿主义状况报告》中，联合国建议志愿者与地方政府联手工作，从而改善常住居民的生活质量；该报告强调了为确保追究责任和履行职责与地方政府、医院、警方以及法院部门合作的重要性，但与此同时，该报告并没有提到全世界任何以警察身份工作的志愿者（United Nations Volunteers，2015）。辅警提供服务往往穿着制服、履行巡逻职责，完成正规警察任务，但是许多警察局采用不同的方式使用辅警。

在英格兰和威尔士，辅警在非巡逻岗位提供服务，包括在国防警察部、社区警务、问题导向警务、情报主导警务、旅游警务以及农村警务。另外，许多英国警察组织已经开始使用特别警员带入警务岗位的技能，并且为特别警员和正规警察都拓展了培训。

在美国，各地使用志愿者的方式差异很大，这取决于地方司法管辖区域和州法律。但是我们在各种方式的例子中，都发现地方、县以及州一级的辅警，包括在州高速公路巡逻队、鱼类和野生动物保护办公室以及海上巡逻机构工作的辅警。另外，许多美国警务机构在使用这些岗位上的志愿者时，不给他们警察职权，但是志愿者在工作上给警察提供帮助，包括志愿者办公室助理、调查员以及人力资源志愿者。志愿者还可以在特殊岗位工作，如旅游警务、搜救队和其他要求具有特殊知识以及/或者训练的工作岗位，而且志愿者可以具有不同水平的培训；一些志愿者接受“不太正规的”警察培训，另一些志愿者则接受全部警察培训并获得证书。

英国警务中志愿者职责的扩展

P40

志愿部门充其量在地方和个人层面与民众产生联系。它能够授权民众在改善生活品质之外，挖掘他们的潜能，创建活跃的社区。这些反映在界定、支持和保持志愿组织的价值观里。志愿部门不是我们“正式”民主的组成部分，但是它丰富了民主生活，途径是关注社区以及管理人员和志愿者的参与。

（Panel on the Independence of the Voluntary Sector，2011，p. 5）

本书成书期间，恰逢英国、美国以及全球大多数国家的经济衰退、不断恶化的时候，而且在一些国家，经济衰退为该国社会及其社区中出现志愿者角色提供了基础。[①]志愿服务不是新生事物，但其重要性一直在增长；在英国，2001 年被定为志愿者国际年（Rochester，2006），五年后，英格兰志愿服务发展委员会建立起一个未来志愿服务委员会。未来志愿服务委员会在其首个出版物（Rochester，2006）（其前言由纽伯格女男爵[②]撰写）中表示，他们计划研究正式和非正式的志愿服务以及所有部门里的志愿服务——换言之，他们要研究的不只是那些在社区和志愿部门工作的志愿者。2008 年 1 月，未来志愿服务委员会确定未来志愿服务的模式并为之提出一些建议（Commission on the Future of Volunteering，2008）。为本书和其他项目开展的研究表明，对警方志愿者的管理和组织并不总是遵循未来志愿服务委员会在《变革宣言》中给出的建议。

然而，最近几年，鼓动使用志愿者的情况在数量和范围上都有增长，而且志愿者在英国警务工作中的重要性于 2012 年表现得尤为突出，当时警察和犯罪总监们正在英格兰和威尔士运作选举事宜。例如，在柴郡，当选的警察和犯罪总监游说，在柴郡的警察局里增加特别警员到 1000 名，与此同时，在许多其他警察局的警察和犯罪总监们也呼吁增加特别警员的人数。托马斯谷的警察局局长于同一时期呼吁在警务中来一场变革。该局长说，在她警察局里的 719 名特别警员，是其警察局有能力维护治安的一个相当重要的原因，而且她质疑为什么社区警务只应由全职警察去做（Whitehead，2012）。（英国）警察联合会，一个以前只代表全职警察的组织，在 2014 年投票第一次允许志愿性质的特别警员加入成为组织成员。警察联合会坚持认为特别警员应该继续作为辅助力量为全职警察提供支持而不是履行警察核心职能，也不能替代警察（Warrell，2014）。

P41

罗切斯特、潘恩和郝莱特（Rochester，Paine& Howlett，2012）指出，在二十一世纪，志愿服务发生的背景已经在很多重要方面发生了变化。他们首次指出英格兰和威尔士的人口是老龄化人口；另外，已经对健康和福利服务产生影响的经济紧缩，导致老年人和弱势群体对救助的需求更高，因为他们经常表现出孤独和被孤立。使这种境况加重的情况是，工作模式已经发生了变化，结果就是，渐渐地，女人和男人一样受雇于有偿工作，有相当比例的工作是有薪金加班和无薪金加班（Smith，2016；Conway & Sturges，2014）。罗切斯特等人（Rochester et al.，2012）简明扼要地概括了现代社会以及过去 20 年已经发生的变化。此外，他们指出，已经被意识到的危险导致出现这样一个社会，即一个不愿承担风险的社会，而且这个社会充斥着一些时刻准备责备政府没有减少风险的个人（Rochester，2001，引用于 Rochester et al.，2012）。这似乎与 1997 年工党政府发布的公告有点相反，该公告介绍了《反社会行为法令》（ASBOs，anti-social behavior orders）。《反社会行为法令》属于民事合同，由警方或地方权力部门签发，以回应公众对一些人的抱怨，因为这些人当时正在骚扰公众。[③]《反社会行为法令》被认为是一种方法，这个方法让一个社区的成员可以被视为维持当地“治安”的力量，并把一定的自主权交到邻里手中。从更加愤世嫉俗的角度来看，你可以认为他们给权力部门提供了一个机会，即把一些责任转嫁给公众的机会。所以，人们会争论说，这是一种志愿服务的形式，那些接受记录反社会行为并将之上报任务的人，实际上是支援警察志愿者的先行者们。但是，最初的结果令人沮丧，继而出现某种程度的混乱，所以在 2011 年，政府宣布改变方向。

但是，在执法部门使用志愿者情况的增长，导致有人批评这是“廉价警务”，尽管这不是什么新提法；根据吉尔和莫比（Gill & Mawby，1990）一篇发表在《警察评论》上的、由一名警察联合会助理秘书撰写的论文，提出这样的担忧：在加班费方面给特别警员带来的消极影响，因为加班费是正规警察可能获得的费用，所以他们能够为这份额外收入工作。同一篇论文继续发表看法：特别警员是“具有公共精神但被完全误导的人们”（Gill & Mawby，1990，p. 51）。吉尔和莫比（Gill & Mawby，1990）同样提出了一系列问题：政府使用特别警员而不是正规警察做一个大型活动的安保工作，政府节省了多少费用。

对特别警员主要职能的看法也已经传到了互联网上。2013 年，在一次在特别警员和正规警察中开展的网络讨论中，一个参与讨论的人写道：

P42

许多年前，我和我师傅有过一次对话。他不喜欢特别警员。我的看法是：有一个人和你一起工作总好过没有人。他告诉我，这是一个开端：老鼠拉木锨——大头在后头；总有一天我们会后悔特别警员的角色。我曾注意到他与一名特别警员聊天。那个人在一个汽车工厂上班，该工厂正在因劳动力过剩裁员。我师傅问那家伙："如果我到你的工厂工作16个小时或者1个多月，不要报酬上班，而你也在上班，你会怎么想？"那位特别警员用这样的话回击我师傅："我们的工作不会有危险。"我师傅回击说："我们的加班时间减少了，因为特别警员来了，还在周末工作到很晚，不然我们就能得到加班费，而这就是老鼠拉木锨——大头在后头。"

（Police UK，2013）

这次网络讨论反映出的这个警察师傅的态度不是个例。特别警员面对来自全职警察的批评有多方面的原因，尽管有的原因对个人来说可能不是真的。米利（Millie，2016）研究了在兰开夏郡警察队工作的志愿者们的经历，因为兰开夏郡警察队实施了一个方案，该方案受到警务中的公民项目资助。这次定性研究被设计用来确定涉及禁止或促进志愿服务、招聘、监督以及管理特别警员和支援警察志愿者的诸多因素。④米利的研究发现，被调查人对志愿服务经历总体上是积极的感受，但是一些人觉得未获充分使用，且与其他志愿者联系不多，没有感觉到自己是警务团队的一分子。本研究中的一些志愿者觉得自己没有价值，研究报告结论中的一个观点是"众多志愿者享受与警察一起工作的时光并且从中收获很多；然而有些人感觉未获充分使用或者所获信息不足，担心志愿者是否会被保留"（Millie，2016，p. 21）。尽管米利在研究报告中说特别警员对他们获得的培训持肯定态度，但米利还是担忧把使用特别警员队作为正规警察潜在申请人的培训阵地。"除了作为廉价劳动力直到成为正规警察，他们可以看到警察所谓的职业特长，这是像我这样的人真心不想进入的职业，应该更好地使用我们"（Millie，2016，p. 14）。

志愿者为公众利益服务

有利他主义精神的人去帮助那些需要帮助的邻居，以及那些常常二话不说帮助陌生人的人，都在展示志愿行为。除了接受他们支持的直接受益人，他们的举动经常被忽视而且未获认可。从十九世纪后半期以来，慈善机构和其他组织更加正式地依赖个人付出的时间和努力（Brewis，2013）。互助运动协会承认"最高形式的慈善是个人服务而非施舍救济"（引用于 Brewis，2013，p. 6）。布雷维斯（Brewis，2013）还发现，在英王爱德华七世时代，当时比较普遍的现象是，慈善机构给那些积极参与"社会服务"运动的人提供培训机会。

P43

在第二次世界大战期间及之后，志愿者角色相当重要。但是，随着 1945 年《家庭补贴法》的出台，福利国家诞生，社会需求由新成立的国家卫生服务部和其他服务部门负责，资金来源是税收和公众提供的普遍支持。英国政治家威廉·贝弗里奇确定了在英国开展重建工作面临的五大障碍：贫困、疾病、无知、邋遢和愚蠢。为了消除这些障碍，贝弗里奇建议制订一个社会保障计划，覆盖全英的卫生服务、免费教育、公共住宅和就业机会。结果是，志愿服务不知怎么就被认为不重要了。但是，志愿服务继续或多或少地存在，有赖于管理的习惯做法。社会服务全国委员会（NCSS，the National Council of Social Service），建立于 1919 年，在开发社会服务和传播社会服务意义方面，它是一个重要机构。1952 年，社会服务全国委员会公布了一份关于志愿服务及其现状的报告。该报告认为，第一次世界大战期间“社会服务”的扩展是一个“转折点”，在两次世界大战之间的几年，“志愿服务”不再是慈善或不再受到资助，而是成为由来自社会各行各业的人们提供的个人服务（Brewis 2013，p. 8）。

但是，直到二十世纪六十年代，政府才再一次开始积极鼓励志愿服务。在七十年代的后半期以及整个八十年代，经济紧缩为保守党政府提供了一个机会，这个机会由保守党政府取自工党首相吉姆·卡拉汉的全国“好邻居”运动，该运动发起于 1976 年。这是一个非正式计划，原本应该鼓励人们自愿照看他们邻里中的弱势居民。当时，人们认识到公共服务不能覆盖所有人，而且志愿者是有益处、有价值的资产，而且全国“好邻居”运动的理念是为了减轻卫生和社会服务部门的压力。随着需求的增加，资源变得更为紧张，后来不论是保守党政府还是工党政府，开始把志愿者视为重要资产。各党派政府这样做的动机不只有一个，原因是多样的，包括特别政治派别的计划。这一点在保守党发起“与众不同”运动时就很清楚了，该运动在 1994—1997 年约翰·梅杰政府期间发起，因为政府需要一个更为全面的计划。该运动一个很重要的特点是，英国的四个联邦首次商讨并达成共识，试图就志愿服务制定一个能让所有参与者满意的政策。令人振奋的是，该运动见证了志愿服务成为一个“参与社会和贡献社会的手段”（引用于 Rochester et al.，2012，p. 90），而不是提供服务的手段。然而，最后，来自政府的资助很有限，这是常有的事。所以，理想很丰满，现实很骨感。

通过使用志愿者，与犯罪有关的组织逐渐发展演变，这方面的一个好例子是被害人救助，开始于英国的英格兰西南部，时间是二十世纪七十年代。起初，一个完全是志愿性质的组织，在 20 年的时间里开始从政府手里获取其收入的一部分。有人可能会认为接受这样的资助，这个组织就存在丧失某些自主权的风险；看来独立问题受到关注，特别是在经济紧缩已经被明确的时候。

根据布拉南、约翰和斯托克（Brannan，John& Stoker，2006）的论文，在英国存在了几十年的政府风气——自上而下的官僚作风，已经变成“如果英国想保留自己的行动能力，好像需要与市民阶层锻造一种新型关系”（Brannan，John& Stoker，2006，p. 994）。邻里守望（NW，Neighbourhood Watch）于 1982 年开始在英国实施，这是展示公民参与犯罪预防的例证。邻里守望获得警察局的支持，通过社区协作威慑和减少犯罪活动以及反社会活动，旨在“让邻里团结起来创建强大、友好和活跃的社区”（Neighbourhood Watch，n. d. ）。在社区参与和犯罪预防的道德框架内，科克霍尔特（英格兰北部罗奇代尔郊区的一个居民区）在二十世纪八十年代末制定了一个减少入室盗窃的计划。该项目开发了“茧（Cocoon）”式邻里守望，即入室盗窃发生后，房屋周边是保持警惕的人们，以此降低入室盗窃的机会和动机，这是该项目得以成功的一个重要因素，也没有证据表明该项目导致犯罪转移（Wakefield & Fleming，2009；参见 Office of Justice Programs，2011）。“茧”式邻里守望在微观层面上起作用：当一个人的财产受到侵害时（在科克霍尔特案例中，案件类型属于住宅盗窃），围绕在被侵害的财产周边的物业住户，自愿去维持自然监视以降低再次被害的风险。

除了这些被认可的志愿服务项目，英格兰和威尔士的警察局在不同场合使用不同种类的志愿者。正如前文提到的，使用支援警察志愿者（包括警官学员）经历了不同的命运；根据全国支援警察志愿者收集的数据以及在 2016 年开展的特别调查，每一个警察局里支援警察志愿者的人数，常常反映高级警官的“意
P45 愿”，即他们是否支持和鼓励支援警察志愿者应聘和提出申请。与一些警察职员的聊天和访谈也表明，在财政紧缩时期，失去志愿者协调员以及类似人员，导致对支援警察志愿者缺少关注和热情。结果就是，支援警察志愿者的评论表明，这些志愿者会觉得他们“被忽视，没什么可做的”，或者“在一般警察队伍里都有，特别是在领导中间也存在，对我们角色和地位的误解；他们同样误解把我们当作别的资源使用的成效。我认为造成这种情况的原因是对我们能够给团队带来什么经验，他们缺少认识”（Britton，2016）。即便不能把这样的评论当作适用于所有警察局里的所有志愿者，但是从年复一年的统计来看，很明显的情况是：志愿者人数正以一个相当惊人的数量在减少。而且，因为数据不能反映活跃水平，所以记载的支援警察志愿者的数据不能反映真实的参与程度。值得注意的是，没

有高级警官为支援警察志愿者代言，但是有高级警官为特别警员代言。

《工作组关于英格兰和威尔士特别警员队的研究报告（1995—1996）》（Home Office，1996）给出的建议多达91条，许多建议涉及给予特别警员补贴。值得注意的是，第二条建议“特别警员不应继续被官方认定为一个警察局建制的组成部分或者警察局的一部分警力，也不应出于工作规划的目的在计算一个特别部门或者地区的警员最佳人数时总是把特别警员计算在内”（Home Office，1996，p. 47）。随后在1997年当选的新一届工党政府，对志愿服务采取了更加稳健的做法。有很多例子表明该届政府为推进志愿服务有点强硬的做法，包括纳入绩效指标。新一届工党政府政策的特别之处在于，在公共政策执行的各个领域，实现目标是中心任务。

志愿服务未来委员会的报告《变革宣言》（Commission on the Future of Volunteering，2008）指出，在一个文化逐步呈现多样性的社会里，公民身份日益重要；在多样性文化的社会里，为了给人一种包容的感觉，需要连接不同信仰、文化和种族。为此，在国家开支紧缩和许多组织重建的时候，《变革宣言》提出六点建议。另一份政府报告建议：“世界一流服务的特点不仅仅是公民与公共服务专业人员之间的协作，而且是给予民众自主权，使他们作出更大的贡献去满足他们自己的需求”（Cabinet Office，2008，p. 22）。该报告还认为这种观点会导致责任分摊。

巴菱基金会与国民交流智库开展合作，于2011年发布了一份报告，题目是《志愿部门的独立性》（Panel on the Independence of the Voluntary Sector，2011）。这份报告由志愿部门独立性调查小组撰写。该调查小组的组长是前监狱总督察长，是一系列关于志愿部门状况及其独立性的出版物的作者。前不久，对公民授权日益成为政府政策的中心，也成为英格兰和威尔士刑事司法系统的密切相关的议题，而且警务中的公民（Citizens in Policing）战略在2016年被披露出来。此战略希望开发一个新的、有创意的方法，从而把在下列三个领域使用警局志愿者的规模最大化：特别警员、支援警察志愿者以及志愿性质的警官学员（VPCs，Volunteer Police Cadets）。此战略提供了一个初步建议去实现愿景：“将社区与警务结合起来以及将警务与社区结合起来”，而且“在适宜之处增加专家数量并把工作标准化，这将提升警察力量并实现物有所值”（Jones，2016，p. 7）。 P46

刑事司法系统里的志愿服务历史悠久，包括地方法官、监狱访客、支援警察志愿者以及教区治安官，还有特别警员。在法院系统内部，在英格兰和威尔士目前约有23000名地方法官（Courts and Tribunal Judiciary，n. d.），苏格兰有450名（Judiciary of Scotland，n. d.），北爱尔兰有21名（Northern Ireland Courts and Tribunals Service，n. d.），不过犯罪简易程序的这种“志愿性质的”管理在不断进行改革，包括在英格兰和威尔士的地方法院已经在大量使用有薪金的地区法官。另一个例子是，英国全境通过志愿性质的警官学员计划，警官学员数量得以增长；13岁至18岁的年轻人，特别是那些来自弱势群体背景的年轻人，受此鼓励加入以武力为基础的机构。

公民加入特别警员队的一个可能原因，由一次在伦敦开展的、对辅警的评估揭示出来。伦敦大都市警察局不仅是英格兰和威尔士最大的警察机构，而且它还有最大数量的特别警员。2016年，伦敦大都会特别警员队（MSC，Metropolitan Police Constabulary）接受了一次战略评审，评审结果令人沮丧（D'Orsi，2016）。高级警官多尔西，是评审小组的负责人，在一次访谈中这样说：“伦敦大都会警察局里的特别警员，十个当中有一个根本没有上过班，而且十个当中有两个在加入警察局后待了不到一年。”（Loeb，2016）评审报告继续指出，在伦敦大都会警察局工作的特别警员中，大约有20%的特别警员不住在伦敦，而且因为住在距伦敦市中心70英里（约为16.1公里）地方的特别警员可以报销差旅费，所以住在离伦敦市中心最远地方的伦敦大都会特别警员们的花销比住得近的要多。在相关财政年度，有646名未住在伦敦的大都会特别警员报销了69640英镑，而2580名住在伦敦的大都会特别警员报销了41340英镑（D'Orsi，2016）。尽管免费旅行可以鼓励那些对志愿服务感兴趣的人承诺付出时间提供服务，但是，罗埃伯
P47 （Loeb，2016）认为，为警务工作提供志愿服务不应成为获得免费旅行的借口。因为伦敦大都会特别警员和伦敦的正规警察被许可乘坐公共交通工具免费旅行，所以有人认为这应该既影响到财政，也影响到问责。[5]

英国的43个司法区域，一个整体力量

大家公认的警务改革开始于1829年，当时罗伯特·比尔，时任英国内政大臣，监督《大都会警察法》的通过。然而，伊姆斯雷（Emsley，2009）的观点是，较1829年的《大都会警察法》早几个星期出台的《柴郡警察法》，见证了首个警察局的诞生，因为地方法官之前想招聘一位名叫乔治·伯格斯的人做有薪金的特别警员，但是由于法律规定他们不能给他发薪水。柴郡警察局是一个大型乡村警察局，但是其职员被集中用在新开发的工业地区；在乡村地区采取集中警

务模式被认为是不必要的。

随着《大都会警察法》的通过，大约 1000 名警察穿着制服并且依据法律，在两位警察总监的指挥下，开始在伦敦的街道上巡逻（Emsley，2009）。在非常短的时间内，警察人数有了明显增长，所以在 1830 年 5 月，在警察诞生后不到一年的时间，警察有 3300 名；然而，人员流动也很快，在被确定的一系列问题中，酗酒是常被提及的一个方面（Emsley，2009）。

尽管大都会警察规模大且发展迅速，但是柴郡警察局被用来作为其他许多县级警察局的榜样。在十九世纪，英格兰和威尔士的警察部门与二十一世纪的警察部门并不相同，由监督委员会负责管理。尽管 1856 年的县与市镇法使警务在英格兰和威尔士得到强势推行，但是直到 1918—1919 年警察机构才树立起国家一体理念，不再是独立的警务机构。因为 1918—1919 年发生了警察罢工，并因此建立了德斯伯勒委员会，通过采用标准化工资形成统一性，才导致警察机构理念的转变。1900 年，有 243 个独立的警察局，这个数字在《1946 年警察法》通过后，减少到 117 个，当时小型镇级警察局被合并到县级警察局。为了提高效率，根据《1964 年警察法》，这个数字被再次减少到 47 个。同样是根据《1964 年警察法》，苏格兰全境建立了 20 个警察局。

1962 年成立的一个皇家委员会促成市和自治市警察局的合并。因此，到 1974 年，英格兰和威尔士处在 43 个警察局的保卫之下。大约在同一段时间里，苏格兰全境的警察局数量被定为 8 个。每个警察局的规模不同，人口和地理位置也不同。因此，在格洛斯特郡、北威尔士以及柴郡乡村面积很大，而大曼彻斯特
P48
警察局（GMP，Greater Manchester Police）、默西塞德郡和大都会警察局都更为都市化，当然也有公园和农业用地。

英格兰最大的警察局是伦敦大都会警察局，它负责保护 720 万人口，辖区面积达 620 平方英里（London Metropolitan Police，n. d.）。然而，其辖区不包括“一平方英里”的伦敦城。伦敦城有居民 11000 人，但现如今容纳 300000 名以上的工人、购物者和游客（City of London，n. d.）。这个地区内其他民众的多样性说明种族的多样性，计算出来大约在 40%—55%之间（Lammy，2014），但是来自这种背景下的警察的百分比却远低于其服务的人口。在伦敦城特别警员队，只有 6%的特别警员明确了自己的种族背景：黑人、亚洲人或者少数族裔（BAME，black，Asian or minority ethnic）。

美国警务中的志愿者

正如本书前文讨论过的，志愿者一直都是美国警务的一部分，而且美国警察局的志愿者目前在全部有薪金警察人数中占比为20%（Dobrin & Wolf，2016），尽管一些州和警察局根本不使用辅警（这里的意思是拥有“宣誓”或“获得认证的”警察权力的志愿者）。早在十七世纪中期，地方县治安官使用来自社区的志愿者组建“保安队”，帮助维持秩序、追捕逃犯以及为打击暴力罪犯提供社区资源。在东部城市的城区里，夜间守卫制度使用志愿者巡逻城市的街巷，直到根据英国《大都会警察法》更加正规的有薪金警察诞生。例如，纽约市警察局建立于1845年，基本上以在伦敦建立的大都会警察局为模板。

然而，美国和英国警察的主要区别是，所有美国警察都配枪。这主要是因为美国社会有大量武器。在美国，许多州有“携枪权利”法律，允许公民拥有枪支（尽管非必须随身携带或者隐藏携带），不用任何类型的许可证或执照。[6]美国和英国警务另一个显著区别是，在美国很难发现一个警察机构有强制退休年龄规定。美国100个最大警察机构里有超过80%的机构没有这样的要求（Pepper & Wolf，2015）。

然而，或许两国警务之间最大的区别在于，英国警察局是全国统一体制，而
P49 美国则有意形成地方分权。在美国超过18000个执法机构里，很难发现任何两个做完全相同事情的机构。这缘于“联邦制”，该原则强调各州的权利和权力，不强调联邦政府的权利和权力。美国宪法的形成赋予了各州模糊的且几乎无限的权力：“宪法不是把权力授予了美国，也不是限制各州的权力，而是为各州单独保留权力，或者给民众保留权力”（Gerstle，2010）。尽管州和地方政府使用宪法赋予的权力规范贸易、制造业以及劳工，但是它们还惩治犯罪活动，如赌博、卖淫以及其他不道德的行为。这也是各州开始产生分歧之处，即它们对一些行为有不同解释，如奴隶制。“政府手里的普通法和宪法赋予的特殊权力，成为‘各州的权利’：这是白种南方人愿意——而且的确——用生命去护卫的信条”（Gerstle，2010，p. 31）。在美国历史的大部分时间里，警察被用于维持政治秩序，而这推动了种族隔离、歧视和奴隶制，注意到这一点同样很重要（Greenberg，2005）。

尽管在美国历史上奴隶制是最不光彩的制度之一，但是奴隶制的确产生了由社区成员组成的、官方的武装队伍，名叫“控奴巡逻队”，这是辅警的一种类型。这些控奴巡逻队在历史上受到不同形式的激励（胁迫、报酬和奖励），负责

搜检奴隶宿舍、驱散未经许可的奴隶集会以及追捕不受控制的奴隶。控奴巡逻队不仅与奴隶发生冲突，而且与奴隶主也发生冲突，因为奴隶主们抱怨控奴巡逻队凶狠残忍、为所欲为地鞭打奴隶。在较大的城市，这种公民巡逻的、松散的组织系统演变成管理良好的、有薪金的警察队伍（Hadden，2001），这当然助长了美国境内非洲裔美国人和其他少数群体与警察机构之间的不良关系，即便在当今社会亦是如此。

当控奴巡逻队在美国内战结束后继续在美国南方存在的时候，辅警角色也在美国其他地方形成。反屋贼协会和侦探社被建立起来，同样被建立起来的还有其他组织。这些组织都得到某种执法职权，如压制恶行联盟。这样的组织在十八世纪九十年代首次出现，在接下来的世纪里甚至更为流行，主要原因是整个美国缺乏有效维护治安的力量。这些官方的和受到法律保护的协会被组建起来以确定并逮捕罪犯。例如，安东尼·科姆斯多克，一个纽约人，从 1872 年到 1915 年在压制恶行纽约社（NYSSV，the New York Society for the Suppression of Vice）担任秘书，几乎是单枪匹马地护卫美国邮件。该组织是一个志愿性质的邮政“特别联邦机构”。科姆斯多克曾参与编撰法律，禁止邮寄淫秽、下流和污秽的物品，后来他最终受命执行这个新法律。他要求不要给他发薪金，以避免来自政治利益的各种干预。在一段短暂的时间内，在十九世纪七十年代中期，科姆斯多克从邮件中没收了超过 300 万件的图片和明信片，科姆斯多克还自夸把差不多 3000 名罪犯送进了监狱（Greenberg，2005；Werbel，2014）。被设计用于侦查并处置犯罪的众多组织，数量上有很大增长，而且几个中西部和东部的州通过法律允许建立志愿性质的组织。这些组织通常被称为反屋贼协会或者公共援助社，而且法律常常把逮捕权授权给这些组织成员（Greenberg，2005）。

P50

然而，在中西部更为荒凉的地区，通过使用县治安官保安队，志愿性质的执法开始成长。在美国边境地区，县治安官可以召集一群人帮助维持和平，允许县治安官召集武装的公民帮助执法。美国人依靠公民来帮助自我管理，而且有人主张：保障公民反对不当的政府权力，产生了地方保安队、[7]人身保护令[8]以及陪审团制度。保安队不论过去还是现在与国民卫队都有明显区别，那就是对保安队没有强制性的培训要求，而且保安队只在被召集的时候才组建起来。国民卫队有正规指挥架构，是由受过训练的成员组成的常设机构（Kopel，2015）。

联邦法院最终能够强制各州承认个人权利的至高无上，一如在宪法、权利法案以及其他宪法修订案里阐述的那样。二十世纪六十年代的民权运动助力把更多的权力转回联邦政府，包括联邦法律禁止各州在分配联邦拨款时采取种族歧视政策。然而，各州及地方权力部门，数量上超过89000个不同司法管辖区域里的部门，现在仍继续抵制联邦政府（Gerstle，2010），而且在2016年选举周期时，这些部门是共和党政治崛起的部分力量。

因为各州之间各自为政，整个美国境内警务演变各不相同，辅警的演变亦是如此。后备警察部门和协警部门开始出现在全美的时间是二十世纪二十年代，地点是美国的大城市。但是，他们很少被召集去履行执法职责，公民常常出于政治偏爱被任命到这些岗位上（Greenberg，2005）。当今有关拥有极其有限权力的协警的例子可以在美国东北部找到。在美国东北部地区，许多城市使用的志愿者被称为“协”警；尽管协警的制服看上去特别像正规警察的制服，但是他们没有执
P51 法职权。美国南部和西部地区更愿意使用“后备”警察。后备警察有全部警察职权，但是接受的培训数量不同。

甚至术语“后备警察”和“协警”在整个美国使用时均有不同的意思。纽约市警察局的协警没有警察权力，而一个反向例子可以在佛罗里达州的协警里找到。佛罗里达州获得认证的协警，是被授权可以携带枪支和实施逮捕的力量，在与获得完全认证的警察一起工作的时候，他们拥有全部警察职权。在美国中西部和中部地区，辅警获得的培训数量和职权都有不同。一些州有后备警察，这些后备警察必须参加培训、身着制服、履行巡逻职责，但是没有权力携带枪支或实施逮捕。另一些州提供相当数量的培训，并授权辅警可以实施逮捕和携带枪支，而且在一些司法管辖区域，他们被授权使用自己的私人汽车作为应急警车。第八章里有各类辅警部门的例子。

因为很难界定美国的“辅警”，所以许多学者把自己的研究局限于那些已经开始或者已经被授权履行各种警务职责的公共组织（职责包括犯罪侦查、逮捕以及处罚），或者局限于那些已经被赋予职权去履行维护治安职能的公共组织（包括交通控制和人群控制以及努力提升见警率）。这些组织还被合法政府的警察局或者政府部门授权（Greenberg，2005）。辅警有一些共性特点。为了本书研究所需，辅警是个人直接为一个政府部门工作，并经授权拥有预防、侦查和处罚犯罪活动以及维护公共秩序的合法职权。辅警提供这些服务未受强制要求也没有获得可观的报酬。然而，合法职权的级别以及可能的报酬数额都是容易改变的方面。

但是，美国辅警有时被视为“工贼”[9]或者“误入歧途的行善者”，这点与他们在英国的特别警员同行们很相像（Greenberg，2005，p. 11）。警察工会现在很

少接纳辅警项目或者辅警，有报道说正规警察对辅警价值的看法各式各样。克拉里（Crary，2015）这样报道：美国国民自由联盟俄克拉荷马州分部的主管认为，志愿者不应履行宣誓警察的职责。“如果有人想自愿在警察局里工作并握住某人的手帮忙过马路……这很好。但是允许某人荷枪实弹履行警察职责，这是不计后果的鲁莽做法。这绝对不应发生”。怀利（Wyllie，2017）报道了在被问到辅警时正规警察表现出的复杂情感，而且众多支持者们指出，一支随时可用的后备力量帮助警察履行日常职责是物有所值的，特别是在预算缩减的年代。但是怀利（Wyllie，2017）还报道了正规警察对辅警的一些消极看法：“我相信‘兼职’警务制度是荒唐透顶的……我们现在苦于应付更多的反警察群体，每天 24 小时、每周 7 天的视频监控，还有比以往更多的指控和法律诉讼。正因如此，做这样的工作却没有全额薪水、没有全部福利，这是脑子有病。”德洛德、布鲁波、香农和斯匹灵（DeLord，Brupo，Shannon & Spearing，2008）考察了警察工会以及后备警察和辅警适应现代警务机构的方法，并探究：警察工会是否努力消除后备警察项目，或者“把后备警察完全整合进警察工会里面”（DeLord，Brupo，Shannon & Spearing，2008，p. 283）。

P52

认可辅警和辅警专业化

在一个财政紧缩和政治意识形态的时代，志愿服务已经成为日益令人向往的服务。不论是美国的还是英国的居民，都受到鼓励在过多的公共服务机构和非营利机构中奉献自己的时间、能力和财富。不论是美国还是英国，使用辅警都说明执法机构有能力提供额外服务来满足公民的期望。

因为辅警获得很少经济报酬或者没有任何经济报酬，所以在美国，通过授予志愿者国家级奖励，志愿者的重要性得到认可，志愿者个人所做工作的重要性得以确定。在美国，国家级奖项有很多，如志愿服务总统奖章，[10]乔治·H. W. 布什颁发的“闪光点”奖，以及巴拉克·奥巴马签发的《爱德华·M. 肯尼迪服务美国法案》（Nesbit and Brudney，2010；Wolf，2013；Wolf，Holmes and Jones，2016）。然而，这些奖项没有一个是专门为辅警设计的；相反，这些奖项是从普遍意义上认可志愿服务，辅警只不过是有资格赢得这些奖励。不过，美国全国县治安官协会（NSA，National Sheriff's Association）创立了一个奖项——后备助理年度奖[11]——认可一个或更多为县治安官办公室的后备警务和志愿警务作出突出贡献的个人。国际警察局长协会给警务志愿者组织设立了奖项——执法志愿者项目领导奖。[12]在英国，勒斯勋爵奖[13]已经在23年的时间里，奖励包括特别警员在内的社会群体所作的突出贡献（Lord Ferrers Awards，2017）。在美国和英国，除了这些国家级奖励，还有警察局范围内举办的仪式，奖励他们自己的志愿者所作的贡献。

认可志愿者服务的奖项为确定并区分志愿者提供了方法，而恶性事件，如2001年9月11日发生在纽约市的袭击，同样对志愿精神产生积极影响。正如在 P53 前文讨论过的，美国在9·11事件之后公民的志愿精神大幅增长，当时县级政府和人口稠密的城市对志愿服务感兴趣的人数飙升（Gazley & Brudney，2005）。民族自豪感同样可以影响志愿精神，例如，2012年伦敦奥运会成功从240000名申请者中录用了70000名志愿者（International Olympic Committee，2012）。然而，这一势头在英国没有保持下来。

随着资源减少以及对个人特殊专业领域的要求持续升高，许多警察机构依赖志愿者来帮助自己降低成本（Hilal & Olsen，2010；Wolf et al.，2016）。然而，在警察机构采用许多方式使用这些志愿者的时候，许多公众并未意识到，美国和英国大量使用志愿者来提高警察在其所服务社区的见警率。在英国，从传统上来说，特别警员被授权到一个特定的警察局，而且他们履行职责往往发挥“万金油”的作用，尽管他们首当其冲的职责是巡逻和安保特别活动。但是，最近特别警员们带入工作岗位里的专业价值得到认可，而且特别警员的专业被日益用在打击网络犯罪和医疗卫生服务领域。例如，大曼彻斯特郡和西约克郡的警察局招聘实习医生进入它们的特别警员队伍，而汉普郡和格洛斯特郡则征募了网络犯罪专家，第五章将论及这个内容。

在美国，警察机构内部的志愿部门常常是专业实体。这些专业实体可以被融入社区功能当中，目的是在社区成员和地方政府之间创建积极的关联（Ren，Zhao，Lovrich& Gaffney，2006）。美国的执法机构使用志愿者的方式多种多样，如宣誓后备警察、协警，或者特别助理，如被害人辩护律师、翻译人员以及其他专业岗位（Hilal & Oslen，2010）。然而，正如第二章详细介绍过的，在美国全部公共安全组织中，仅有30%的公共安全组织使用志愿者（Brudney & Kellough，2000），而且甚至更少的公共安全组织允许警察局里的志愿者拥有全部逮捕权以及/或者在工作时配枪的权力。为辅警提供的专业培训将在第六章里讨论。

注释

①在经济衰退的时代，对服务的需求常常会出现一个增长，而满足这些需求

的资金却更少。类似无家可归、精神健康和犯罪这样的社会问题会增多，而通常自愿提供这些服务的人或者捐款资助提供服务组织的人，可能不再有时间或者不再有金钱这样做了，因为他们自己还要努力拼搏满足自己的个人需求（Ellis，2008）。

②茱莉亚·纽伯格女男爵在1977年成为英国第二位女性拉比，即犹太教经师。她在伦敦担任拉比，还担任利昂·巴埃克学院的教授级别的职位，她在被任命为英帝国女爵士（DBE，Dame of the British Empire）之前，在该学院任职达20年之久。在随后那一年，她被晋升为女男爵。

③反社会行为法令出现在1988年出台的《犯罪与无序法案》第一部分的条款里。该法案在1999年4月1日正式生效。此后，该法案被修订了好几次，分别在2002年、2003年和2005年。在2014年10月，《犯罪行为法令》（CBO，criminal behavior order）颁行，替代了《反社会行为法令》。《反社会行为法令》属于民事法令，意图保护社会免受反社会行为的侵害。反社会行为是如骚扰和非法侵入这样的行为。这样的行为给不与违法者在同一家庭里的任何对方或者任何他人必然造成或者很可能造成骚扰、恐慌或者痛苦。该法令实质上不是刑事法令，旨在起到预防作用而不是惩罚作用（Crown Prosecution Service，n. d.）。

④支援警察志愿者在二十世纪九十年代开始在英格兰和威尔士出现（Bullock，2017）。最初的理念是允许志愿性质的角色履行特殊职责，这会使获得认证的警察有时间去一线工作。支援警察志愿者包括以提供支持的员工的身份向被害人和目击证人提供案件信息，作为警方和公众的桥梁纽带，或者做警察的牧师或者警察总部的志愿者（Millie，2016）。支援警察志愿者自愿做未获认证的"公民"警察员工。2014年1月，英格兰和威尔士有大约9000名支援警察志愿者（Bullock，2017）。

⑤在2013年2月至2015年1月，58件来自官员（特别警员和伦敦大都会正规警察）的投诉被《每日邮报》披露在一个请求刊登《信息自由法》的信件里。根据该报道，伦敦大都会警察局审查过职员不当使用警察证出入酒吧和夜总会、现场观看足球比赛以及免费乘坐火车旅行的情况。在查处的一个案子里，一名特别警员被开除，因为他在乘坐火车被发现没有该车车票时，他出示了自己的大都会警察局（MPS，Metropolitan Police Service）警察证。为了使用大都会警察局免费旅行的福利，警察和特别警员们必须同时持有他们的警察证和一张配发的警察旅行通用卡（Boyle，2015）。不幸的是，这样的新闻报道引发公众的负面议

论，让那些没有享受制度利好的人很难继续享受应该拥有的福利。

⑥例如，佛罗里达州的法律允许任何没有被判重罪的公民（否则法院会剥夺他们的携带枪支的权利）持有武器。在佛罗里达州，拥有或持有武器不用获得许可证，而且事实上，政府不可以追踪是谁拥有武器。但是，为了能随身隐秘携带武器，公民必须申请并获得“隐秘携带武器许可证”。为了获得隐秘携带武器许可证，申请人必须是美国公民（不用必须是佛罗里达州公民），年龄在 21 岁及以上，并且通过了有限犯罪背景调查。另外，申请人必须有能力展示有体能使用武
P55 器（这可以通过一个非常短的手把手培训来实现，培训费用不高），而且要交费至少 $ 100。但是，其他州在允许携带武器方面采用相反的规定。一些州禁止在未获特别许可证的情况下携带武器，这个许可证很难获得。其他 14 个美国州与佛罗里达州有协议互认许可证，所以，佛罗里达州的隐秘携带武器许可证在这 14 个州被接纳作为本州的隐秘携带武器许可证。

⑦保安队的发源地在盎格鲁-撒克逊时代的英格兰。当时的郡最高司法长官的一个核心权力是召集公民保卫辖区，而且在美国殖民地时期，社会生活当中的一个常见现象是参加保安队。“就像参加陪审团一样，人们愿意参加保安队是因为把它视为民主社会负责任的公民的义务和责任”（Kopel，2014）。召集公民保卫辖区这项权力现在仍然存在，而且全美国的县治安官均使用这项权力，召集志愿者去满足县治安官办公室的各种需求。

⑧人身保护令：是一个书面命令，要求把已经被逮捕的人带至一名法官面前即法庭上，除非有合法证据表明他或她应该被监禁，否则就要释放该人。

⑨“工贼”是指一个工人，在别的工人参加罢工的时候，他或她仍在工作或开始工作。在十六世纪初，该术语最初的意思是指皮肤受伤后形成的结痂，后来意思得到扩展，开始指流氓或无赖，而这可能是由于他们坏习惯和不做清洁。到十八世纪后期，该术语开始有了现在的意思：不愿意加入罢工或者参加有组织劳作的工人。

⑩志愿服务总统奖是由国家和社区服务局管理的奖项。该局是一个联邦机构，这个联邦机构认证在社区和基于信仰的组织提供的服务。任何人，只要他或她加入一个经认证的组织做志愿者，就可以被认可为一定的志愿等级，志愿等级根据志愿者的年龄确定。另外，志愿者在一生当中做志愿者奉献的时间超过 4000 个小时，就可以被授予总统志愿服务奖（the President’s Volunteer Service A-ward，n. d.）。

⑪美国全国县治安官办公室后备助理年度奖由全国县治安官办公室的后备执法官员委员会创设于 2013 年。该机构认可那些作出“直接与志愿者执法有关的突出贡献或成就”的个人。尽管有功行为或英勇行为是在考虑范围内，但是该奖项是为了认可不同寻常的倡议而设立的。只有在县治安官办公室工作的志愿者助理才有资格评奖（National Sheriff’s Association，2017），那些在警察局工作的志愿者没有资格评奖。

⑫执法志愿者项目领导奖，是国际警察局长协会颁发给这样的项目，即“在扩大宣誓或公民职员以及/或者完善提供给社区的服务方面，有创新和有效实践”；颁发给那些志愿者项目，即明显为多用途的项目，而且包含越多的志愿服务成分越好，包括非宣誓的支持性服务（International Association of Chiefs of Police，n. d.）；仅仅被用于警务职责的志愿性质的后备警察项目以及协警项目没有资格申请该奖励。不论是地方警察机构的还是县治安官办公室的志愿者项目都有资格申请，因为这些机构是州级别的警务部门。

⑬勒斯勋爵奖之前被称为特别警员和支援警察志愿者奖。该奖项认可在警察局工作的志愿者对英国警务发挥的重大作用。2013 年，该奖项被重新命名为勒斯勋爵奖。勒斯勋爵是英国前内政部部长，是他在 1993 年创设了该奖项。该奖项不仅认可以个人名义和团队形式履职的特别警员、支援警察志愿者、警官学员，而且认可出资人对警务组织的资助以及在支持警务科技方面所作的贡献（Lord Ferrers Awards，2017）。

P56

参考文献

Boyle，D.（2015，April 29）（博伊尔〈2015 年 4 月 29 日〉）. Let me through，I’m a cop! Dozens of police officers disciplined for abusing their warrant cards to get into bars and football matches and blag free train travel（“让我进去，我是警察！因滥用警察证进入酒吧、观看足球比赛和享受免费乘车待遇，数十名警察受到纪律处罚”）. *Daily Mail*（《每日邮报》）. 2017 年 8 月 13 日检索网址 www. dailymail. co. uk/news/article-3060513/let-m-cop-dozens-police-officers-discplined-abusing-warrant-cards-bars-blag-free-train-travel. html.

Brannan，T.，John，P.，& Stoker，G.（2006）（布拉南、约翰和斯托克尔）. Active citizenship and effective services and programmes：How can we know what really works?（“积极的公民意识与有效的服务以及项目：我们怎样知道什么真正有

用?”）*Urban Studies*（《城市研究》），43（5/6），993—1008.

Brewis, G.（2013）（布雷维斯）. *Towards a new understanding of volunteering in England before* 1960?（《对 1960 年之前英格兰志愿服务的新理解》），Working Paper 2（工作报告 2）. London：Institute for Volunteering Research（伦敦：志愿服务调查研究所）. 2017 年 4 月 14 日检索网址 http：//eprints. ioe. ac. uk_/18258/1/ivr_workingpaper_two_history__of_volunteering. pdf.

Britton, I.（2016）（布里顿）. *National survey of special constables and police support volunteers*：*Initial findings report*（《对特别警员和支援警察志愿者的全国性调查：初步调查报告》）. Northampton, UK：University of Northampton, Institute for Public Safety, Crime and Justice（北安普顿，英国：北安普顿大学，公共安全、犯罪和司法研究所）.

Brudney, J. L., & Kellough, J. E.（2000）（布鲁德尼和克拉夫）. Volunteers in state government：Involvement, management and benefits（“州政府里的志愿者：参与、管理和待遇”）. *Nonprofit and voluntary sector quarterly*（《非营利性志愿部门季刊》），29（1），111—130.

Bullock, K.（2017）（布洛克）. Shoring up the “home guard”? Reflections on the development and deployment of police support volunteer programmes in England and Wales（“支持‘民兵’？关于英格兰和威尔士支援警察志愿者项目开发部署的思考”）. *Policing and Society*（《警务与社会》），27（4），341—358.

Cabinet Office（2008）（内阁办公室）. *Excellence and fairness*：*Achieving world class public services*（《卓越与公平：实现世界一流的公共服务》）. London：HMSO（伦敦：英国皇家文书局）.

City of London（n. d.）（伦敦城〈日期不详〉）. Police authority（“警察职权”）. 2017 年 4 月 14 日检索网址 www. cityoflondon gov. uk/about－the－city/how-we-make-decisions/Pages/policeauthority. aspx.

Commission on the Future of Volunteering（2008）（未来志愿服务委员会）. *Report of the Commission on the Future of Volunteering and manifesto for change*（《未来志愿服务委员会报告和变革宣言》）. London：Commission on the Future of Volunteering（伦敦：未来志愿服务委员会）. 2017 年 4 月 14 日检索网址 www. fairpalyforchildren. org/pdf/1216564640.

Conway, N., & Sturges, J.（2014）（康韦和斯特金斯）. Investigating unpaid overtime working among the part-time workforce（“在兼职工作人员中调查加班工作未支付报酬的情况”）. *British Journal of Management*（《英国管理》），25（4），755—771.

Courts and Tribunal Judiciary（n. d.）（法院和特别法庭〈日期不详〉）. Magistrates' court（“治安法庭”）. 2017 年 4 月 14 日检索网址 www. judiciary-gov. uk/you-and-the-judiciary/going-to-court/magistratescourt.

Crary, D. （2015, April 13）（克拉里〈2015 年 4 月 13 日〉）. Amid tight budgets, use of police reserve officers is common. *The San Diego Union-Tribune*（“在预算紧缩之时，使用后备警察是普遍现象”）. 2017 年 8 月 13 日检索网址 www. sandiegouniontribune. com/sdut-amid-tight-budgets-use-of-policereserve-officers-2015apr13-story. htmL.

Crown Prosecution Service（n. d.）（皇家检察总署〈日期不详〉）. Anti-social behaviour orders on conviction（ASBos）（“反社会行为法令生效”）. 2017 年 8 月 13 日检索网址 www. cps. govuk/legal-guidance/anti_social behaviour-orders-conviction-asbos.

DeLord, R., Burpo, J., Shannon, M., & Spearing, J. （2008）（德洛德、布尔珀、山农和斯柏灵）. *Police union power, politics, and confrontation in the 21st century: New challenges, new issues*, 2nd Edition［《二十一世纪警察工会的权力、政治与现实：新挑战、新问题》（第二版）］. Springfield, IL: Charles C. Thomas Publishing（斯普林菲尔德，伊利诺伊州：查尔斯·C. 托马斯出版社）.

Dobrin, A., & Wolf, R. （2016）（多布林和沃尔夫）. What is known and not known about volunteer policing in the United States（“我们知道的以及我们不知道的美国辅警管理”）. *International Journal of Police Science Management*（《警察科学与管理国际期刊》），18（3），220—227.

D'Orsi, L. （2016）（多尔西）. *Metropolitan Special Constabulary: Strategic review*（《大都会特别警员队：战略评论》）. London: Metropolitan Police（伦敦：大都会警察局）. 2017 年 2 月 9 日检索网址 www. metpolice. uk/foi/pdfs/priorities_and_how_we_are_doing/corporate/msc_strategic_review. pdf.

Ellis, S. J. （2008, November）（埃利斯〈2008 年 11 月〉）. How will the economic crisis affect volunteering?（“经济危机怎样影响志愿服务?”）Energize（激励）. 2017 年 8 月 13 日检索网址 www. energizeinc. com/hot-topics/2008/no-

P57

vember.

Emsley, C. （2009）（伊姆斯雷）. *The Great British bobby*：*A history of British policing from the*18*th century to the present*（《大英帝国警察：从十八世纪至今的英国警务历史》）. London：Quercus（伦敦：栎树出版公司）.

Gazley, B. , & Brudney, J. L. （2005）（盖兹雷和布鲁德尼）. Volunteer involvement in local government after September 11：The continuing question of capacity（“9/11之后志愿者加入地方政府：一直存在的能力问题”）. *Public Administration Review*（《公共管理评论》）, 65（2）, 131—142.

Gerstle, G. （2010）（盖斯特勒）. Federalism in America：Beyond the Tea Partiers（《美国联邦制：茶党除外》）. *Dissent*（《异议》）, 57（4）, 29—36.

Gill, M. L. , Mawby, R. I. （1990）（吉尔和莫比）. *A special constable*：*A study of the police reserve*（《特别警员；关于警方后备人员的研究》）. Aldershot, UK：Avebury Publishing（奥尔德肖特，英国：阿维伯里出版社）.

Greenberg, M. A. （2005）（格林伯格）. *Citizens defending America*：*From colonial times to the age of terrorism*（《保卫美国的公民：从殖民地时代到恐怖主义年代》）. Pittsburgh：University of Pittsburgh Press（匹兹堡：匹兹堡大学出版社）.

Hadden, S. E. （2001）（哈德）. *Slave patrols*：*Law and violence in Virginia and the Carolinas*（《控奴巡逻：在弗吉尼亚州和卡罗莱纳州的法律和暴力》）. Cambridge, MA：Harvard University Press（剑桥市，马萨诸塞州：哈佛大学出版社）.

Hilal, S. M. , & Olsen, D. P. （2010）（希拉尔和奥尔森）. Police reserve officers：Essential in today's economy and an opportunity to increase diversity in the law enforcement profession（“后备警察：在当前经济中地位至关重要且是增强执法职场多元化的一个机会”）. *The Police Chief*（《警察局长》）, 77（10）, 92—94.

Home Office（1996）（英国内政部）. *Report of the Working Group on the Special Constabulary in England and Wales* 1995—1996（《工作组关于英格兰和威尔士特别警员队的研究报告1995—1996年》）. London：Home Office Communications Directorate（伦敦：英国内政部通信理事会）.

International Association of Chiefs of Police（n. d.）（国际警察局长协会〈日期不详〉）. IACP/Body Worn Leadership in Law Enforcement Volunteer Programs Award（国际警察局长协会/随身佩戴执法志愿者项目领导奖）. 2017 年 8 月 27 日检索网址 www. theiacp. org/lacp-aWaRd-For-OutstaNding-achievement-in-law-Enforcement-Volunteer-Programs.

International Olympic Committee（2012, July 21）（国际奥林匹克委员会〈2012 年 7 月 21 日〉）. Volunteers: Helping to make the games happen（“志愿者：帮助奥运会举办”）. 2017 年 3 月 13 日检索网址 www. olympic. org/news/volunteers-helping-to-make-the-games-happen.

Jewish Women's Archive（n. d.）（犹太妇女档案馆〈日期不详〉）. Women rabbis: Julia Neuberger（“女拉比：茱莉亚·纽伯格”）. 2017 年 9 月 9 日检索网址 https: /jwa. org/rabbis/narrators/neuberger-julia.

Jones, D. (2016)（乔恩思）. *Citizens in policing strategy* 2016-2019（《警务战略中的公民 2016—2019》）. London: National Police Chiefs´ Council Judiciary of Scotland（伦敦：苏格兰司法部全国警察局长委员会）.

Justices of the Peace（n. d.）（治安法官〈日期不详〉）. 2016 年 12 月 15 日检索网址 www. scotland-judiciary. orguk/38/0/justices-of-The-peace.

Kopel, D. B. (2015)（科佩尔）. The *posse comitatus* and the office of the sheriff: Armed citizens summoned to the aid of law enforcement（“保安队和县治安官办公室：武装公民被召帮助执法”）. *The Journal of Criminal Law and Criminology*（《刑法与犯罪学》）, 104 (4), 761—850.

Lammy, D. (2014, January 13)（拉梅〈2014 年 1 月 13 日〉）. Does the Metropolitan Police reflect London's ethnic diversity?（《大都会警察局反映了伦敦的种族多样性吗?》）. *Daily Mirror*（《每日镜报》）. 2017 年 4 月 14 日检索网址 https: //fullfactt org/crime/does-metropolitan-police-reflect-londons-ethnic-diversity.

Loeb, J. (2016, April 8)（罗埃伯〈2016 年 4 月 8 日〉）. Specials not complying with 16 hours per month volunteering role（“不符合每月 16 个小时志愿服务的特别警员”）. Police Oracle（警察网上论坛）. 2016 年 4 月 11 日检索网址 www. policeoracle. com/news/special_constabulary/2016/apr/08/-specials-notcomplying-with-16-hours-per-month-volunteering-rule-_91506. html.

London Metropolitan Police（n. d.）（伦敦大都会警察局〈日期不详〉）. Who we are（“我们是谁”）. 2017 年 4 月 14 日检索网址 http: //

P58

content. metpoliceuk/site/About.

Lord Ferrers Awards（2017，August 18）（勒斯勋爵奖〈2017 年 8 月 18 日〉）. Lord Ferrers Awards 2017（勒斯勋爵奖 2017 年）. 2017 年 3 月 13 日检索网址 www. gov. uk/government/publications/lord-ferrers-awards-2017.

Millie，A.（2016）（米利）. *Volunteering within the police：Experiences of special constables and police support volunteers*（《警方内部志愿行为：特别警员和支援警察的志愿者的经历》）. Ormskirk，UK：Edge Hill University，Department of Law and Criminology（奥姆斯柯克，英国：艾奇·希尔大学，法律和犯罪学系）. 2016 年 5 月 25 日检索网址 https：//repository. edgehill. ac. uk/8206/1/MILLIE%20-%20police%20volunteers%20report%20-%20FINAL. pdf.

National Sheriffs' Association（2017）（全国县治安官协会）. 2017 awards（"2017 年奖励"）. 2017 年 8 月 27 日检索网址 www. sheriffs. org/sites/default/files/nsa%20awards%202017.

Neighbourhood Watch（n. d.）（邻里守望〈日期不详〉）. About us（"关于我们"）. Retrieved February 20，2017，from www. ourwatch. org. uk/about-us.

Nesbit，R.，& Brudney，J. L.（2010）（奈斯比特）. At your service？Volunteering and national service in 2020（"听候吩咐？2020 年的志愿行为和国家服务"）. *Public Administration Review*（《公共管理评论》），70（S1），S107-S113.

Northern Ireland Courts and Tribunals Service（n. d.）（北爱尔兰法院和法庭服务〈日期不详〉）. Judiciary of Northern Ireland（北爱尔兰司法部）. 2016 年 12 月 15 日检索网址 www. courtsni. gov. uk/en-gb/AboutUs/OrganisationalStructure/Pages/Judiciary-of-Northern-Ireland. aspx.

Office of Justice Programs（2011，June 10）（司法项目办公室〈2011 年 6 月 10 日〉）. Program profile：Kirkholt（England）burglary prevention project（"项目方案：科克霍尔特〈英国〉减少入室盗窃计划"）. 2017 年 5 月 24 日检索网址 www. crimesolutions. gov/ProgramDetails. aspx？ID=71.

Panel on the Independence of the Voluntary Sector（2011）（志愿部门独立性调查小区）. *Voluntary sector independence*（《志愿部门的独立性》）. London：Baring Foundation（伦敦：巴陵基金会）. 2017 年 4 月 14 日检索网址 http：//baringfoundation. org. uk/wp-content/uploads/2011/03/POIreport2011. pdf.

Pepper，I. K.，& Wolf，R.（2015）（帕珀和沃尔夫）. Volunteering to serve：

An international comparison of volunteer police others in a UK north east police force and a US Florida sheriff's office（“志愿提供服务：将英国东北部一家警察局和美国佛罗里达州的一个县治安官办公室的辅警进行国际对比”）. *The Police Journal：Theory，Practice and Principles*（《警察学报：理论、实践与原则》），88（3），209—219.

Police UK（2013，July 6）（英国警察〈2013 年 7 月 6 日〉）. General police discussion（讨论普通警察）. 2017 年 6 月 7 日 检索网址 www. policeuk. com/forum/index. php? /topic/18198-specials.

President's Volunteer Service Award（n. d.）（总统志愿服务奖〈日期不详〉）. The award（该奖项）. 2017 年 8 月 27 日检索网址 www. presidentialserviceawards. gov/the-award.

Ren，L.，Zhao，J.，Lovrich，N. P.，& Gaffney，M. J.（2006）（任、赵、洛夫里奇和加夫尼）. Participation community crime prevention：Who volunteers for police work?（“参加社区犯罪预防：谁志愿做警察工作?”）*Policing：An International Journal of Police Strategies and Management*（《警务：关于警察战略与管理的国际期刊》），29（3），464—481.

Rochester，C.（2006）（罗切斯特）. *Making sense of volunteering：A literature review*（《理解志愿行为：文献综述》）. London：Commission on the Future of volunteering（伦敦：未来志愿服务委员会）.

Rochester，C.，Paine，A. E.，& Howlett，S.（2012）（罗切斯特、帕伊内和豪莱特）. *Volunteering and society in the 21st century*（《二十一世纪志愿服务与社会》）. Basingstoke，UK：Palgrave Macmillan（贝辛斯托克，英国：麦克米伦出版公司）.

Smith，A.（2016）（史密斯）. “The Magnificent 7 [am]?” Work-life articulation beyond the 9（am）to 5（pm）“norm.”[“‘壮丽的（早晨）7 点’：超过（上午）9 点到（下午）5 点‘标准’的工作生活方式”] *New Technology，Work and Employment*（《新科技、工作和雇用》），31（3），209—222.

United Nations Volunteers（2015）（联合国志愿者）. 2015 *state of the world's volunteerism report：Transforming governance*（《2015 年世界志愿服务现状报告：转变治理》）. Washington，DC：United Nations Volunteers（华盛顿特区：联合国志愿者）. 2017 年 8 月 12 日 www. unv. org/sites/default/files/2015%20State %

20of% 20the% World% 27s% 20Volunteerism% 20Report% 20% 20Transforming% 20Governance. pdf.

Wakefield, A., & Fleming, J. (Eds.) (2009) (韦克菲尔德和弗莱明主编). *The Sage dictionary of policing* (《赛格警务词典》). London: Sage (伦敦：赛格出版公司).

Warrell, H. (2014, November 7) (沃莱〈2014 年 11 月 7 日〉). Special constables take bigger role as budget cuts hit police ("在警方遭受预算削减的时候，特别警员承担更重要的角色"). *Financial Times* (《金融时报》). 2017 年 8 月 20 日检索网址 www. ft. com/content/edcb8282-3409-11e4-8832-00144feabdc0.

Werbel, A. (2014) (韦尔伯尔). The crime of the nude Anthony Comstock, the Art Students of New York, and the origins of modern American obscenity ("裸体安东尼·康斯托克犯罪、纽约艺术生群体以及现代美国淫秽起源"). *Winterthur Portfolio: A Journal of American Material Culture* (《温特图尔证券：美国材料文化学报》), 48 (4), 249—282.

Whitehead, T. (2012, October 9) (怀特海姆〈2012 年 10 月 9 日〉). Police cuts mean more specials and volunteers, chief signals ("警方人数削减意味着更多的特别警员和志愿者加入警方，重要信号"). *The Daily Telegraph* (《每日电讯报》). 2017 年 8 月 13 日检索网址 www. ttelegraphco uk/news/uknewslaw-and-order/9643289/Police - cuts - mean - more - specials - and - volunteers - chief - signals. html.

Wolf, R. (2013) (沃尔夫). An exploratory study of the utilization of volunteer law enforcement officers by American sheriffs ("美国县治安官使用志愿性质执法人员研究"). In *Proceedings of the International Conference of Forensic Sciences and Criminalistics Research*, Volume I (《法医学和犯罪学研究国际会议议程，卷1》), pp. 37—41. Singapore: Global Science and Technology Forum (新加坡：全球科技论坛).

Wolf, R., Holmes, S. T., & Jones, C. (2016) (沃尔夫、赫尔摩斯和乔恩思). Utilization and satisfaction of volunteer law enforcement officers in the office of the American sheriff: An exploratory nationwide study ("美国县治安官办公室志愿性质执法官员的使用及其满意度：一项全国性研究"). *Police Practice and Research: An International Journal* (《警察实践与研究：国际期刊》), 17 (5),

448—462.

Wyllie, D. （2017, August 8）（怀利〈2017 年 8 月 8 日〉）. The reserve officer's role in law enforcement（“后备警察在执法中的角色”）. PoliceOne（警察一号）. 2017 年 8 月 13 日检索网址 www. policeone. com/patrol-issues/articles/4239138-The-reserve-officers-role-in-law-enforcement.

P60

第四章　辅警的历史发展

在英国，特别警员的使用在打击犯罪和恢复混乱的社会秩序方面有着长期而不可或缺的作用，在全职、“正式”警察之前几百年就出现了。警务自身的历史是从志愿者开始的，很多书都写过（Mawby，1999；Seth，2006；Greenberg，2015），但还是值得在本书再次写一写，当然篇幅不长。历史上，在社区里开展警务的实践，可以说与一千年前“太兴（tithing）”[1]的建立紧密相关。大约十户为一太兴，每户都处在十户长（tithingman）的领导之下。十户长是领头人，是太兴的领导或发言人。太兴是根据地域划分的，后来成为众所周知的“镇”（Seth，2006）。术语“百户（hundred）”被用来指大约十个太兴，即一百户。十户长则对百户长（hundredman）负责。

在太兴和百户内，法律和秩序（或称为“国王的治安”）得以维持的方式系使用成年公民：这些成年公民在无报酬的情况下，负责“压制小偷、追回被盗财物以及互相保障免遭小偷带来的损失”（Seth，2006，p. 31）；而且这些成年公民可以被视为英国首支正式建立的辅警力量。“千户（shire）”由几个百户组成（后来就是众所周知的县或教区），而且有一名千户长（shire reeve）［就是后来众所周知的郡最高司法长官（sheriff）］。千户长负责为国王维持治安，而且是行政首长。在后来的封建制度下，千户长还负责确保收割庄稼和出售粮食、强制偿还债务以及收款和付款。

术语“constable”在这一时期（以及在后续几个世纪里）与警务没有关系，它是指军队里的人（Giblin，2007）负责维护保管国王的武器。在十三世纪中期，非军事性质的constable出现，当时这个头衔给予了被任命为封建领地首席代表的人物。他们的角色经历了这般演变后，到十三世纪末期，他们被赋予权力以
P61 确保国王的治安得到维护。当然，一如莫比（Mawby，1999）所指出的，我们更愿意承认“警务”职能仅在1285年的《温彻斯特法案》中出现的。该法案规定

了“守望和守卫”制度，依据此规定“在天黑的时间里，所有身体健壮的乡镇男性居民必须轮流保卫乡镇”（Mawby，1999，p. 29）。由国王查尔斯二世在1673年通过的一部法案规定，当出现巨大骚乱危险时，任何公民均有可能被赋予临时警察的权力（City of London Special Cosntabulary，2011）。这种警务制度，由无薪金的、志愿性质的教区治安员构成，在英格兰②一直存在下去，直到1829年《大都会警察法》颁行。《大都会警察法》以及后来于1839年颁行的《县警察局法》，导致全职、有偿的职业警察建立起来。《大都会警察法》授权成立新型警务组织：“国王陛下可以在大都会及其周边地区建立一支新型警察队伍，而且可以任命两人担任法官，在国务大臣的管理下，处理司法事务”（Legislation. gov. uk，n. d. ）。根据《大都会警察法》，罗伯特·比尔爵士的“警察（bobbies）”被建立起来，他们的职能是打击“骚乱、暴乱和重罪”，工作地点在“任何教区、乡镇或者任何位于上述法官各自开展工作的范围或限制范围内的地方，而且这样的法官应该知道，受命维护治安的普通官员是不能满足需要的”（Kettiby Rickards，1931，p. 254）。

现代志愿性质的特别警员的角色由一部法案创建。这部法案修订了与任命特别警员有关的法律，而且这部法案出台的目的是更好地维护国王的治安。通常这部法案被称为《特别警员法案：1831年》。因为《特别警员法案：1831年》，警察局聘用的辅警的人数增长不少。这个法案允许在不安定时期挑选辅警，而且授权他们拥有全部逮捕权。这个法案还授予这些没有薪金的辅警于特殊时期，在相邻县工作的职权。警察局还给特别警员配发了履职所需的必要物品和武器（Seth，2006）。这个法案使治安法官有能力给付出劳动的特别警员发放合理的津贴，这个规定到现在还有效，发放用餐补助和其他报酬以换取志愿者履职。最后，这个法案有一个有趣的规定，要求那些被确定做特别警员的人必须履职，如果拒绝就要被罚款5英镑（在当时这是相当可观的一笔钱）（Seth，2006）。

尽管特别警员现在基本上被用于为全职警察提供支持，但是他们还被大量使用在英格兰的动荡和战争时期。1848年，在法国处于政治斗争高潮期间，至少85000名男子自愿并宣誓在伦敦大都会警察局做特别警员。1914年，在英德爆发战争的时候，20000名特别警员被招聘入警察局工作。因为第一次世界大战，政府被迫修订了《特别警员法案：1831年》。修订后的法案包括准予发放津贴，用以补偿时间损失费、医药费以及被杀害特别警员家属的抚恤金，而且如果被任命的特别警员想辞职，就给他补偿金以便他可以辞职（Seth，2006）。

P62

下一个特别警员在全国范围内被召集的时间是 1926 年的大罢工，[3]而且到 1930 年，特别警员增长到 136000 名。但是，正如在所有其他时期里那样，最终人数是另一回事。因为“志愿精神”的本质，所以个人如果被要求在没有经济报酬的情况下为了他人的利益奉献自己的时间和精力，都不能被强制去工作。

在第二次世界大战期间（1939—1945 年），因为全职警察被征召入伍或者自愿入伍，他们的工作岗位被大约 130000 名特别警员替代，许多特别警员是以正规警察身份退休的。与其他紧急事件后出现的迫切需求一样，在第二次世界大战结束阶段，特别警员的人数明显下降。1949 年，在特别警员队现代组织架构建立起来后 100 多年的时候，女性最终被允许进入特别警员队。

虽然英格兰和威尔士相对来说地方不大却人口众多，但是有一半以上的面积都是乡村，而乡村地区警务多年来都是一个棘手的问题。乡村地区被认为有田园诗般的宁静，犯罪更少、危险不多。但是，实际上，成本估算表明，在类似地区的犯罪成本要比之前预想的切切实实明显高出很多。全国乡村犯罪网（NRCN，the National Rural Crime Network）已经估算出乡村犯罪成本在 2015 年是 8 亿英镑，而不是之前由英国全国农场主协会互助委员会（NFU Mutual，the National Farmers’Union Mutual）在 2014 年估算的 3840 万英镑（BBC，2016）。保卫这些人烟稀少的地区，给英格兰和威尔士的 43 个警察局中的众多警察局带来挑战。每个警察局面临的乡村等级不同，但是一些地方，比如德文郡和康沃尔郡以及北威尔士郡主要是农村地区。

从历史上看，城市区域和乡村区域的治安维护有很大不同，因为城市里的警察一起工作，而那些辖区是乡村区域的警察很大程度上是其所在社区的组成部分，通常独立工作（Cain，1973）。但是，正如莫比和亚伍德（Mawby & Yarwood，2016）明确指出的，技术进步和机动性增强减少了工作方法和工作模式方面的不同。英国的警察局以新颖且经济的方式解决了这些方面存在的一些差异。自从 2009 年赫特福德郡警察局招聘并使用特别警员——这些特别警员骑着自己的马去巡逻乡村地区，从而使巡逻范围覆盖了车辆不能到的区域（Hertfordshire Constabulary，n. d. ）。

1993 年，内政大臣（Southgate，Bucke& Byron，1995）提出《教区特别警
P63 员方案》，借此方案增加乡村地区特别警员的招聘人数，以期改善警察局与乡村地区感到被忽视的居民之间的关系（Southgate，Bucke& Byron，1995）。

北爱尔兰的特别警员

北爱尔兰特别警员的演变与大不列颠岛本土的特别警员的发展有点不同。爱尔兰在二十世纪的大多数时间里是一个充斥着痛苦和动荡的地方，这也体现在其军事性质的警务形式上——明显区别于其没有武装的英格兰同行。

在 1920 年之前，在爱尔兰（当时的爱尔兰与大不列颠是一个国家，由来自欧洲大陆的威斯敏斯特议会统治着）有两个警察局：一个是爱尔兰皇家警察局（RIC，the Royal Irish Constabulary），大约有 10000 人，装备了手枪和步枪；另一个是都柏林大都会警察局（DMP，the Dublin Metropolitan Police），没有武装，大约有 1100 人。因为爱尔兰南部地区寻求独立，政治动荡加剧，没有武装的都柏林大都会警察发现自己日益处在被攻击的状态之下，所以他们关闭了许多乡村地区的警察署，从而使这些地方的警察可以被重新调配到城市地区（Hezlet，1972）。

爱尔兰北部地区许多警察署被关闭后，迫切需要有一支特别警员队伍去帮助爱尔兰皇家警察局。在 1920 年，阿尔斯特特别警员队（USC，the Ulster Special Constabulary）在北爱尔兰建立，并且其组织结构调整为政治/军事结构（Farrell，1983）。

北爱尔兰的特别警员队实际上由三个单独部分组成："A""B""C"特别警员队。"A"特别警员队是全职性质，由身体健壮、年龄在 21 岁至 45 岁的男人组成（政府希望他们是有经验的退役军人）。他们一次被聘用的时间是六个月，得到与爱尔兰皇家警察局的警察们同样的报酬加额外赏金，在解聘时支付。这样的报酬甚至比技术工人的报酬还要高很多。他们要携带武器，穿着与爱尔兰皇家警察局的警察相似的制服，而且有相同的合法权力。他们接受自己的高级官员的领导，而且被授权只在北爱尔兰的六个县里提供服务（Farrell，1983）。所以，尽管他们被称作"特别警员"，实际上他们的聘用条件与英国大陆辅警的不一样。

"B"特别警员队是一支由兼职警察组成的队伍。兼职警察通常被用在类似这样的勤务方面，如搬动路障（一种常见的现象）、骑马巡逻以及在夜晚时间警卫大楼。他们被要求每周工作一个晚上而且没有报酬，尽管他们可以获得的合法津贴是每六个月 5 英镑，每次他们工作的时候还有一个小额餐费补贴。他们还得参加定期培训课程，他们提供服务的一个条件是在紧急情况下他们可以被调用至全职岗位。他们被授权只在自己当地提供服务，而且他们在提供服务的时候，仅

P64

仅用帽子和臂章把他们和其他人加以区别。1922年，他们配发了全套制服。他们在岗工作时全副武装，但是当他们不在岗时，他们被要求把武器放在警察署里。对此规定的反对导致部分规定被推翻，乡村地区的“B”特别警员被允许居家时携带武器，而城市地区的“B”特别警员不得不继续把武器放在警营里（Farrell，1983）。

下文是对“B”特别警员的活动一个比较好的描述，节选自甘博（Gamble，2009，p. 2）记载的比尔·巴尔梅尔的回忆：

1953年10月，我加入B特别警员队的“巴利马尼排”，当时约翰·穆尼斯少校负责B特别警员队。

卡尔·卡顿是B特别警员队的建立者。他去世后，约翰·穆尼斯少校接替他的位置。约翰·穆尼斯少校是巴利马尼地区最后一位县指挥官。他在1970年加入阿尔斯特防卫团，就在这一年B特别警员队被撤销了。约翰·穆尼斯的平民身份是一家位于科尔雷恩的狄克逊鞋店的经理。

在穆尼斯少校被晋升为县指挥官的时候，汤米·姆马兰接管“巴利马尼排”，担任副排长，得到威廉·希尔和阿尔菲·韩纳的支持。当汤米·姆马兰去英格兰生活后，我被晋升为“巴利马尼排”的副排长……

……当时我在邮局工作。邮局希望我在每天早晨4点钟开始工作，6点钟开始投递邮件。一些事件发生后，我仍然在外面街道上巡逻，去邮局工作的时间就晚了。一天，我迟到很久，我的主管把我叫到一边，说了我一顿。当我告诉他我在街上巡逻而且巡逻后就直接到邮局上班时，他就让我回家，并且说他不希望我在邮局工作了。他威胁要当场解雇我。但是对他来说不幸的是，邮局有许多职员是退伍兵。这些人中的一个，把主管顶到墙上并告诉主管，如果没有像我这样的人保卫他，他不可能像一个自由的人一样走在巴利马尼的大街上。那个人放开了主管，而主管也明白了，如果他把我解雇，他很可能要面对一个“严重问题”。

第三支队伍，即“C”特别警员队，完全是后备力量，没有正式职责，只是偶尔参加演习和培训练习。他们的角色是在紧急情况下履行一些本地化职责，类似于那些“B”特别警员履行的职责或者短期履行某些全职职责。他们没有制服，仅仅有帽子和臂章，与那些在早期配发给“B”特别警员们的帽子和臂章相似。他们没有报酬，只有津贴，这个津贴在他们被召集时才会发放，并且只有他们在岗工作时才配备武器。但是，他们被鼓励提供自己的武器，而且会被一次性颁发适用的许可证，在这样的证书几乎不可能得到的情况下（Farrell，1983）。 P65

爱尔兰正式分裂了，其北部和南部边界最终在 1925 年确定下来。结果，“A”特别警员队首次被撤销，之后招聘“C”特别警员的工作也很快终止了，目的是减小特别警员队伍的规模。1926 年 4 月，“B”特别警员领取的津贴减少到每年 3 英镑，而且他们只被要求从事演习工作，不再是一支活跃的警察力量（Hezlet，1972）。

政治动荡和暴乱在北爱尔兰持续不断。在二十世纪三十年代，“B”特别警员队，这支从二十年代中期以来备受忽视的队伍，突然又引发争议，因为他们被用作警察的替代物，履行正规警察职责，同样要保卫军事建筑物。这更符合日常治安，与“B”特别警员队仅仅被用于镇压骚乱相反（Hezlet，1972）。“B”特别警员队继续在动乱和激进的氛围中历经磨难，当时，即 1969 年，《亨特报告》提出了一些建议，这些建议与北爱尔兰的警务有关，包括解散“B”特别警员队（Advisory Committee on Police in Northern Ireland，1969）。“B”特别警员队在接下来的那一年被解散了，代之以阿尔斯特皇家警察局（RUC，the Royal Ulster Constabulary）后备队，这是根据 1970 年《警察法（北爱尔兰）》的规定。阿尔斯特皇家警察局在 2001 年被北爱尔兰警察局（PSNI，the Police Service of Northern Ireland）取代。但是，自 1970 以来，北爱尔兰就没有特别警员队；相反，北爱尔兰警察局雇用了一支小规模的、大约 450 名“兼职”警察，这些“兼职”警察被要求每年最少工作 144 个小时（*Belfast Telegraph*，2015）。

苏格兰使用特别警员的情况

北爱尔兰的警务同英格兰和威尔士的警务存在的显著不同已经被明确了一样，唐纳利和斯科特（Donnelly & Scott，2002）对苏格兰在警务方面的做法也有同样的描述。苏格兰是英国的一部分，但是其法律系统和刑事司法系统一直根植于自己的历史。

在苏格兰，系统性警务组织在比尔建立伦敦大都会警察之前就建立起来了，依据是 1800 年在格拉斯哥颁行的地方议会法案。根据这个法案，户主选举警察总监监督警察局，这一组织架构迅速在苏格兰各地普及，结果，在 1890 年，《警察自治市（苏格兰）法案》颁行。此法案确定在苏格兰全境建立警察自治市。[4] P66
在苏格兰，特别警员被使用的方式与在英格兰和威尔士的相似，在乡村地区尤其如此，而乡村地区是苏格兰的一个显著地理特点（Donnelly & Scott，2002）。

因为在英格兰和威尔士，特别警员队数量明显下降，所以在2014年，一个飞行员计划出台，因此在格兰扁和泰赛德的特别警员每年可以获得1000英镑的酬金。重要的是，这笔钱不应被视为报酬，否则就偏离了“志愿者”的定义。这笔钱也不能被用于补偿额外开销，因为对额外开销的补偿已经发放了。2005年，这一制度被扩展至苏格兰全部八个警察局。两年前，这个“赏金”制度在英格兰和威尔士开始实施。2013年4月1日，根据2012年颁行的《警察和消防改革（苏格兰）法案》，苏格兰的八个警察局被联合起来成为一体。作出这种调整的部分原因是在需要考虑经济利益的时期减少重复。在苏格兰特别警员中，女性特别警员的比例比全职警察里的女性比例还要高（分别是37%和28%），比在英格兰和威尔士的比例也略高。至于苏格兰特别警员的年龄，5%的特别警员在55岁以上，50%的特别警员在25岁至45岁。

美国辅警的演变

美国辅警演变的轨迹，要追溯到英国模式。在北美殖民地以及土地上，对志愿者的使用最早出现在十七世纪中期，当时志愿性质的“保安队”，是被地方郡最高司法长官召集起来辅助执法、维持秩序以及拘捕逃犯的一群人。政府使用武装公民辅助执法的做法，“在盎格鲁-撒克逊的法律制度中根深蒂固，开端不晚于公元九世纪”（Kopel，2015，p. 763）。在美国从东部到西部大规模扩张时期，新的领土和州被组建、占据、统治。这些司法管辖地区由若干县组成，而且很多时候美国人民效仿盎格鲁-撒克逊的郡最高司法长官的样式塑造县治安的维护者。保安队拥有的普通法权力使美国的县治安官可以为了履行维护治安的职责，召集身体健壮的公民（而妇女历来被排除在外）来帮助执法，而且县治安官可以全权决定怎样武装那些公民（Kopel，2015）。殖民地时期的美国人直接模仿源于英格兰的盎格鲁-撒克逊郡最高司法长官的模式，只有一个例外。新殖民地的县治安官们是通过选举产生的，因而比其英国同行们能更加积极地拘捕逃犯、把逃犯送上法庭并通过执行法律来维护治安（Kopel，2015）。在美国，尤其是在美国南
P67 部和西部，县治安官在职能方面的扩展在现代警务中随处可见，而且甚至在当今出现对辅警的使用大规模增长的情况。尽管现在美国东北部许多州把县治安官办公室的职责仅定为保卫法庭、社区矫正和发放许可证，[5]但是美国南部和西部的州把县治安官用作经选举产生的警察机构领导者，拥有全部警察权力并承担全部

警察职责。

美国陆军国民警卫队的建立可以追溯到十七世纪早期民兵组织的建立。在1636年12月13日，根据马萨诸塞湾殖民地法院的一道命令，北美首支民兵组织被组建起来。民兵组织需要年龄在16岁至60岁的所有身体健壮的男性（法官和牧师除外）服役。该命令宣布，公民士兵在需要的时候会被用于保卫马萨诸塞殖民地。此后不久，民兵组织很快在其他殖民地建立起来，如康涅狄格和罗德岛。各殖民地的民兵组织都有相似的部门，而且同样的部门被其他地方的民兵组织复制，这些地方是佛罗里达、弗吉尼亚以及新墨西哥（Boehm，2011）。

在北部地区，民兵组织还被用于履行守夜职责（Greenberg，2015）。在美国东北部以及在许多人口众多的大城市地区，守夜制度被用来帮助同犯罪活动作斗争。这一守夜制度——后来因为在遏制犯罪方面的无效和无能而闻名于世——使用公民志愿者，他们基本上是在夜晚，针对犯罪活动开展巡逻。这种守夜制度首先出现于十七世纪早期的波士顿和十七世纪晚期的纽约市。守夜巡逻的职责是报告火情、公告时间和天气情况、保护街灯、协助处理讨厌的动物以及警惕任何类型的犯罪活动。

在十八世纪早期，南方法律人还使用相似的群体，以控奴巡逻的形式执行奴隶制法律。这些巡逻队通常用烟叶或现金的形式向白人公民支付报酬，由其负责将逃跑的奴隶抓回来还给奴隶的主人。后来，这些巡逻队由从州民兵组织中挑选出来的民兵组成。尽管这些巡逻队不是真正的辅警部门，而辅警是本书研究的核心，但是在研究美国警务历史的时候，这些巡逻队不能被忽略。这些巡逻队惯常对待奴隶的残暴方式以及这些巡逻队被用来镇压奴隶暴动和打断奴隶集会的事实，至少对美国有色人种社区对警察缺乏信任负有部分责任，而且特别是，对美国有色人种社区对选择参与辅警持有警惕态度负有部分责任。

十九世纪的美国警务是由政客们控制的，常常是残暴、腐败而且无能。警方被谴责很少预防犯罪，反而是当权政党的执法武器。政客们决定谁可以被任命做警察这一高薪职业。政客们还决定警界里谁可以被提拔至更高的级别。因为腐败盛行，所以警察经常成为犯罪问题的一部分。公民通常不喜欢警察而且表面上也不尊重警察，而这反过来也使警察恼火进而行为残暴，所以警察挥舞棍棒来掌控局面。西奥多·罗斯福，[6]从1895年至1897年担任纽约市警察委员会的委员长，致力于提升警察的职业化水平。罗斯福经过斗争，提升了录用警察的标准，并且处罚不诚实的警察。罗斯福努力工作改革纽约市的警察，但是因为当时警务中存

P68

在的强力政治干预，他的许多努力均以失败告终（Dempsey & Forst，2008）。

在二十世纪早期美国政府的进步开明时代，更多改革警察的努力被尝试，但是那些改革都是由来自警察机构之外的改革者发起的。政府进步开明运动旨在消除政府中的腐败。但是，在这些改革中，有许多改革再次失败，腐败、无能和残暴的警务继续存在下去（Dempsey & Forst，2008）。

随着美国进入第一次世界大战和第二次世界大战，使用志愿者帮助维护日常公共安全的做法不断增多。1941 年，美国公民服务公司正式组织成立。1950 年，《联邦民防法案》出台。战时征兵导致缺少能干的人来担任警察，许多富有经验的警察被招募到军队中履职。公民服务公司因此被建立起来，为的是在第二次世界大战期间，公民志愿者可以负责领导对抗社区里的不安全和糟糕的卫生状况。任何“身体健壮的”人都被鼓励加入公民服务公司，并且被组织进入地方防卫委员会。后来，在美国处在“冷战”威胁的那几年里，辅警项目百花齐放，部分是因为有可用的联邦拨款项目帮助这些辅警项目，为其提供资金。这包括空袭防护局以及协警局，这两个机构负责保卫容易成为蓄意破坏者侵害的目标并在这些目标周边巡逻，这些目标包括电站、公共工程设施以及煤气罐（Greenberg，2015）。

二十世纪六十年代美国政治骚乱，约翰 · F. 肯尼迪总统（1963 年）、罗伯特 · 肯尼迪议员（1968 年）以及马丁 · 路德 · 金博士（1968 年）被暗杀就是这种政治骚乱的表现。这个时期的美国社会动荡不安，反战游行、非暴力反抗以及警方与公众之间的暴力冲突不断。1968 年在芝加哥的民主党全国代表大会选举总统候选人时发生的暴力冲突就是例证。大学校园成为示威的主阵地，也见证了警方和示威者之间发生的更多暴力冲突。其中被最广泛报道的冲突发生在纽约市哥伦比亚大学：学生占领了自己的学校。在哥伦比亚大学大约有 2000 名警察试图清除校园楼宇中的示威者。预备役军官培训公司（ROTC，Reserve Officer Training Corps）的办公大楼位于威斯康星大学校园内，在 1970 年被燃烧弹攻击，导致全国大学校园里发生 500 起爆炸和纵火案件。在此期间，警方和学生示威者之间的冲突，在国民心目中留下了持久的负面印象（Dempsey & Forst，2008）。

二十世纪八十年代和九十年代美国警务有了积极发展，包括大量使用科技、完善沟通以及暴力犯罪大幅度下降。许多不同因素导致九十年代早期暴力犯罪减少，包括采用社区导向警务、问题导向警务以及甚至更为激进的“零容忍”警务。“零容忍”警务应记入时任纽约市警察局局长威廉 · J. 布莱顿的政绩，布莱顿局长通过实施CompStat[⑦]倡导情报引领警务。但是，这一时期犯罪降低的成果却被几个事件抹黑。这几个事件包括残暴对待罗德尼·金案件[⑧]以及审判O. J. 辛普森案，[⑨]它们令全美公众都认为警方“对黑人另眼相看”（Dempsey & Forst，2008）。

美国许多现代辅警组织可以将其历史追溯至二十世纪四十年代和五十年代的国民防卫组织。随着犯罪和暴力增长、国内秩序动荡不安以及遏制犯罪巡逻的增多，许多司法管辖区域转而使用志愿者以提高人力水平，而且许多政府扩展使用志愿者，经常在警方的支持下使用国民防卫部门。但是，美国东北部明显是一个例外。在美国东北部，这些使用辅警的倡议受到强大的警察工会和警察协会的阻挠。在一些州，由这些警察协会挑起的法律行动以及合法性挑战，已经导致强烈反对雇用没有薪金的警察职员（Wolf，Albrecht& Dobrin，2015）。尽管这些州可能有活跃的辅警组织，但合法性挑战已经导致在这些岗位上工作的辅警所拥有的职权和职责大幅度减少。例如，许多辅警没有逮捕权（没有超越任何公民）。

对犯罪增多和国内不稳定的同样关注，使全国邻里守望（NNW，the National Neighborhood Watch）[⑩]计划在1972年出台，该计划由全国县治安官协会制定，资金来源是美国司法部的司法协助局的司法项目办公室。虽然根据本书的定义，全国邻里守望不能被归类为辅警组织，但是全国邻里守望不断吸纳公民成为警方的“眼睛和耳朵”，有助于理解在全美建立这类组织的原因。[⑪]为了减少引发犯罪的机会，邻里守望还可以用来降低犯罪，方法是提升社区凝聚力以及与政府警务机构之间进行更多的对话。邻里守望始终与犯罪的降低有关，但是“邻里守望是否能威慑罪犯或者提升警察的调查工作，这就不清楚了”（Holloway，Bennet，& Farrington，2013）。 P70

2001年9月11日恐怖袭击以来美国的志愿精神

2001年纽约市遭受袭击后，志愿者数量在美国攀升了28.8%，对政府机构的支持也是数十年之内处在最高值（Zherka，2014）。美国人寻求机会在许多政府或非营利性社区服务机构内提供服务，包括社区应急团队、美国红十字会、人类家园以及其他组织。美国人觉得在这样一个时期，他们理所应当帮助那些没有能力的人，应该为他人提供服务，并且与其他美国人团结在一起。9.11事件发生后，上千名来自美国各地的美国人很快前往纽约市，希望成为志愿者，提供力所能及的帮助（Steffen & Fothergill，2009）。然而，这种最初的增长不可能持续下去，后来许多志愿者离开并不再提供服务。

但是，2007年的经济大衰退迫使政府机构把志愿者当作补充服务的方法。经济下滑迫使21%的美国警务机构辞退文职人员和警察，另外有56%的美国警务机构故意收缩规模，方法是不再招聘新人填补因为员工流失出现的岗位空缺。这种在职业警务方面出现的人员流失情况受到谴责，因为这导致犯罪率提升和警察逮捕减少（Yoder，2012）。志愿者被招聘去帮助警务机构完成很多与社区和生活质量有关的任务。然而，这些志愿者中的许多人没有任何执法权或者受到任何培训。许多志愿者被用在非执法岗位，包括犯罪现场处理、提取指纹、在接待区工作、案件登记和管理、由警察管理的游客信息中心以及其他更多岗位（Greenberg，2015）。

使用没有报酬的志愿者，不论是宣誓岗位还是非宣誓岗位（非宣誓岗位也被称为“文职”岗位），从此以后在全美国发展起来，当然，不是所有警察机构也不是所有州都使用志愿者，或者采用相同的方式使用志愿者。许多机构使用后备警察和协警，他们没有任何执法权或者执法权极其有限。志愿者扮演着重要角色，因为他们使警力成倍增长而且他们向全职警察报告犯罪活动和有嫌疑的活动。正如在前文概述的，这导致在怎样使用志愿者方面出现很大的地域差异。在美国西部和南部，志愿者基本上被用在执法岗位，拥有全部或部分警察权，而且被用在各种警务岗位上、发挥各种警务作用。

警务角色文职化

P71 除了吸纳志愿者支持警察履职，警察组织还通过将过去由警察占据的岗位用非宣誓的（或“文职”）人员来代替。警察组织已经成功地将一些宣誓警察岗位变成文职岗位，包括接待人员、沟通人员、饮酒驾车（DUI，driving under the influence）或者证据技术员、人力资源人员、研究和制订计划人员以及其他可以更有效率地用不那么昂贵的雇员来从事的岗位（Cordner & Scarborough，2010）。例如，犯罪现场勘查岗位，过去只有那些有警察工作经验和警察权的人才能做；但是，现在许多警务机构用不那么贵的（因为薪水，但是很大程度上还因为福利降低了）受过训练的文职人员来做。“通过使用文职人员承担通常由宣誓职员承担的职责，警察局能够省钱，主要通过更低的报酬、降低培训要求以及更小的经费需求来实现省钱的目的”（Greenberg，2015，p. 37）。

在警察机构中使用志愿者和文职人员履职的一个优势，就是它“让不同类型的人进入警察组织”（Cordner & Scarborough，2010，p. 272）。非宣誓志愿者岗位即文职岗位，可以给那些可能对执法岗位不感兴趣、没有资质承担执法岗位或者身体不够健壮不能胜任执法岗位的人去承担。这些工作可能尤其吸引上年纪的人、身体不太健壮的人，或者那些没有能力为必要的警察培训花费时间的人（Cordner & Scarborough，2010）。一些警察局使用有报酬的社会志愿服务官员、穿制服的文职人员履行警察日常职责。这些岗位与英国的社区服务警察（PCSO，police community support officer）的岗位相似，其职责是报告轻罪，并通过处理打给警察的非执法类型的求助电话来支持一线警务，提供轻微病症急救，提供预防犯罪信息并给公民提出预防犯罪的建议。这些穿制服的人员也被当作全职警察的一个招募来源（Travis & Langworthy，2008）。

注释

①关于太兴（tithings）的早期历史，参阅莫比的著作（Mawby，1999）。

②弓街捕快也是被雇用的全职人员，而且不在志愿制度之内，因为志愿制度在当时主要依赖于无报酬的治安员。官方将弓街捕快称为弓街“首席官员”。弓街捕快成立于 1749 年，被称为伦敦首支职业警察力量。当有人报告犯罪发生时，弓街捕快被长官派出去查明嫌疑人并将之抓捕归案（Old Bailey Proceedings Online，n. d.）。但是，到十九世纪二十年代，伦敦无法无天的状况呈指数级增长，有报酬的治安员人数已经完全不够了（Seth，2006）。 P72

③1926 年发生在英国的大罢工从 5 月 4 日持续到 12 日。此次大罢工由工人的工会发起，目的是迫使英国政府阻止周薪降低以及矿工状况恶化。为了帮助警方并恢复公共秩序，政府让大批特别警员宣誓就职。罢工波及的工人超过 300 万名，但是，尽管罢工人数众多，然而罢工结束时，出乎意料地没有多少暴乱也没有人死亡；最著名的事件是警察和罢工工人在普利茅斯踢了一场足球赛（Pugh，2006）。

④自治市是苏格兰的自治城市委员会，相当于城市的行政区或镇，而警察自治市是指政府采用“警察体制”的自治市。这些地方自治市有委员会、经选举产生的管理者以及警察局局长。警察自治市在苏格兰存在的时间为 1833 年到 1975 年。

⑤例如，纽约市（NYC，New York City）县治安官办公室是纽约市财政局下属的一个处级部门。县治安官由纽约市市长任命（尽管纽约州其他县治安官是

由选举产生的)。县治安官助理主要开展民事执法驱逐、签发搜查令和发送传票工作，并且确保判决被取走。纽约市县治安官过去监管纽约市的监狱，但是现在不再监管了；监管监狱的职责现在由纽约市社区矫正局承担。与此相反，奥兰治县（佛罗里达州）县治安官主要负责全部执法职能，执法范围是奥兰治县的县域，奥兰治县不在自治市的司法管辖范围内。奥兰治县县治安官经选举产生，但是不负责管理县监狱，县监狱的管理由奥兰治县社区矫正局负责；这在佛罗里达州是特例，因为佛罗里达州大多数县治安官的主要职责是监管县监狱。

⑥西奥多·罗斯福后来成为纽约州的州长（在 1898 年）并随后成为美国第 26 届总统（1901—1909 年）。在第 25 届总统威廉·麦金利被暗杀、罗斯福从副总统之位升任总统时，罗斯福还不到 43 岁。“说话轻柔但手持大棒”可以说是他最著名的语录。

⑦CompStat 要么是“Computer Statistics（计算机统计）”的缩写，要么是“Compare Statistics（对比统计）”的缩写。CompStat，是指一个用来减少犯罪的流程，方法是强调分享信息、管理者的责任以及提升效率。CompStat 有四个核心内容：(1) 及时、准确的情报；(2) 迅速调配人员和资源；(3) 有效使用警方策略；(4)“没完没了”地跟进（Bureau of Justice Assistance，2013）。

⑧罗德尼·金事件指的是 1991 年洛杉矶市警察局的警察殴打一名非洲裔美国人被拍摄下来。录像是由一名旁观者拍摄的，他拍摄了警察以每小时 115 英里的速度在洛杉矶市追逐罗德尼·金之后的高潮部分。四名警察被逮捕并被控杀害罗德尼·金，而且最初刑事法庭陪审团认定四人无罪，但是后来联邦法院认定四人有罪，因为他们侵害了罗德尼·金的公民权利。

P73

⑨O. J. 辛普森是一位美国职业橄榄球运动员和电影明星。辛普森被指控犯下两宗谋杀罪，被害人为其前妻及其好友。审判持续了七个月，可以说是历史上最公开化的刑事审判。辛普森的辩护团队把洛杉矶市警察局描绘成在调查中失策并且有系统性种族主义。

⑩全国邻里守望授权公民积极参与社区打击犯罪的工作，方法是参与社区组织从而获得培训、技术支持、资源以及其他来自地方警察机构和全国县治安官协会的帮助。另外，全国邻里守望计划为注册的组织提供标志，从而标记参与全国组织的社区。

⑪全国邻里守望成员以及地方组织没有任何警察权，但是他们要受到必要的教育以使他们可以报告可疑的、犯罪的或者危险的活动。这个计划还在二十世纪

八十年代传到英国，而在2000年，在英格兰和威尔士，大概有600万户或者说超过155000个活跃的组织参与邻里守望“方案”。

参考文献

Advisory Committee on Police in Northern Ireland (1969)(位于北爱尔兰的警察咨询委员会). *Report of the Advisory Committee on Police in Northern Ireland*(《位于北爱尔兰的警察咨询委员会的报告》). Belfast: HMSO(贝尔法斯特：英国皇家文书局).

BBC (2016, September 15)(英国广播公司〈2016年9月15日〉). Rural crime: Cost in England and Wales “reaches more than? 800m.”(“郊区犯罪：在英格兰和威尔士的犯罪成本‘高于800m’”). 2017年4月15日检索网址 www.bbc.co.uk/news/uk-34250455.

Belfast Telegraph (2015, April 22)(《贝尔法斯特电信报》〈2015年4月22日〉). Concerns over part-time officers(“对兼职警察的担忧”). 2018年1月10日检索网址 www.belfasttelegraph.co.uk/news/northern-ireland/concerns-over-parttime-officers-31161970.html.

Boehm, B. (2011, December 13)(博埃姆〈2011年12月13日〉). National Guard marks its 375th birthday(“国民警卫队迎来375岁生日”). US Army(美国军队). 2017年1月4日检索网址 www.army.mil/article/70758.

Bureau of Justice Assistance (2013)(司法协助局). *Compstat: Its origins, evolution, and future in law enforcement agencies*(《Compstat：在执法机构中的起源、演变和未来发展》). Washington, DC: Police Executive Research Forum(华盛顿特区：警察高级官员研究论坛).

Cain, M.E. (1973)(凯恩). *Society and the policeman's role*(《社会和警察角色》). London: Routledge & Kegan Paul(伦敦：劳特利奇和开根·保罗出版公司).

City of London Special Constabulary (2011)(伦敦城特别警员队). *City of London Special Constabulary*, 1911—2011(《伦敦城特别警员队，1911—2011年》). London: City of London Special Constabulary(伦敦：伦敦城特别警员队).

Cordner, G.W., Scarborough, K.E. (2010)(科尔德纳和斯卡伯勒). *Po-*

lice administration, 7th Edition [《警察管理》（第七版）]. New Providence, NJ: Lexis Nexis（新普罗维登斯，新泽西：律商联讯集团）.

Dempsey, J., & Forst, L. S. (2008)（德姆普瑟和福斯特）. *An introduction to policing*, 4th Edition [《警务概论》（第四版）]. Belmont, CA: Wadsworth（贝尔蒙特，加利福尼亚州：沃兹沃思出版公司）.

Donnelly, D., & Scott, K. B. (2002)（唐纳利和斯科特）. Police accountability in Scotland: (1) The "new" tripartite system（"苏格兰追究警察责任：(1)'新'三方系统"）. *The Police Journal*（《警察》）, 75 (1), 1—12.

Donnelly, D., & Scott, K. B. (2010)（唐纳利和斯科特）. *Policing Scotland*, 2nd Edition [《维护苏格兰治安》（第二版）]. Cullompton, UK: Willan Publishing（卡伦顿，英国：威兰出版社）.

Farrell, M. (1983)（法雷尔）. *Arming the Protestants: The formation of the Ulster Special Constabulary and the Royal Ulster Constabulary* 1920—1927（《武装新教徒：阿尔斯特特别警员队和阿尔斯特皇家警察局的形成 1920—1927 年》）. London: Pluto Press（伦敦：普鲁托出版社）.

Gamble, R. (2009)（甘博）. *My service life* (1939—1979): *William "Bill" Balmer*（《我服兵役的时光（1939—1979）：威廉·"比尔"·巴尔梅尔》）. Coleraine, UK: Causeway Museum Service（科尔雷恩，英国：铜锣博物馆服务部）.

Giblin, J. (2007)（吉布林）. *The office of constable: An historical perspective of the "old" and "new" police*（《警察局：历史视角下的"新""旧"警察》）. Leatherhead, UK: Police Federation（莱瑟黑德，英国：警察联合会）. 2018 年 1 月 10 日检索网址 www.scribd.com/document/54427522/183-the-office-ofConstable-An-Historical-Perspective-of-the-Old-and-New-Police.

Greenberg, M. A. (2015)（格林伯格）. *American volunteer police: Mobilizing for security*（《美国辅警：为安全动员起来》）. Boca Raton, FL: CRC Press（博卡-拉顿，佛罗里达州：CRC 出版社）.

Hertfordshire Constabulary (n. d.)（赫特福德郡警察局〈日期不详〉）. Rural special constabulary（"郊区特别警员队"）. 2016 年 10 月 14 日检索网址 www.herts.policeuk/hertfordshire_constabulary/specialconstabularyrural_specials.aspx.

Hezlet, A. (1972)（赫兹勒特）. *The "B" Specials: A history of the Ulster*

Special Constabulary（《“B”特别警员：阿尔斯特特别警员队历史》）. London：Stacey（伦敦：斯塔塞出版公司）.

Holloway, K., Bennett, T., & Farrington, D. P. (2013)（霍洛维、本奈特和法灵顿）. *Does neighborhood watch reduce crime?*（《邻里守望减少犯罪了吗?》）, Crime Prevention Research Review 3（犯罪预防研究综述 3）. Washington, DC：US Department of Justice, Office of Community Oriented Policing Services（华盛顿特区：美国司法部，社区导向警务服务办公室）.

Kettilby Rickards, G. (1831)（凯提尔拜·理查兹）. *The Statutes of the United Kingdom of Great Britain and Ireland*, 1 &2 *William IV*（《大不列颠及爱尔兰联合王国法规，1 和 2 威廉四世》）. London：His Majesty's Statute and Law Printers（伦敦：国王陛下的法令及法律印刷厂）.

Kopel, D. B. (2015)（科佩尔）. The posse comitatus and the office of the sheriff：Armed citizens summoned to the aid of law enforcement（“保安队和县治安官办公室：武装公民被召帮助执法”）. *Journal of Criminal Law and Criminology*（《刑法与犯罪学》）, 104 (4), 761—850.

Legislation. gov. uk (n. d.)（日期不详）. Metropolitan Police Act 1829（“1829 年大都会警察法”）. 2018 年 1 月 12 日检索网址 www. legislation. gov. uk/ukpga/geo4/10/44/contents.

Mawby, R. (1999)（莫比）. *Policing across the world：Issues for the twenty-first century*（《世界警务：二十一世纪面临的问题》）. London：UCL Press（伦敦：UCL 出版社）.

Mawby, R. I., & Yarwood, R. (2016)（莫比和亚伍德）. *Rural policing and policing the rural：A constable countryside?*（《郊区警务和维护郊区治安：一个稳定的乡间》）Farnham, UK：Ashgate（法纳姆，英国：阿什盖特出版公司）.

Old Bailey Proceedings Online (n. d.)（老贝利诉讼在线〈日期不详〉）. Policing in London（“伦敦警务”）. 2018 年 1 月 10 日检索网址 www. oldbaileyonline. org/static/policing. jsp.

Pugh, M. (2006)（皮格）. The General Strike（“大罢工”）. *History Today*（《当今历史》）, 56 (5), 40—47.

Seth, R. (2006)（塞斯）. *The specials*（《特别警员》）. Trowbridge, UK：Cromwell Press（特洛布里奇，英国：克伦威尔出版社）.

Southgate, P., Bucke, T., & Byron, C. (1995)（索斯盖特、布克和毕荣）. *The parish special constables scheme*（《教区特别警员队方案》）, Home Office Research Study 143（“内政部调查研究 143”）. London: Home Office Research and Planning Unit（伦敦：内政部调查和规划部门）.

Steffen, S. L, & Fothergill, A. (2009)（斯蒂芬和福瑟吉尔）. 9/11 volunteerism: A pathway to personal healing and community engagement（“9/11 志愿服务：个人康复和社区参与的途径”）. *The Social Science Journal*（《社会科学期刊》）, 46 (1), 29—46.

Travis, L. F., & Langworthy, R. H. (2008)（特拉维斯和兰沃思）. *Policing in America: A balance of forces*（《美国警务：警察力量的平衡》）. Upper Saddle River, NJ: Pearson Publishing（上鞍河，新泽西：培生出版集团）.

Wolf, R., Albrecht, J., & Dobrin, A. (2015)（沃尔夫、阿尔布雷希特和多布林）. Reserve policing in the United States: Citizens volunteering for public service（“美国后备警察管理：公民志愿参与公共服务”）. *The Police Chief*（《警察局长》）, 82 (10), 38—47.

Yoder, S. (2012, August 7)（约德〈2012 年 8 月 7 日〉）. As police budget are cut, citizens step in（“因警察预算削减，故公民介入”）. *The Fiscal Times*（《财经时报》）. 2017 年 1 月 2 日检索网址 www.thefiscaltimes.com/articles/2012/08/07/Police-Budget-Cut#page1.

Zherka, I. (2014, November 11)（宰尔卡〈2014 年 11 月 11 日〉）. Volunteering and service are more than a temporary response to tragedy（“志愿行为和服务不仅仅是一个临时性的战略对策”）. *The Huffington Post*（《赫芬顿邮报》）. 2017 年 1 月 2 日检索网址 www.huffingtonpost.com/ilir-zherka/volunteering-and-service-_b_5805286.html.

第五章　辅警的当代角色与作用

P75

在美国和英国，在现代警界开启有偿、全职、正规执法职业生涯，需要具有为社区服务的理念。申请人必须愿意长时间轮班工作，在危险或者至少可疑的环境中工作，同时暴露在身体危险和心理危险之中，而且通常得到低于中等收入的工资。执法官员要承担被诉风险（不论其是正确的一方还是错误的一方）以及公民监督群体的调查（Walker，2001），而且可能是种族主义或贬损性评论的对象，而种族主义或贬损性评论的发表者是那些社区里不喜欢警方的人（Greenberg，2005）。在英格兰和威尔士，还有警察监察局开展的正规监督；在美国，存在两种可能性：民事诉讼以及由职业标准部门或内部调查部门发起的调查。

但是，成为志愿性质的执法官员则把这些要求提升到了一个新的水平。美国辅警必须"考虑如下这些职业危害：有可能死亡、身体伤害、压力、愤世嫉俗、酗酒、离婚以及其他严重问题"（Berg & Doerner，1988，p. 82），还有必须喜欢与人共事，并喜欢学习和使用新技术，目的是接受这样的挑战却没有经济奖励，或者甚至要用个人经济支出。在美国许多司法管辖区域，他们还必须愿意维持警察认证，即维持某种培训水平，而这可能需要无数个小时的准备，却没有报酬，而且他们必须愿意在警察机构半军事化的组织框架内从事必要的工作。强制出庭或者听证可能会使辅警无法正常工作，或者无法与家人见面（Arwood，Hilal，Karsky& Norman，2005）。在英格兰和威尔士也存在相似的情况。在英格兰和威尔士，警务学院监督警务的方方面面，包括认证特别警员。在2016年召开的英国特别警员队大会上，大会的焦点是警务中的志愿服务。这个焦点凸显了特别警员仍然在经受的来自正规警察的非难，因为正规警察对辅警的看法常常是一成不变的东拉西扯和贬低轻蔑，尽管志愿者们自愿贡献自己的精力和时间。然而，这种情况不只出现在英国的特别警员身上；美国辅警要经常面对全职正规警察把辅警看作"周末斗士"或者"想当警察之人"。在美国的一些地方，辅警遭到全职 P76

警察和主管的蔑视，这些人抱怨：对日日维护治安的“真”警察来说，辅警是个“累赘”。

虽然要找到一个没有任何金钱奖励又愿意付出许多的志愿者不太容易，但是在地方政府层级业已存在不少对志愿者的需求。政府开支降低、人口增加以及公众对服务质量更佳的期盼不断增长，已经使地方政府和地方警察机构把目光投向志愿者，用志愿者填补重要的岗位（Sharpe，1986；Fredericksen & Levin，2004）。在英格兰和威尔士，使用特别警员以及最近以来使用服务社区警察，已经被人谴责是“廉价警务”（Whitehead，2012）。警务机构还可以应对日益增长的犯罪，途径是“扩展各种志愿者可以提供服务的角色”（Sharpe，1986，p. 86）。辅警“有助于拉近警察局和全职警察之间的距离，这是一个方面，另一方面，有助于拉近和社区之间的距离”（Fredericksen & Levin，2004，p. 121）。除了志愿者的社区警务角色，美国更常见的是，警务中的志愿者能成为下列工作的重要组成部分：国土安全、预防青年人犯罪计划、缉毒执法（Greenberg，2005）以及犯罪侦查。志愿者还可以被用在应对天灾或人祸上。在英国，专业化角色虽然不常见，但是正在上升，而且是一个正在慢慢发生变化的议题，本章后文将讨论这个议题。

人们普遍认可的是，维护治安以及整个刑事司法系统，在察觉和侦查犯罪活动方面要依赖公众的参与（Gill & Mawby，1990；Roberg，Novak& Cordner，2009）。类似“见到什么就说什么”这样的公众犯罪预防运动，有赖于公民参与察觉犯罪活动并将之报告给警方，而类似英国的《犯罪监视》计划则表明警方和公众之间的协同增效作用。没有公众的协作和善意，犯罪不会被报告给警方，常规侦查工作也不会破案；因此，在文献资料中，警察和公民之间的关系是经常被考察和探讨的问题（Weitzer & Tuch，2005；Myhill & Beak，2008；Sindall，Sturgis& Jennings，2012；Perkins，2016；Sprott & Doob，2014）。有人可能会认为，英国特别警员及其美国同行辅警，与支援警察志愿者和警官学员一样，可以被看作最接近罗伯特·比尔的“警务中的公民”原则（College of Policing，n. d.）。
P77 这些志愿者所做的事情，常常远不只是街面上的另一双“眼睛”；辅警尤其被赋予权力并承担在“警界”积极履职的责任。尽管部署这些辅警可以获得积极成果，如警方和社区之间更好的关系、更好的责任感以及节省同等数量全职警察的成本，但是没有研究认为增加辅警是对犯罪活动的一种威慑，而且当然也不会超过增加同样很少数量的正规警察可能产生的效果（Gill & Mawby，1990）。

辅警来自不同的背景。他们可以有全职工作，如医生、护士、水暖工、商人、教育工作者、企业商业领袖、律师或者职业运动员（Williams，2005；Volunteer Special Constabulary，1998；*Special Impact*，2015a）。他们在年龄、种族、性别、宗教以及文化方面呈现多样化（Gravelle & Rogers，2009）。多样化问题十分重要，因为当代警务内部的多样化，在确保提升少数族裔之间的关系以及为犯罪女性被害人提供帮助方面，被认为相当重要（Police. uk，2015）。警察机构使用辅警的方式多种多样。辅警可以提供基本的警察服务，如步行巡逻，即在辖区内走动。但是，有其他方式使用宣誓辅警，而且美国警务机构尤其在如下岗位使用辅警：海上巡逻、航空系统、交通运输系统、特别武装团队或特别应对团队、骑马巡逻以及警犬巡逻。但是，在英格兰和威尔士，专业人员的职责范围有点受限。

特别警员的优势之一是专业和知识，这些专业和知识是他们中许多人从自己的有偿岗位上带过来的，可以被用于为警察局带来好处。这方面一个特例是大都会特别警员队在 2013 年 2 月实施的一个方案。该方案招聘有资质的注册会计师，以身着便服的特别警员身份，在大都会警察局犯罪专家组工作。注册会计师们没有像现在的特别警员那样完成相同的培训，但是受到犯罪专家组的培训，帮助侦查员扣押犯罪所得。

（Seth，2006，p. 257）

从历史上看，将志愿者掌握的技术转用到警方的形式在英国被有意避开了，但是还是有运用志愿者之前获得的经验和接受过的教育的形式出现。1995 年，在英格兰东南部的一个警察局，在奇切斯特海港部署巡逻时，使用一艘完全由特别警员驾驶的船。这替代了在 12 年前因为高昂的成本被废弃的类似巡逻工作，因为当时用的是正规警察（Howe & Graham，1995）。

志愿者使用从警务工作之外所获专业技能的另一个例证是，位于英国朴次茅斯的汉普郡警察局，已经开始招聘经验丰富的信息技术（IT，Information Technology）工作人员到警察局作为特别警员和提供支持的志愿者工作。志愿者被用于侦查网络犯罪，包括互联网诈骗、勒索软件攻击以及剥削儿童。志愿者凭借之前接受的专业培训，每月最低工作时间 16 个小时，为有关犯罪侦查工作提供帮助，并提供数字取证支持。志愿者组成的侦查员团队被称为“网络专家”，他们

P78

拥有与正规警察一样的侦查职权（Fishwick，2016）。领航员计划出台，目的是扩展与警方的其他合作以巩固全职警察的职能并为之提供支持。领航员项目的评估工作由朴次茅斯大学负责，朴次茅斯大学管理着一个新建立的法医创新中心。领航员项目在汉普郡警察局的辖区内实施。在这个辖区，汉普郡专家主管汤姆·哈耶是一个广播公司的首席执行官，因而该项目处于数字技术的前沿。在格洛斯特郡，即政府沟通总部（GCHQ，the Government Communications Headquarters）所在地，网络专家的招聘工作同样一直在进行。

英国的国家犯罪局（NCA，National Crime Agency）还招聘辅警身份的专业人员，运用他们在网络安全、金融服务与市场、会计以及语言技能方面的专长。英国的国家犯罪局与美国的联邦调查局（FBI，the Federal Bureau Investigation）十分相似，在 2013 年成立，代替有组织犯罪局去侦查贩卖人口、武器和毒品、网络犯罪以及经济犯罪。这一做法与美国相反，因为美国的辅警不被用在国家级别的联邦警察机构里，尽管地方全职警察或州全职警察因侦查犯罪需要可以同时向联邦机构宣誓。

伦敦城警察局是一个独立的警察局，与伦敦大都会警察局不是一体的。伦敦城警察局建立了一个非常成功的经济犯罪主管处，这个经济犯罪主管处在英国是侦查这些类型犯罪的领头羊。经济犯罪主管处因为其盛名远播而获得国际认可，它是欧洲最大的诈骗侦查部门，侦查地方、国家和国际各个层级的犯罪（Field，2007）。经济犯罪主管处在很多领域使用志愿性质的特别警员，包括经济犯罪领域。

> 使用跨部门背景的专业知识，从而增强了我们的网络技术能力、经济专长，并且增强了我们打击经济犯罪和网络犯罪的能力。
>
> （City of London Police，2016）

但是，另外一个非常特别的角色是，伦敦城警察局是英国第一个在专业标准的侦查工作中培训并使用特别警员的警察局。伦敦城警察局培训特别警员处理对
P79 警察的投诉，包括所谓的歧视案件、使用武力、误用机动车以及其他被质疑的政策或者伦敦城警察局官员实施的违法犯罪行为。特别警员队的指挥官杨·米勒对其特别警员们所做的专业工作感到非常自豪，担任特别警员使这些人有机会“利用自己的技能在更多更广的领域对社区产生价值并为社区提供服务”（Robinson

& Miller，2016）。伦敦城有大约 75 名特别警员，即特别警员占有 700 人的正规警察力量的 10%多一点。

接受了适当水平培训的辅警，能够被召集去做任何全职警察能做的事情，但是使用辅警还有另外一个好处：在自然灾害或者人为灾害中，警察队伍的规模可以（几乎）迅速倍增。在一个需要当班职员作出相对迅速反应的事件里，辅警可以被召集“填充”警察局的常规巡逻岗位。[①]一些司法管辖区域可能使用辅警组成特别应对团队或者补充特别应对团队，这样的团队可以快速应对国内动荡或者大规模灾难。另一些司法管辖区域可能需要辅警处理大量涌入的人口，这些涌入的人口增加了正常人口数量。这可能包括体育赛事、春假和休假，或者其他需要切实增加警察在现场以及提升见警率的时段。[②]

下面这个例子，对获得正确培训和适当机会的辅警来说，可能算是一个配置类型的示例：2015 年，贝德福德郡特别警员巡官约翰·鲍尔成为英国首位由特别警员成为一名警察警犬训练员的人。约翰及其警犬（查尔利）在向其指挥团队分享了思路后，参加了全国培训课程。约翰及其警犬参加的是一个为期 8 个星期的住校学习课程，培训班开办地点是萨里警犬学院，培训重点是爆炸物探测。约翰及其警犬一经局长协会（ACPO，the Association of Chief Police Officers）认证为一个经过认证的爆炸物探测警犬团队，就开始贡献自己的时间，确保贝德福德郡卢顿机场具备安全的旅行环境。然而，约翰及其警犬还为一个反恐联合小组提供支持，为到访的皇室成员、达官贵人以及外国首脑进行爆炸物检查（*Special Impact*，2015）。贝德福德郡大约有 250 名特别警员，他们在 2015 年实施了超过 500 次的逮捕，提供了超过 82000 个小时的志愿服务（Bedfordshire Police，n. d.）。

除了在英格兰和威尔士的 43 个警察局内部的特别警员，辅警还可以被用在专业警务服务工作中，包括附属于铁路系统的英国交通警察总队（BTP，the British Transport Police）。英国交通警察总队由英国交通警察管理局监管，而英国交通警察管理局是一个独立部门，向铁路公司和公众负责。它们还任命特别警员主管以及其他高级职位，它们还要反馈对英国交通警察总队的投诉。英国交通警察从 1830 年就开始为保护铁路资产以及火车运行开展巡逻工作，《特别警员法案：1831 年》又给特别警员授权。特别警员完成的工作对正在建设的新铁路特别重要，因为大量的“筑路工”[③]为新出现的工作机会蜂拥而至，导致出现大量棚户区。在这样的环境下，犯罪成为主要问题。所以，特别警员被用来维护治安

P80

来解决这个问题。但是，所有这些特别警员的费用，最初落到了地方税纳税人头上，直到1838年一部法案出台，让铁路公司承担特别警员的费用（British Transport Police，n. d.）。就像全英国的警察局一样，英国交通警察总队特别警员还被授权拥有全部警察权，尽管他们维护治安的区域十分特别。英国交通警察总队的警察和特别警员不但被用在英格兰和威尔士的铁路火车站上，而且他们还跟车工作，特别是在举办大型体育赛事和音乐活动的时候，届时人数众多的粉丝使用铁路系统去比赛场地、集会地点和音乐会场。

佛罗里达州奥兰多的奥兰治县县治安官办公室，根据后备警察接受的培训，只要有可能就使用后备警察。后备警察一完成他们最初的学院培训以及后续的实战培训评估项目（FTEP，Field Training Evaluation Program），就被要求在巡逻部门工作以完成一个月的志愿服务小时数。但是，就像警察机构里的全职助理一样，他们被允许请求特殊培训以便在特殊部门工作。获得适当证书和培训的后备警察，能够加入骑马工作部门、海上巡逻部门、自行车巡逻部门或者其他特殊巡逻部门。另外，根据后备警察获得的培训、经历以及兴趣爱好，他们被授权为侦查工作提供帮助，而且他们可以参与抓捕逃犯、犯罪侦查工作，或者参加培训部门的工作。

P81

同样的，洛杉矶县县治安官部（LASD，the Los Angeles County Sheriff's Department）的后备队伍局有超过700名后备警察，这些后备警察都接受过各种培训、拥有职权（*Monrovia Weekly*，2015）。洛杉矶县县治安官部的后备助理们，为服务自己的社区每年获得的报酬是1美元，而且他们还经常被派往巡逻点去履行日常执法职责，包括接听要求服务的电话、交通管制以及犯罪侦查。但是，超过150名后备助理还参加了搜救队，包括水上快速救援队。在2015年，洛杉矶县县治安官部的搜救队参与的搜救任务超过450个，使该搜救队成为这个国家最活跃的搜救队之一。“航空救援队5”是洛杉矶县县治安官部的直升机组，机组成员是后备助理（Alfonso，2015），该机组每天24小时、一周7天均在岗执勤。洛杉矶县县治安官部的特别队伍局的所有助理，包括那些在搜救队和“航空救援队5”工作的助理，都是有资质的急救护理人员和救生员（*Monrovia Weekly*，2015）。另外，根据洛杉矶县县治安官部的辅警接受的骑马培训，他们还被授权参加骑警执法队、骑警搜救队以及后备骑警治安队。2014年，洛杉矶县县治安官部的辅警，志愿服务时间累计超过450000个小时，估计能给洛杉矶县县治安官部节省超过100万美元的费用（Wright，2015）。

英格兰和威尔士的特别警员多年来证明了自己在时间、专长、努力和可靠性方面的价值，但是乡村地区的警务直到最近仍被视为次于城市地区，很大程度上是因为人们认为人口密度不高的地方犯罪率很低。但是，最近在类似地区发生的事件和犯罪类型呈现上升趋势，而且在一些区域，地方警察局已经采用警务创新方式。例如，在英格兰的一些警察局，自己有马匹的特别警员们被派到乡村地区履职；这使他们有机会到达开阔地区和其他不好操控车辆的区域。

尽管火灾救援队使用留用消防人员已经有很多年了，但是只在 1996 年，英国内政部才建议研究是否可以让有意应聘特别警员的新人与雇主协作。雇主受到鼓励让其雇员带薪（时薪）为其社区提供服务，雇员接受所需培训之后，以特别警员或者支援警察的志愿者身份在社区发挥积极作用。在这个计划经历了一个有些摇摆不定的开端之后，现在积极支持为警察提供志愿服务的雇主们既有银行和电信部门，还有超市和市政委员会。这样的合作关系能够给雇主、警察局和个人带来好处。在 2015 年，一个“付出和收获”日活动在大曼彻斯特举行。当天，参与雇主支持警务（ESP，Employer Supported Policing）项目的特别警员和支援警察的志愿者，全天参与一些有针对性的倡议活动。一些参与其中的雇主对特别警员和支援警察的志愿者进行了一整天的观察，观察特别警员和支援警察的志愿者与正规警察同事一起工作的情况以及不与正规警察同事一起工作的情况。在当天活动取得的成果中，有缴获一件航空武器、没收大麻以及找回一辆被盗机动车，还有处置相当数量的轻微违法行为（Greater Manchester Police，2015）。

P82

对辅警的领导、管理和认可

辅警来自各行各业的全职岗位或者经历丰富，而且甚至在决定自愿担任警务角色之前，他们可能就是成功的领导者、企业家或者公共部门的雇员。他们致力于为自己的社区提供服务，在社会上扮演积极的角色。警察系统采用的特色鲜明的自上而下的半军事化组织架构，可能会招致某些辅警的抵触。例如，在美国一些地方，退休的执法官员在辅警队伍中服务，其之前的经验、知识和领导能力需要获得培养和认可。成为辅警的前全职正规警察不仅可以把在前任角色中获得的丰富领导经验带到辅警岗位上，而且可以不在辅警岗位上担任正式领导职位。因为辅警贡献自己的时间，获得有限的奖励或者没有正式奖励，警察机构必须思考能够满足个人需求、动力以及技能的方法；这种方法可以包括建立一个内部管理组织，包括建立一个等级架构。

尽管美国的一些机构成功实施了一些志愿者项目，这些项目仅由一个或两个带薪的雇员来管理（通常是正规执法官员），另一些机构则创建了组织结构，类似或者复制机构中全职成员的组织结构。在英国，这样的制度被广泛采用，同时由特别警员高级主管指挥警察局的特别警员，但是在美国则情况变化很大，就像其他许多警务方面一样。

尽管不是完全一致，众多英国警察局为辅警使用一个等级架构。国家警务改进局已经就辅警的等级架构给出了建议，这个等级架构包括特别警员、特别警佐、特别督察、特别总督察、特别警司、特别总警司（如有需要），以及特别警员队总队长。其他警察局额外增加了高级管理级别，包括特别警员队副总队长、
P83
特别警员队总队长助理。英国众多警察局使用特别警员等级徽章，而这不是国家警务改进局建议做的（国家警务改进局 2012 年被警务学院取代），而且这与正规警察局采用的等级也不一致。高级别特别警员仍是志愿者，但是他们拥有的职权多寡，警察局与警察局之间有不同的规定。

在最近开展的一项研究中，一份调查问卷被发放给英格兰和威尔士全部 43 个警察局中的所有高级特别警员，39 个警察局提交了答卷；3 个警察局未能提供高级特别警员的性别信息，因此被排除在下列统计之外。在剩下来的每一个警察局中，男性特别督察的比例高出女性的比例为 65%—100%。在特别总督察的数据中，13 个警察局说它们局里没有这样的级别，而余下的警察局中，除了 1 个警察局，其他的男性特别总督察的人数比女性多。根据调查发现，在一个有十名特别总督察的警察局里，该级别没有女性。数据显示，在特别警员方面，级别越高，女性的可能性就越低。至于每一级别的性别，尽管女性特别警员在所有特别警员中占了几乎三分之一的比例（31. 3%），但女性官长只占全部特别警员的 8. 1%（Britton，Knight& Maloney，2016）。

最近，对正规警察和辅警之间的级别高低问题存在很大争议。例如，在正规警员和特别警佐同时在现场的情况下，谁的级别更高？警务学院的领导关系评论指出，在正规警察和辅警之间“继续存在‘我们和他们’的问题”（College of Policing，n. d. ）。尽管在特别警员队中有等级制度，但是这一等级制度仍然与正规警察等级制度分离，因此，即使一个特别警员可能有强大且久经考验的领导能力和知识，而在警务“家庭”内部，正规警察照例要接管这样的特别警员。

美国警察机构使用等级架构的一个例证是，佛罗里达州奥兰治县县治安官办

公室将后备助理的级别与机构内全职警察的级别相匹配。奥兰治县县治安官办公室的后备助理的级别有：后备下士、后备中士、后备中尉、后备上尉、后备少校、后备县治安官助理。后备助理等级的徽章与这些级别的全职同事的徽章一样；但是，后备助理级别徽章的颜色是银色的，不是金色的。[④]另外，全职下士和中士在衣袖上缝制的级别徽章是金色的，后备下士和中士佩戴着相同标志的银色镶金边领章。奥兰治县县治安官办公室的全职成员还有别的级别，包括第一助理级别以及高级助理。[⑤]但是，这些级别通常不是管理性质的级别，都是被用作机构内正规成员的晋升机会。所以，辅警部门没有将自己融入指挥架构。但是，奥兰治县县治安官办公室任一级别的后备助理在职衔方面没有超过该机构的全职成员。尽管具有管理级别的后备警察与具有相同级别的全职县治安官助理获得同样的尊重，但是他们在履行职责的过程中，在职权方面没有超过任何全职警察或正规助理。在与全职助理执行职能部门工作的时候，拥有级别的后备助理不能佩戴他们的徽章，这样做的目的是不让公众（或者全职助理）对管理权产生歧义。但是，当工作小队中的成员只有后备警察或者在举办仪式的场合，后备警察被授权可以佩戴他们的级别徽章。 P84

来自佛罗里达州的另一个例证是圣露西县县治安官办公室的后备部门。该部门规模小，只有 15 名后备助理，这些后备助理同时具有全职执法证书和协助执法证书，两种证书作用相等。但是，这个机构选举产生的级别只有两个，即后备助理和后备中士。这个机构没有别的级别，而且后备中士没有超越后备助理的管理权。哈密尔顿警察局（加拿大）的协警遵循同样的领导模式：协助职员中士和协助中士以及协助警员要向哈密尔顿警察局的正规全职管理领导汇报工作。协助中士负责在指定区域巡逻、参与犯罪预防团队以及培训部门的工作。协助中士负责管理协助警员，协助警员向所在地区报告工作。

后备警察、协警和特别警员中的名人

埃尔维斯·普雷斯利（1935—1977 年）

“摇滚乐之王”不仅是一名歌星和电影明星，他还是一名执法后备人员。在他的职业生涯中，众所周知，他喜爱执法工作，而且经常与警察和安保部门保持联系，出于其地位和安保需要。他收集警察徽章和纪念品，而且人们常说，如果他没有成为一名著名摇滚明星的话，他就会在警察局工作。他在成名前，与孟菲斯警察局里很多人是好朋友，他曾宣誓做孟菲斯警察局的上尉，而且作为谢尔比县县治安官部的一员，他担任该部门的代言人，还担任丹佛警察局的名誉上尉（Troedson，2013）。1970 年 12 月 21 日，埃尔维斯会见理查德 · 尼克松总统，当
P85 时埃尔维斯展示了自己收集的警察徽章并且询问是否有可能得到麻醉药品和危险药品局的徽章。尼克松总统满足了他的要求。在埃尔维斯 1977 年因过量吸食毒品致死后，埃尔维斯与尼克松总统在椭圆形办公室的合影非常受欢迎（Carlson，2010）。

贝比 · 鲁斯（1895—1948 年）

贝比 · 鲁斯在 1914 年开始了他为巴尔的摩奥里奥勒斯做棒球投手的职业生涯。他在 1948 年去世，去世前与癌症作斗争，但他仍然是闻名遐迩的美国最伟大的棒球运动员。在大萧条时期，他给数百万的棒球迷以希望，也使他们得到精神慰藉。鲁斯曾宣誓成为纽约市警察局的一名后备警察，而且纽约市警察局给他配发了一套制服和中尉警衔（Garvey，2004），尽管他好像从来没有参加过任何培训或者执法工作。他在纽约市警察局里的角色是仪式性的，为的是促进积极的公共关系（Wagenheim，2014）。

埃里克 · 艾斯特拉达（1949 年至今）

埃里克 · 艾斯特拉达闻名遐迩，因为他主演了弗兰克 · 庞切雷洛或称为“庞克”这个角色。这个角色是二十世纪七十年代末和八十年代初一部名叫《加州公路巡警》（*ChiPs*）的电视剧里的人物。艾斯特拉达在美国许多城市当后备警察。2006 年，艾斯特拉达和其他社会名流接受培训，成为印第安纳州曼西警察局（MPD，the Muncie Police Department）的后备警察。这些展示在一档电视真人秀节目里。这个节目就是《枪手真人秀》（*Armed and Famous*），2007 年年初由哥伦比亚广播公司（CBS）录制。艾斯特拉达在 2006 年 12 月 5 日宣誓成为曼西警察局的后备警察，在 2009 年成为弗吉尼亚州贝德福德县治安官办公室的一名全职县治安官助理，但是 2009 年以后，艾斯特拉达还宣誓在爱达荷州圣安东尼警察局工作。艾斯特拉达宣称他甚至在成为一名演员之前就希望自己能当警察（Real，2016）。

沙奎尔 · 奥尼尔（1972 年至今）

这位有七英尺一英寸高（约 2.16 米）的美国前职业篮球运动员，还参演过

许多电影。作为演员、说唱明星和电视真人秀明星，他声名鹊起。然而，他还在洛杉矶县县治安官后备警察学校学习，并成为洛杉矶港口警察局一名后备警察。他在许多辅警岗位上工作过，包括坦佩（亚利桑那州）后备警察、贝德福德县（弗吉尼亚州）后备警察助理、迈阿密海岸（佛罗里达州）后备警察、佛罗里达州多拉尔警察局后备警察以及位于南佛罗里达州戈尔登比奇警察局的后备警察（Wyllie，2009）。他还被授予美国名誉副元帅，还因为帮助盖恩斯维尔的警察与邻居几名小孩打篮球而获得公众赞誉，因为在此之前有人打电话投诉这些孩子吵闹。他与警察和地方年轻人玩接球游戏的视频走红（Karimi，2016）。媒体多次报道“大鲨鱼”（奥尼尔的外号）表示有朝一日很有可能在佛罗里达州参加需要选举产生的执法岗位，比如县治安官。

P86

斯蒂文·西格尔（1952 年至今）

功夫大师和电影明星斯蒂文·西格尔在长达 20 多年里志愿为路易斯安那州杰斐逊教区县治安官办公室做后备警察助理。西格尔在路易斯安那州拥有第二套房子，他在各地工作、拍电影，而这使他成为名人，而且他开始为县治安官办公室工作，当后备警察。他的电视真人秀节目——主题是他在杰斐逊教区的工作情况——《斯蒂文·西格尔：法律人》在 2009 年 12 月 2 日首次播出。这档节目在 2010 年 4 月停播，当时县治安官办公室给出的解释是该档节目第二季不再录制，原因是诉讼界反对该演员的性骚扰行为（Lemons，2011）。在离开杰斐逊教区的岗位后，媒体报道由于诉讼问题，西格尔成为亚利桑那州马里科帕县县治安官乔·阿尔派诺的保安队的一员。保安队队员未经亚利桑那警察标准认证，主要被用在为警察提供支援的岗位，不是执法官员（Lemons，2011）。西格尔在政坛一直相当活跃，他公开呼吁弹劾总统巴拉克·奥巴马。2016 年，西格尔被弗拉基米尔·普京总统授予俄罗斯公民身份（Walker，2016）。

卢·费里格诺（1951 年至今）

卢·费里格诺最为人所知的是他饰演的“神奇绿巨人”，由哥伦比亚广播公司在二十世纪七十年代末和八十年代初播出。卢·费里格诺还获得连续两届“健美运动世界先生”头衔。在加利福尼亚州接受培训后，他在 2006 年宣誓成为洛杉矶县县治安官部的一名后备警察助理。费里格诺在三岁的时候就被诊断出听力严重丧失，而且因为这个情况，洛杉矶县县治安官派他执行不会导致逮捕的工作，包括录用新助理和在特殊被害人局工作。他还在 2010 年宣誓进入马里科帕县（亚利桑那州）县治安官的志愿保安队，随后在 2012 年，他宣誓进入加利福尼亚州圣路易斯奥比斯波县县治安官办公室（Linn，2012）。2013 年 9 月，他宣誓成为俄亥俄州特拉华县县治安官的一名特别助理。在俄亥俄州当特别助理期间，费里格诺没有逮捕权，但是他的工作岗位是促进社区和警察之间的积极联系。“他说，太多人认为警察和警察助理不是好人。他想与这样的偏见作斗争”（Arenschield，2013）。费里格诺坚定认为他对警务的兴趣源自他的父亲。他的父 P87 亲曾是纽约市警察局的一名中尉。

卡尔·爱德华（1979 年至今）

卡尔·爱德华是一名改装赛车的赛车手，在汽车比赛协会举办的斯普林特杯系列赛事中竞技，在 2016 年最后一次参加比赛。作为一名密苏里州哥伦比亚市当地人，他在 2007 年 28 岁的年纪，赢得了汽车比赛协会举办的布施系列比赛的冠军。爱德华在密苏里州布恩县担任县治安官的后备助理，而且他用自己的明星效应为“100 以下”运动提供支持。该项运动是在全美开展的、旨在将美国在一个年份里于执法方面发生的死亡人数降低到 100 以下。这位汽车比赛协会的赛车手，在 2004 年将自己的圣诞假期用于身着制服为他的社区提供服务（Walljasper，2005）。

查尔斯·狄更斯（1812—1870 年）

查尔斯·狄更斯身为作家，因为写出《大卫·科波菲尔》《雾都孤儿》以及《圣诞颂歌》这些作品而闻名于世。他在利物浦曾经短暂待过一段时间，对这座城市的警务工作表现出兴趣。他在利物浦宣誓成为一名特别警员，可能只有一个晚上。人们认为在他出版的几部作品里，他使用了角色描述以及其“执勤”场地。据说他担任特别警员为他撰写《不做生意的旅行者》所做的资料搜集工作提供了帮助（O’Keefe & Hull，2012）。

伊萨姆巴德·金德木·布鲁奈尔（1806—1859 年）

布鲁奈尔是英国最杰出的工程师之一；他一生中设计并建造了许多桥梁和隧道，这些建筑在建成后几乎 200 年的今天仍被使用着。在他于英格兰西南部布里斯托建造横跨埃文河的克利夫顿斜拉桥的过程中，布里斯托发生了政治动荡和骚乱。在 1831 年布里斯托发生骚乱的过程中，布鲁奈尔报名成为一名特别警员，由于大桥的建设受到了严重影响，因此工期被延误（Brunel200，n. d.）。

尼格尔·曼塞尔（1953 年至今）

尼格尔·曼塞尔曾是 F1 世界杯比赛的冠军。在他担任赛车手的职业生涯中及之后，他做过特别警员。他生活在英国西海岸一个小小的马恩岛上，该岛是一个自治的皇家属地。因此，该岛的刑事司法系统，包括警务，都与英国本土的法律和传送的方式不同；尽管马恩岛没有特别警员，但是尼格尔·曼塞尔作为该岛 P88 居民，以特别警员的身份服务了数年。他还在英格兰西南部的德文郡和康沃尔郡做过特别警员，在此期间，他因为在一条英国公路上超速被抓，但是他没有被迫辞掉其志愿服务角色（BBC，1998）。

拿破仑三世皇帝（1808—1873 年）

路易·拿破仑·波拿巴王子，即法国未来的拿破仑三世皇帝，在 1848 年宣誓成为伦敦的一名特别警员。由于整个英国工人运动高涨以及整个欧洲革命浪潮涌动，当时很多人特别害怕可能会有一场巨大的革命到来。为了应对这些情况，成千上万的军队驻扎在伦敦的众多桥梁上，英格兰银行的墙壁也得到加固。当时大约 85000 名特别警员被录用并被登记造册，包括波拿巴（Working Class Movement Library，2016）。

注释

①例如，2005 年在中佛罗里达大学警察局（UCFPD，University of Central Florida Police Department）的官员马里奥·詹金斯，因为工作时身着便服，结果其身份被误判，被一名奥兰多警察局的官员射杀。该大学的警察局在当时拥有的宣誓警察职员不足 50 人，马里奥是该局因为在一线工作而亡的首位官员。这一损失对该局产生了相当大的影响。奥兰治县县治安官的后备警察部门接管了中佛罗里达大学警察局所有警务工作，时长两天，因为当时来自中佛罗里达大学的官员们参加马里奥的葬礼以及其他纪念活动。

②佛罗里达州沃卢西亚县代托纳比奇警察局（DBPD，Daytona Beach Police Department）在警察局需要大量人手的时候使用后备警察提供帮助，包括自行车周、春假以及其他重要活动举行的时候。但是，代托纳比奇警察局给其后备警察

支付报酬从而帮助后备警察履行职责。另外一个在海滨地区使用后备警察的例证是博因顿比奇警察局，同样是在佛罗里达州。博因顿比奇警察局拥有一支无报酬志愿者队伍，这支队伍全部是获得认证的志愿性质的协警，他们在需要人手的时候作为一支增援力量工作（Keegan，2015）。

③“筑路工”（navvy）是十九世纪早期对单词“navigator”的缩写。“筑路工”指的是为铁道、隧道和道路建设工作的劳工。

④奥兰治县县治安官办公室，给所有高于下士衔级的全职县治安官助理配发金色衔级徽章和统一徽章。

⑤这些级别的衔级，处在助理和下士之间。

参考文献

Alfonso，M. （2015，October 30）（阿方索〈2015 年 10 月 30 日〉）. LASD Air Rescue 5 completes humanitarian mission，saves people（“洛杉矶县县治安官部空中救援 5 大队完成人道救援任务，拯救人民”）. South Pasadena Patch（南帕萨迪纳片区）. 2016 年 9 月 23 日检索网址 http：//patch. com/california/southpasadena/lasd-air-rescue-5-completes-humanitarian-mission-saves-people.

Arenschield，L. （2013，September 21）（阿伦希尔德〈2013 年 9 月 21 日〉）. “Hulk” actor Lou Ferrigno to be strong arm of law here（“‘绿巨人’扮演者卢·费里格诺在本地成为法律的有力武器”）. *The Columbus Dispatch*（《哥伦布快讯》）. 2016 年 11 月 15 日检索网址 www. dispatch. com/content/stories/local/2013/09/21/hulk-actor-lou-ferrigno-to-be-strong-arm-of-law-here. html.

Arwood，D. E. ，Hilal，S. M. ，Karsky，J. ，& Norman，M. （2005）（阿尔伍德、希拉尔、卡斯凯和诺曼）. Police reserve officers：Structural embeddedness of self-role merger and volunteering（“警察：自我角色整合者与志愿服务的结构嵌入性”）. *Great Plains Sociologists*（《大平原地区社会学家》），17（2），36—60.

BBC（1998，January 23）（英国广播公司〈1998 年 1 月 23 日〉）. Former racing champion banned from the road（“前赛车冠军上路被禁”）. 2017 年 9 月 3 日检索网址 http：//news. bbc. co. uk/1/hi/uk/49787. stm.

Bedfordshire Police（n. d. ）（贝德福德郡警察局〈日期不详〉）. Bedfordshire Police：Protecting people and fighting crime（“贝德福德郡警察局：保卫人民、打击犯罪”）. 2016 年 9 月 23 日检索网址 www. bedfordshire. police. uk/recruitment/

special_constables. aspx.

Berg, B. L., & Doerner, W. G. (1988)(伯格和多尔奈尔). Volunteer police officers: An unexamined personnel dimension in law enforcement(“辅警：未经审查的执法人员”). *American Journal of Police*(《美国警察》), 7 (1), 81—89.

British Transport Police (n. d.)(英国交通警察总队〈日期不详〉). Our history: The first railway police(“我们的历史：首支高速公路警察队伍”). 2017年2月13日检索网址 www. btp. police. uk/about_us/our_history/detailed-history. aspx.

Britton, I., Knight, L., & Maloney, D. (2016)(布里顿、耐特和马龙内). *Citizens in policing: National benchmarking exercise -phase one*(《警务中的公民：国家基准测试——第一阶段》). Northampton, UK: University of Northampton, Institute for Public Safety, Crime and Justice(北安普顿，英国：北安普顿大学，公共安全、犯罪与司法研究所).

Brunel200. com (n. d.)(日期不详). Brunel biography(“布鲁奈尔个人传记”). 2017年9月3日检索网址 www. brunel200. com/1820s. htm.

Carlson, P. (2010)(卡尔松). When Elvis met Nixon(“埃尔维斯进见尼克松的时候”). *Smithsonian* (December)(《史密森学会》(十一月)). 2016年11月23日检索网址 www. smithsonianmag. com/history/when - elvis - met - nixon-69892425.

City of London Police (2016)(伦敦城警察局). *National policing lead for economic crime: Annual review* (2015—2016)(《经济犯罪国家警务领导：年度回顾(2015—2016)》). London: City of London Police(伦敦：伦敦城警察局).

College of Policing (n. d.)(警务大学〈日期不详〉). Special constables and volunteers in policing(“特别警员和警务中的志愿者”). 2017年1月8日检索网址 www. collegepoliceuk/what-wE-do/development/Promotion/the-leadership-review/Pages/Current-topics. aspx.

Field, M. (2007, December 18)(菲尔德〈2007年12月18日〉). The future of the City of London Police(“伦敦城警察局的未来”). Mark Field MP(马克·菲尔德议员). 2016年9月22日检索网址 http://markfieldmp. com/speeches/freedom-a-security-speeches/the-future-of-the-city-of-london-police.

Fishwick, B. (2016, January 20)(菲什威克〈2016年1月20日〉).

Hampshire Police want "geeks" to volunteer for cyber crime fight（"汉普郡警察局希望'电脑怪杰们'志愿打击网络犯罪"）. *The News*（《新闻》）. 2016年9月22日检索网址 www. portsmouth. co. uk/news/crime/hampshire - police - want - geeks-to-volunteer-for-cyber-crime-fight-1-7170191.

Fredericksen, P. J., & Levin, D. (2004)（弗雷德里克森和勒文）. Accountability and the use of volunteer officers in public safety organizations（"追责与公共安全组织使用辅警"）. *Public Performance and Management Review*（《公共绩效和管理评论》）, 27 (4), 118—143.

Garvey, J. (2004)（加维）. *Images of America: San Francisco Police Department*（《美国印象：旧金山警察局》）. San Francisco: Arcadia Publishing（旧金山：阿卡迪亚出版社）.

Gill, M. L., & Mawby, R. I. (1990)（吉尔和莫比）. *A special constable: A study of the police reserve*（《特别警员：关于警方后备人员的研究》）. Aldershot, UK: Avebury Publishing（奥尔德肖特，英国：阿维伯里出版社）.

Gravelle, J., & Rogers, C. (2009)（格拉维勒和罗格斯）. Your country needs you! The economic viability of volunteers in the police（"你的国家需要你！警方志愿者的经济生存能力"）. *Safer Communities*（《更安全社区》）, 8 (3), 34—38.

Greater Manchester Police (2015)（大曼彻斯特警察局）. Give and Gain Day, 2015: Debrief document（"得失日，2015年：汇报文件"）. Manchester: Greater Manchester Police（曼彻斯特：大曼彻斯特警察局）.

Greenberg, M. A. (2005)（格林伯格）. *Citizens defending America: From colonial times to the age of terrorism*（《保卫美国的公民：从殖民地时代到恐怖主义年代》）. Pittsburgh: University of Pittsburgh Press（匹兹堡：匹兹堡大学出版社）.

Howe, S., & Graham, V. (1995, September 29)（豪和格拉哈姆〈1995年9月29日〉）. Special duties（"特别职责"）. *Police Review*（《警察评论》）.

Karimi, E. (2016, January 24)（卡里米〈2016年1月24日〉）. Shaq, Florida officer surprise kids with a basketball game（"佛罗里达警察'鲨鱼'与孩子们玩篮球让孩子们惊奇"）. CNN. 2016年11月2日检索网址 www. cnn. com/2016/01/24/us/florida-shaq-police-officers-game.

P90

Keegan, C. （2015, December 21）（基甘〈2015 年 12 月 21 日〉）. Boynton Beach Police Department expanding reserve officer program: Unpaid volunteers serve as police officers（“博因顿比奇警察局拓展后备警察项目：无报酬志愿者以警察身份工作”）. WPTVC. com. 2017 年 8 月 20 日检索网址 www. wptv. com/news/region-s-palm-beach-county/boynton-beach/boynton-beach-police-department-expanding-reserve-officer-program.

Lemons, S. （2011, March 18）（勒蒙斯〈2011 年 3 月 18 日〉）. Steven Seagal resigned rather than face IA investigation, according to Sheriff Newell Normand（“根据县治安官纽维尔·诺曼德，斯蒂文·西格尔辞职而不是面对 IA 调查”）. *Phoenix New Times*（《凤凰城新闻时报》）. 2016 年 11 月 2 日检索网址 www. phoenixnewtimes. com/blogs/stevenagal-resigned-rather-than-face-ia-investigation-according-to-sheriff-newell-normand-6499604.

Linn, S. （2012, June 15）（林〈2012 年 6 月 15 日〉）. Lou Ferrigno, aka The Hulk, sworn in as reserve deputy for Sheriffs Office（卢·费里格诺，亦称绿巨人，宣誓成为县治安官办公室后备助理）. *The Tribune*（《论坛报》）. 2016 年 11 月 15 日检索网址 www. sanluisobispo. com/news/local/article39205230. html.

Monrovia Weekly（2015, October 7）（《蒙罗维亚周刊》〈2015 年 10 月 7 日〉）. L. A. Sheriff Search and Rescue prepares for swift water rescues during rainy El Nino（“洛杉矶县县治安官部搜救队准备在厄尔尼诺现象导致的雨季实施快速水中救援”）. 2016 年 9 月 23 日检索网址 www. monroviaweekly. com/current-news/-a-sheriff-search-and-rescueprepares-for-swift-water-rescues-during-rainy-el-nino.

Myhill, A. , & Beak, K. （2008）（米希尔和比克）. *Public confidence in the police*（《公众对警方的信心》）. London: National Police Improvement Agency（伦敦：国家警务改进局）.

O'Keefe, J. , & Hull, R. （2012）（欧基和赫尔）. Charles Dickens's Liverpool（“查尔斯·狄更斯在利物浦”）. *The Merseysider*（2）[《默西塞德杂志》（2）]. 2017 年 9 月 3 日检索网址 www. merseysidermagazine. com/site/local-history/charles-dickenss-liverpool.

Perkins, M. （2016）（珀金斯）. Modelling public confidence of the police: How perceptions of the police differ between neighborhoods in a city（“塑造公众对

警察的信心：城市不同社区对警察看法是如何变化的”）. *Police Practice and Research*：*An International Journal*（《警察实践与研究：国际期刊》），17（2），113—125.

Police. uk（2015，October 22）（2015 年 10 月 22 日）. How diverse are the police?（“警察多元化程度有多大?”）2017 年 1 月 2 日检索网址 www. police. uk/news/how-diverse-are-police.

Real，E.（2016，July 6）（雷亚尔〈2016 年 7 月 6 日〉）. “CHiPs” alum Erik Estrada is a real-life police officer now!（“《加州公路巡警》主演埃里克·艾斯特拉达在现实生活中成为一名警察啦!”）*US Weekly*（《美国周刊》）. 2016 年 11 月 23 日检索网址 www. usmagazine. com/celebrity-news/news/chips-alum-erik-estrada-is-a-real-life-police-officer-now-w212275.

Roberg，R.，Novak，K.，& Cordner，G. W.（2009）（罗伯格、诺瓦克和科尔德纳）. *Police and society*，4th Edition（《警察与社会》（第四版））. New York：Oxford University Press（纽约：哈佛大学出版社）.

Robinson，D.，& Miller，I.（2016，September 21）（罗宾森和米勒〈2016 年 9 月 21 日〉）. Specials making their mark in the professional standards department（“特别警员在专业标准部有了一席之地”）. Police Oracle（警察网上论坛）. 2016 年 9 月 22 日检索网址 www. policeoracle. com/news/investigation/2016/sep/20/specialsmaking - their - mark - in - professional - standards - department _ 92962. html. html.

Seth，R.（2006）（塞斯）. *The specials*（《特别警员》）. Trowbridge，UK：Cromwell Press（特洛布里奇，英国：克伦威尔出版社）.

Sharpe，M. E.（1986）（夏珀）. Volunteering in municipal police departments：Some hypotheses on performance impacts（“市警察局中的志愿行为：对绩效影响的若干假设”）. *Public Productivity Review*（《公共生产力评论》），10（2），77—92.

Sindall，K.，Sturgis，P.，& Jennings，W.（2012）（辛代尔、斯特吉斯和詹宁斯）. Public confidence in the police：A time-series analysis（“公众对警方的信心：采用时序分析法”）. *British Journal of Criminology*（《英国犯罪学学报》），52（4），744—764.

Special Impact（2015a）（特殊影响）. Newcastle Falcons rugby player joins

Special Constabulary（“纽卡斯尔猎鹰橄榄球运动员加入特别警员队”）. *Special Impact*（《特殊影响》）（21），2016 年 9 月 22 日检索网址 www. dutysheet. com/special_impact/special_impact_Issue_21. pdf.

Special Impact（2015b）（特殊影响）. UK’s first special constable dog handler（“英国首位特别警员警犬训练员”）. *Special Impact*（《特殊影响》）（21），16 –17. Retrieved September 22，2016，from www. dutysheet. com_/specialImpact/Special Impact_Issue_21. pdf.

Sprott，J. B.，& Doob，A. N.（2014）（斯普罗特和杜伯）. Confidence in the police：Variation across groups classified as visible minorities（“对警方的信心：被归类为显明少数族裔的不同群体间的差别”）. *Canadian Journal of Criminology and Criminal Justice*（《加拿大犯罪学与刑事司法学报》），56（3），367—379.

Troedson，D.（2016，July 24）（特罗埃德森〈2016 年 7 月 24 日〉）. Elvis Presley and the police（埃尔维斯·普雷斯利与警方）. Elvis Australia（澳大利亚猫王）. 2016 年 11 月 23 日检索网址 www. elvis. com. au/presley/police-elvis-presley. shtml.

Volunteer Special Constabulary（1998）（志愿特别警员队）. *Service to the nation：50 years of the Volunteer Special Constabulary*（《为国家服务：志愿特别警员队的 50 年历史》）. Singapore：Volunteer Special Constabulary（新加坡：志愿特别警员队）.

Wagenheim，K.（2014）（瓦根海姆）. *Babe Ruth：His life and legend*（《贝比·鲁斯：生平与传奇》）. New York：Open Road Media（纽约：公路媒体）.

Walker，S.（2001）（沃克）. *Police accountability：The role of citizen oversight*（《追责警察：公民监督的作用》）. Belmont，CA：Wadsworth（贝尔蒙特，加利福尼亚州：沃兹沃思）.

Walker，S.（2016，November 3）（沃克〈2016 年 11 月 3 日〉）. Steven Seagal granted Russian citizenship by Vladimir Putin（“弗拉基米尔·普京批准斯蒂文·西格尔入籍俄罗斯”）. *The guardian*（《卫报》）. 2016 年 11 月 15 日检索网址 www. theguardian. com/culture/2016/nov/03/steven-seagal-granted-russian-citizenship-vladimir-putin.

Walljasper，J.（2005，February 16）（瓦尔贾斯珀〈2005 年 2 月 16 日〉）. The ride of his life：Columbia driver can′t stop smiling on his way to the top（“飞驰

人生：哥伦比亚赛车手一路顺意直抵巅峰”）. *Columbia Daily Tribune*（《哥伦比亚每日论坛报》）. 2016 年 11 月 15 日检索网址 http：//archive. columbiatribune. com/2005/feb/20050216spor007.

Weitzer, R. , & Tuch, S. A. （2005）（魏特泽和图克）. Racially biased policing: Determinants of citizen perceptions（“警务中的种族歧视：公民认知的决定因素”）. *Social Forces*（《社会力量》）, 83（3）, 1009—1030.

Whitehead, T. （2012, October 9）（怀特海德〈2012 年 10 月 9 日〉）. Police cuts mean more specials and volunteers, chief signals（“警方人数削减意味着更多的特别警员和志愿者加入警方，重要信号”）. *The Daily Telegraph*（《每日电讯报》）. 2017 年 7 月 15 日检索网址 www. telegraph. co. uk/news/uknews/law-and-order/9643289/Police-cuts-mean-more-specials-and-volunteers-chief-signals. html.

Williams, G. （2005）（威廉姆斯）. Special report: Reserve officers on bikes（“特别报道：后备警察骑自行车”）. *Law and Order*（《法律和秩序》）, 53（4）, 82—87.

Working Class Movement Library（2016, December）（工运图书馆〈2016 年 12 月〉）. A special constable is sworn in（“一名特别警员宣誓加入”）. 2017 年 9 月 3 日检索网址 www. wcml. org. uk/our-collections/object-of-the-month/objects-of-the-month-2016/a-special-constable-is-sworn-in.

Wright, T. （2015, March 12）（怀特〈2015 年 3 月 12 日〉）. LASD volunteers log 450, 000 hours（“洛杉矶县县治安官部志愿者们贡献 450000 个小时”）. *The Malibu Times*. （《马里布时报》）2016 年 9 月 23 日检索网址 www. malibutimes. com/news/article ea5ddfca-c84a-11e4-8136-7ff750f42c9a. html.

Wyllie, D. （2009, October 29）（怀利〈2009 年 10 月 29 日〉）. Shaquille O'Neal may be Ohio's next deputy sheriff（“沙奎尔·奥尼尔有可能成为俄亥俄州下一位县治安官助理”）. PoliceOne（警察一号）. 2016 年 11 月 2 日检索网址 www. policeone. com/police-recruiting/articles/1960007-Shaquille-ONeal-may-be-Ohios-next-deputy-sheriff.

第六章　辅警培训

P92

不论是在美国还是在英国，公民个人成为辅警的原因多种多样，其所接受的培训量也各不相同。尽管英国的警察队伍是全国统一体制，而且对警察的培训在全英的标准化程度也很高，但是对特别警员的培训，直到最近，更多地是由当地警察部门决定。在英格兰和威尔士所有地方，在警察局中提供常规服务的警察，从 2010 年 1 月开始，要按国家职业标准配置并且要参加新警学习和开发项目（IPLDP，the Initial Police Learning and Development Programme）。该项目为期两年，培训新警并最后给他们颁发警务文凭（College of Policing，n. d. -a）。

在美国，每个州有不同的法规涉及全职警察和辅警。对于后备警察和协警或者正规警察，在录取、聘用、背景审查或者培训方面，根本没有统一规定。要想成为一名正规警察，许多州要求被录取者完成一个警察学院的培训课程，这样的课程针对执法官员的标准都是最低要求（Discover Policing，n. d. ）。2006 年，在全美有 648 所州和地方执法学院，其中 213 所是县级、地区级或者州级学院，292 所是技术学校、学院或者大学的学院，143 所是城市或自治市学院（Bureau of Justice Statistics，2009）。尽管在许多州完成的学院培训可以在其他许多州被认可为申请人已经完成的培训，但是在这个方面同样缺乏统一性。尽管一名在一个州获得全部认证的警察，可能在所获证书通过审查、证明其获得最少的培训量或者在接受教育的同时有培训经历，可以转岗到别的州当警察，但是对未获全部认证的辅警来说，这种情况不可能发生。

为了更好地理解与正规警察培训的不同和相同之处，下文将通过对比辅警培训，对全职警务职责所要求的培训加以简短描述。正如前文指出的，要给美国的培训标出界线是相当困难的，因为不单是州与州之间，甚至是州内的地方司法管辖区域之间都不一样，这使人们很难理解培训需求以及辅警的角色。但是，在英格兰和威尔士，正如警务学院所界定的，对正规警察的培训和对特别警员的培训 P93

都采纳更加同质化的结构。

正规警察培训

英国

警务学院被指定为信息交换之所，以及为在英格兰和威尔士开展的警察培训设定标准之地。警察局配备了培训模块，学习这些培训模块都会有效果，而且警察局能够选择使用国家提供的资料，或者开发本地资料以取代或者完善国家提供的资料。警察局的教员、勤务辅导员、执法一线的管理者以及监督者全部参与对录用人员的培训工作。

在英格兰和威尔士，空缺岗位都在网上展示，申请者一次只能向一个警察局提出申请。除了基本的年龄要求（18 岁及以上，没有上限规定）以及具有在英国居住的合法资格，在具备过得去的书面表达能力和计算能力，对申请者没有别的正式申请要求。许多警察局目前或之前与大学和继续教育学院合作，通过将警察教员聘用进入大学工作的方式，提供部分培训或者全部培训。在过去，其他更高端的教育机构鼓励警察局的教员采用培训模块作为其培训课程的一部分。但是，许多这样的合作方式都是短期的，因为培训模块适应性差或者双方在实际合作过程中存在误解。但是，在警察局和大学之间成功合作的范例还是有的。在这个成功的合作里，参训警察获得一个学位，这个学位是在两年的学习基础上被授予的，这个学位表明一名正规警察在为期两年的试用期间于理论方面收获的知识。学员（自费）被要求在学习期间以特别警员的身份工作，在成功完成学业的时候，学员毕业并获得国家认可的学位（警务知识证书）并且被认定具备独立巡逻的能力。[1]其他警察机构和大学之间的协作取得成功的程度参差不齐。尽管英国在警察培训方面目前没有国家学位，但是警察培训正在朝着大学学历教育专业化方向发展，学员在接受学历教育的同时要经受高水平的警务训练。这样的学历教育在 2018 年 4 月开始，2018 年 9 月开始要求申请者加入警察机构之前要获得专业学位。

在 2016 年的前四个月，警务学院编写了一份咨询文件，即“警务教育资格评定标准体系”（PEQF，Policing Education Qualifications Framework）。该文件呼吁回应警察培训标准化以及公众对警察培训的认可。过去，警察在接受工作所需的基础培训的同时接受一定范围的专业培训。但是，到一个警察退休的时候，这些技能和专业培训，尽管是从事警务工作必须的和必要的，却没有得到来自国家的资格证明（在过去，培训不等同于一个教育学位）。结果就是，卸职的警察无法用简单的方式向广大世界展示他们的能力和力量，尽管他们在技能和专业上是行家里手。当然，即便是作为警务的硬性要求以及在警务岗位上成功履职所需的基础知识，的确也需要继续扩展，以适应日益发展的技能、公众的要求以及经济的挑战。

国家警务课程（NPC，the National Policing Curriculum）规定了每个警察局所要求的标准："该课程提供了警务内部开发知识、理解、技能、态度以及行为举止的标准体系和基本准则，途径是教育和培训，采用多种方法和培训方式"（College of Policing，n. d. –b）。

在历史上，每个警察局负责对其新成员进行教育和培训。正规警察培训的时间明显比特别警员培训的时间要长，而且不包括可能为顺应当时不同警察局要求所需的任何专家培训。培训被设计成确保成功入职的候选人适合在英格兰和威尔士境内的任何警察局执行独立巡逻。这是因为，不同于美国，国家警务课程在英国全境建立起了统一的警察培训标准。在苏格兰，培训不断实施的地方是苏格兰警察培训和招聘中心、位于塔利阿兰的苏格兰警察学院以及私人机构内部（Police Scotland，n. d. ）。英格兰和威尔士的培训由一些组织机构提供，每一个组织机构都必须满足国家警务课程以及"警务教育资格评定标准体系"的要求。

现在，英国警察职业化和培训正处在一个复杂的变革时期；在内政部部长布兰登·刘易斯于 2017 年 3 月发表的一次讲话中，他宣布，2012 年建立起来的警务学院，现在负责高标准的警务工作。这个在"警务教育资格评定标准体系"会议上发表的演说，强调了警察道德规范、持续职业开发文化以及教育标准的重要性。刘易斯强调警务学院的重要性，是为了确保警察局是灵活机动的、职业化的而且有很强的适应性。而且，他建议"警务教育资格评定标准体系"和警务学院合作，为在如此重要领域工作的警察签发许可证和普遍认证。刘易斯提到的重要领域包括警察与易受侵害的人群工作。最后，他认为警务学院和"警务教育资格评定标准体系"应该设法对技能进行认证，使警察能够获得将来成功所需的知识和技能。他强调应该继续拓展进入警察职业的多种途径。他还强调了通过警务训练获取学位这一途径的重要性，因为这使各色各样的人们有机会提升在工作场地实施培训的水准（Lewis，2017）。 P95

2016 年，警务学院发布了一个报告，题目是《制定并发布警务教育标准体系》。该报告的结论是"对获得认证的资格证明应该有一个国家级的标准体系"

（College of Policing，2016）。简而言之，该报告的总结是：未来所有从事警务工作的职员将获得与其受教育水平对等的资格证明，从而使社区服务警察达到 4 级水平。[②]警员获得 5 级[③]或者 6 级，[④]这种级别相当于本科生的水平。为了在国家警务课程中成功取得所要求的级别，要么以警务训练的方式完成培训，要么申请者在加入警察机构之前从一个获得认证的研究机构获得专业警务学位。

正规警察的录取过程与特别警员不同，但是现在有一个快速通道评价方式，这个快速通道开放的对象有特别警员、警察职员以及那些可能给警察角色带来多种新视角的大学本科毕业生。通过快速通道方式获得成功的申请者们，有望在三年后获得督察的职位，所以，他们的培训更多聚焦在管理和领导方面。可能会有候选人申请加入特别警员队，也会有候选人已经具备领导和管理才能；这些候选人可以考虑转到正规警察岗位，他们或许可以在某一岗位上发现自己的能力，因为在这个岗位上他们可以用自己精通的技能促进自身的提升。但是在他们做特别警员期间，他们对自己所处的岗位可能只能忍受一点或者根本无法忍受。

快速通道评价方式包括大约 35 周的课堂教学，同时有一个内容广泛的培训，这个培训是实操性的，而且培训人员要在指导下完成。不管谁来提供培训，所有课程都经过“资格评定与学分标准体系”（QCF，the Qualifications and Credit Framework）的质量评估。新成员在成功完成初始培训之后，要经历为期两年的见习时期，这意味着，尽管新成员已经适合进行独立巡逻，但是他们必须继续接受培训并完成一个职业发展计划（PDP，professional development portfolio），以表明他们到岗后能够胜任工作。

美国

美国警察院校为正规警察提供的是中等时长的培训，大约 19 周（或者说 761 个小时），其中 60 个小时用于枪支教学，44 个小时是自我防卫教学（Bureau of Justice Statistics，2009）。按培训课程中等时长递减顺序，其他教学课程包括：调查（45 个小时），健体（40 个小时），巡逻流程和技术（40 个小时），刑法（40 个小时），应急车辆驾驶（36 个小时），基本急救护理和心肺复苏（24 个小时），基本外语技能（16 个小时），家暴（12 个小时），使用非致命武器（12 个小时），宪法（11 个小时），人际关系（11 个小时），国内备战/恐怖主义（8 个小时），仇恨犯罪/偏见犯罪（8 个小时），社区警务（8 个小时），有关少年犯的法律和程序（8 个小时），道德和正直（8 个小时），文化多样性（8 个小时），计算机和信息系统（8 个小时），警察民事/刑事责任（6 个小时），压力预防和

P96

管理（6 个小时）以及解决问题（6 个小时）（Discover Policing，n. d.）。

进入院校进行基础培训的女性在被录取者中仅占大约 16%。毕竟，在全美范围内，开始警察基础培训的被录取者中，大约 86%能完成这个培训。在完成警察院校学习之后，被录取者要在一名培训教官的指导下完成实战培训，即在职培训。尽管对怎样实施这样的培训，美国全境做法各种各样，被录取者用在这种在职培训上的中等时长大致是 8 周，或者说 320 个小时（Discover Policing，n. d.）。

正如在前文提到的，在一个州里开展的院校培训可能或者不可能被别的州接受作为一名执法官员的资格证明。例如，佛罗里达州在大多数情况下会认可执法官员在别的州接受的培训，只要有资格证明的申请者，在别的信誉良好的州作为获得认证的执法官员已经工作至少一年。但是，来自其他州的要在佛罗里达州申请资格证明的申请者，还必须完成一个为期两周的培训课程，以表明其胜任某些方面的工作（诸如攻击战术、使用枪支、急救和车辆驾驶）。其他州有类似的资格证明转认规定，但是不是所有的州都有；一些司法管辖区域可能要求：一名来自别的州的已经获得认证的执法官员个人，参加警察院校的培训并通过全部课程考试。另外，资格证明在一个州的要求可能与另一个州的不同，因此，申请者可能没有满足最低/最高年龄要求，或者无法满足资格证明的某些背景要求。

即便是在一个州，将资格证明从一个司法管辖区域转认到另一个司法管辖区域，可能也是困难重重。一般情况下，如果一名申请者在一个州内从一个执法机构转到另一个执法机构，那么院校和州的资格证明都不是问题；但是，申请者可能发现自己不得不放弃衔级和资历，常常还要放弃他们的退休福利。另外，一些机构要求所有的宣誓雇员必须完成他们的院校培训，而且不会接受其他任何培训。例如，作为一名申请者，不论你在别地拥有多少经验或者经历多少培训，你都不能在下列警察机构工作：纽约市警察局、洛杉矶市警察局、佛罗里达高速公路巡逻队，除非你已经成功完成这些警察机构自己的院校培训。

在美国许多地方，全职警察转岗成为一名辅警，不论是在他们自己的机构内部，还是到一个外部警察机构，都不是少见的事情（尽管如前所述，这在美国东北部不常发生，因为在那里辅警通常没有警察权）。如果新机构在别的州而该州辅警又拥有全部警察权和职权，那么作为全职警察转岗为辅警通常要完成所需的必修培训。如果他或她在同一个州里转岗，那么资格证明的转认通常不成问题，然而在新机构里，警察好像将不得不完成某类缩短了时间的实战培训。但是，就算在同一机构内部从全职警察转为后备警察，警察可能不得不放弃所有已经获得的衔级；当然实际情况不都是这样，警察局局长和县治安官能够就这些类型的转岗作出自己的决定。

许多州有“内部”培训项目和院校，因此申请者们被挑选，受训者开始以雇员身份工作并且在院校开始培训的第一天就开始领取薪水。但是，美国现在更为常见的情况是，在警察作为雇员开始第一天工作之前，地方院校和地区院校收取学费并且“证明”警察的资格。来自美国各地的52%的培训院校收取学费，以帮助满足运营成本（Discover Policing，n. d.），这意味着学员必须从自己的腰包里掏钱去上学，期待在将来得到一个警务岗位。警察院校学费昂贵：一个可能成为警察的人在犹他州上警察院校的花费可能超过6000美元（Utah Valley University，n. d.）。但是，其他州报告的花费要少一些，包括佐治亚州和佛罗里达州，这两个州收取的学费和费用大约是3800美元（Georgia Public Safety Training，n. d.；Valencia College，n. d.）。

各州之间的这种差异从院校开始培训新的被录取人员时就存在了。在一些州（像佛罗里达州、新泽西州以及密歇根州），学员要么向一个地方警察机构提出准入申请，要么直接向院校提出准入申请。被录取者可能在院校培训开始前就被一个警察机构雇用成为“受训者”（此类学员被称为“定向生”[5]），因此这样的学员是公费上学，上学期间领取图书、制服而且经常有时薪。而那些在上学前没能成功被雇用的被录取者，就必须自费上学，要自己准备图书、制服（此类学员被称为“非定向”受训者）。这些学员经常要依赖助学贷款来完成资格证明，或者必须在外面干活来偿还债务并满足生活开销。

并不是所有这些类型项目的院校毕业生都能找到当警察的工作，因为许多接
P98 受学员进入他们警察院校培训项目的院校实施粗略的背景审查，而警察机构更为详细的背景审查可能使一名院校毕业生在法律上不符合当警察的要求或者降低他们当警察的愿望。那些把自己背景中的问题视为小瑕疵的候选人，可能无法找到当警察的工作，这些小瑕疵通常包括信用报告或者交通罚单。

整个佛罗里达州有39所警察院校，而且在佛罗里达州，基础执法（BLE，basic law enforcement）资格证明的基础是：成功完成院校学习，成功通过一个州级考试，并且在成功通过州级考试的四年内被一个警察机构雇用。在佛罗里达州，这些院校的学员可能要么是自费学习，要么是由一个警察机构资助学习。犹他州将公费被录取者与自费被录取者区分对待：用院校的附属机构为没有被犹他州执法机构雇用的自费学员提供治安官员培训；用犹他州治安官员标准和培训学

院为被警察机构雇用的申请者提供培训。科罗拉多州采用警察机构院校为公费被录取者提供培训，同时采用社区大学院校给自费学员提供自费参加培训的机会（Utah Department of Public Safety，n. d.；Colorado Peace Officer Standards and Training，n. d.）。

罗德岛要求申请者首先完成申请一个警察机构的程序，而且申请者不能在未获资助的情况下直接进入一所学院。被录取者可以进入一所警察院校学习，只有在一个警察局雇用了该候选人作为见习警察才可以。在申请者在警察院校登记之前，警察机构开展所有的背景调查并且组织考试（State of Rhode Island Municipal Police Training Academy，n. d.）。路易斯安那州也是这样操作的。该州要求所有候选人受雇在一个警察局，然后参加一个国家承认的警察基础培训学习，培训时间大致为 360 个小时，由此他们获得路易斯安那州治安官员标准和培训委员会颁发的资格证书（Louisiana Commission on Law Enforcement and Administration of Criminal Justice，n. d.）。

辅警培训

英国

当今许多英国警察局已经采用特别警员国家招录评估流程，这是一个标准化申请流程，供那些有意愿当辅警的人使用。候选人被要求完成一个考查能力水平的问卷调查（CBQ，competency based questionnaire）、形势判断考试（SJT，situational judgement test）、一个写作技能考试以及参加一个考查能力水平的访谈。一些警察局选择对被录取者采取附加的背景调查。候选人还必须成功完成一个标准化的身体素质测试以及一个医学筛查。英格兰和威尔士的所有警察局提供培训和教育的依据是新警学习和开发项目（IPLDP，Initial Police Learning and Development Programme）的核心要求，而特别警员的培训依据的是特别警员队基础学习（IL4SC，the Initial Learning for the Special Constabulary）国家项目（Pepper，2014；College of Policing，n. d. -a）。

P99

特别警员基础学习的核心要素包括道德、多样性、健康和安全以及急救。特别警员基础学习为特别警员履职提供了操作和法律要求的基础。不像美国的警察机构，在英国，一旦申请者申请特别警员这样的辅警岗位获得通过并开始接受培训，新被录取者即宣誓就职并获得他的警察证。警察证让持有者拥有逮捕权，与正规警察拥有的逮捕权完全一样。这一情况甚至在培训开始前就出现了。但是，新被录取者直到完成基础培训才会上街巡逻。然而，即便他们完成了基础培训，他们还是被要求在上街巡逻时要有警察随行，直到他们被视为有能力独立巡逻。后续培训不论在内容还是在时长方面，各个警察局都有不同，新招录的特别警员受训以满足地方警务的需要。

特别警员队基础学习要求大约3.5周的现场直接学习，尽管提供学习的方式在警察局之间各有不同。为了成功完成这部分培训，特别警员学员被认为适合在警察陪伴下开展巡逻。为正规警察和特别警员提供的培训在警察局之间各不相同。这已经导致内政事务委员会在一份政府报告中提出建议，该份政府报告还有关于国家标准的内容（Home Affairs Committee，2016）。

美国

在整个美国，因为各州和单个警务机构赋予辅警的职权的方式不同，所以对于他们能够提供的培训，没有单一的标准或者直截了当的观点。下文叙述的例子是美国警务机构培训其辅警的许多不同方式。但是，美国既存在一些警务机构对辅警不要求任何特别培训，也存在一些警务机构要求辅警完成与正规警察一样的高层次培训；其他警务机构则要求上述两种方式之间的任意一个层次。这种在培训方面的变化，很大程度上取决于最终怎样使用辅警。那些赋予辅警很小职权的州，大多数情况下提供最少量的培训。那些赋予辅警全部警察职权的州，大多数情况下提供大量广泛的培训，常常与全日制院校培训一样或者类似全日制院校培训。

一些州不要求培训的具体小时数，也不要求给辅警颁发任何类型的州级资格
P100 证明。通常的原因是（与全职警察相比）辅警拥有的权力被大大减少了，或者根本没有任何警察权力。在那些后备警察以及/或者协警不能携带枪支或者执行逮捕的州，常见的现象是，每个警察机构负责根据岗位任职对辅警的要求来决定培训。正如本书前文所述，纽约市警察局就是一个不给其协警任何职权的警察局的例子。纽约市警察局协警被要求执行着装步行巡逻、机动车巡逻或者自行车巡逻，但是没有任何职权对现行犯罪活动采取行动。这些辅警作为辅助警方的“眼睛和耳朵”工作，他们接受培训要注意突发状况并且要向正规的、全职警察报告该状况，他们还在非执法工作中提供帮助（New York City Police Department，n. d.）。纽约市警察局协警未被视为警察，他们不携带枪支，而且没有逮捕权。他们接受54个小时的教导，学习以辅警身份履职（Kelly，Grasso，Esposito，Giannelli，and Maroulis，2008；New York City Auxiliary Police，2012），这样，

他们就成为“未受枪支培训的治安官员”。纽约州的治安官员有某种执法职权，但是他们与警察不一样。

蒙大拿州允许后备警察宣誓入职并马上开始以辅警身份工作，但是要求他们必须在头两年完成 88 个小时的基础培训，目的是继续当后备警察。蒙大拿州的警方后备人员被看作“治安官员”而不是警察。作为“治安官员”，他们只有在蒙大拿州的搜查令以及在其他州签署的重罪令下才有逮捕权。后备警察经授权在蒙大拿州携带枪支（如果他们通过了由蒙大拿执法学院开设的枪支课程，而且获得其警察机构主要执法官员的授权），而且他们被看作宣誓警察。后备警察可以在巡逻、安全检查或者类似工作方面提供帮助。蒙大拿州另外一种辅警是协警，然而，他们是非宣誓的、兼职辅警，可以担任的工作有“搜救、办公室工作、人群和交通控制以及犯罪预防活动”（Montana Code Annotated 7-32-201，2015），而且他们没有逮捕职权，无异于给任何一位在蒙大拿州的公民的授权。

明尼苏达州是另一个后备警察没有警察职权的州的例子。明尼苏达州的州法规把后备警察界定为“公民个人提供的服务被执法机构使用，在特殊大型活动、交通或人群控制以及管理或文案协助方面为执法机构提供辅助，而且应该包括后备助理、特别助理、骑马巡逻或非骑马巡逻人员以及所有发挥后备警察作用的其他雇员或者志愿者。一名后备警察的职责不包括执行明尼苏达州一般刑法，而且后备警察没有全部逮捕权或者没有携带枪支工作的职权”（Minnesota Statute 626.84）。明尼苏达州的后备执法警察不被允许携带枪支，而且明尼苏达州不要求后备警察获得任何许可或者教育资质，但是明尼苏达州允许各个警察机构制定自己的培训要求。 P101

得克萨斯州（像其他许多州一样）使用术语“治安官员”，这与蒙大拿州和纽约州不同。因此得克萨斯州的所有警察都必须获得治安官员认证并成功完成一个州级许可考试；所有的辅警也要参加这个考试。在 1989 年，得克萨斯州改变了担任辅警的要求，所有后备警察现在必须完成与其全职同事完全一样的培训。得克萨斯州执法委员会从 1989 年开始，就要求后备警察接受与全职正规警察一样数量的培训，即 640 个小时以上，尽管各个警察机构可以要求自己的后备警察做更多培训（Hallman & Martin，2015）。达拉斯城警察局把这个培训等同于在一年之内培训时长超过 1000 个小时，包括在职培训（Dallas Police Department Reserves，n. d. ）。

佛罗里达州有两种不同类型的辅警执法官员。第一种是拥有资格证明的“协助”执法官员。这些官员已经接受了“涉及重大责任”培训（包括枪支使用、防守战术、巡逻技术、犯罪侦查、急救以及应急车辆驾驶），但是还没有完成全州执法资格证明要求的所有佛罗里达州课程（390 个课时）。第二种是州法规分类的“兼职”官员，他们拥有全部执法权力。这些官员接受与其正规、全职警察同事一样的培训（790 个小时），并且拥有与其正规、全职警察同事一样的职权，但是他们通常以辅警身份工作。在佛罗里达州，不论是获得协助认证的辅警还是获得基本执法（BLE，Basic Law Enforcement）认证的辅警，都要完成“涉及重大责任”培训。这种培训涉及方方面面，这些方面可能在法庭上会受到细致审查。这种培训包括急救、执法车辆驾驶、枪支使用、防守战术以及麻醉飞镖射击眩晕枪。在佛罗里达州，因为协警必须经常处在获得基本执法认证官员的监管之下，所以协警接受附加的、有限的培训：巡逻战术、交通控制以及调查。佛罗里达州获得基本执法认证的辅警接受与其全职同事一样的培训（而且经常参加与那些申请全职岗位的人一样的院校培训），这样的培训还包括下列教学内容：关于法律问题、沟通、犯罪现场勘查、交通违例叫停、醉酒驾驶调查、交通撞击事故调查以及人的问题。

加利福尼亚州的培训在制定培训标准的方式上与佛罗里达州的培训最为相
P102 似。在加利福尼亚州，后备岗位的申请者必须自己支付学费，因为加利福尼亚州法律规定培训开销补贴只发给全职固定工资雇员。一级后备警察在加利福尼亚州是获得完全认证的警察，拥有与其全职同事一样的职权。为了具备加利福尼亚州治安官员标准和培训（POST，Peace Officer Standards and Training）这个称号，他们必须接受 727 个小时的培训，培训花费大约是 2000 美元（College of the Desert，n. d. ）。而二级后备警察拥有有限的职权，而且只能在一名加利福尼亚州警察的直接监管下工作。这一级别的培训要求是 333 个小时。三级后备警察接受的培训是 144 个小时，但是可以履行的只是特殊帮助职责。获得当一名二级后备警察或者三级后备警察的资格证明，花费大约是 1000 美元（College of the Desert，n. d. ）。其他州有类似的二级或三级体系分类的辅警，分类依据是辅警所接受的培训数量以及他们被赋予的职权数量。

俄勒冈州为即将成为后备警察的候选人提供后备警察院校培训。这个院校培训时长要比全职警察院校短。在俄勒冈州，一些警察机构免费提供后备警察院校培训，其他警察机构要求参加培训人员支付学费以抵消运行学院培训项目的花销。例如，在马里恩县（俄勒冈州），后备助理院校项目在 2017 年的学费是 400

美元（Marion County，Oregon，n. d.）。这些后备院校是业余性质的，通常一个星期有几个晚上上课以及周末上课。后备院校课程时长大约是375个小时（而全日制院校大约是640个小时），培训课程包括防卫战术、使用武力、枪支使用、急救和心肺复苏术以及应急车辆驾驶。后备警察被允许在完成院校培训后与正规全职警察一起工作，但是不能作为个体单独工作，直到他们完成了附加培训才可以单独工作。例如，俄勒冈州的达拉斯城，要求后备警察在获得合法资格能够独立工作之前，在一名实战培训教官的指导下，承担一个附加的960个小时的巡逻活动。达拉斯城允许后备警察获得授权独立履行大多数交通执法职责，但是还可以处理反映小问题的电话并为其他巡逻之需提供帮助（City of Dallas，Oregon，n. d.）。

南加利福尼亚州的辅警培训与俄勒冈州的相似。在南加利福尼亚州，一名后备警察是一名由警察机构首脑任命的并投其所好的志愿者，但是后备警察还必须成功完成南加利福尼亚州后备警察培训项目。该项目包括一个期末笔试。院校培训时长为162个小时，而且由警务机构免费提供。这个院校培训包括下列课程：南加州法律、伦理、宪法、城镇条例、巡逻流程、防守战术、人际关系、枪支使用以及其他内容的课程。个人在成功完成后备警察院校学习并通过州级考试，才有资格在南加利福尼亚州当后备警察。南加利福尼亚州后备警察被分配给全职警察一起工作，后备警察必须总是与该全职警察保持联络状态，要么使用无线电通信装置要么使用别的设备，但是只要他们完成最低的附加的240个小时的实战培训并且获得警察机构首脑的批准，他们就可以独立工作。南加利福尼亚州法律的确允许那些积极工作至少两年的后备警察为成为一名全职执法警察接受附加培训（South Carolina Code of Laws §23-28-10；South Carolina Criminal Justice Academy，2012）。 P103

专业培训

警察机构还允许辅警参加专业部门，或者允许辅警携带特种装备，这可能同样需要附加培训。一个能说明这种类型培训的例子就是为履行自行车巡逻职责设置的培训。许多美国司法管辖区域采用自行车这个交通工具让全职警察和辅警履行巡逻职责，但是可能要求履行这些职责的人员参加附加培训。培训警察自行车技术的课程可以教授警察和辅警组队骑行、骑过障碍物、从台阶上骑下去、十分缓慢地骑行以及从自行车上下来。对于有执法职权的辅警来说，这些课程还可以包括快速骑上自行车并追踪、骑自行车时瞄准和射击以及靠近嫌疑物和事故的安全方法（Mroz，2001）。另一个例子就是应急车辆驾驶。在美国，尽管大多数辅警拥有全部执法职权，应该已经在院校培训中接受过车辆驾驶训练，但是大多数英国辅警必须参加额外培训，以便获得授权为其警察局驾驶某些车辆。

但是，正如本章前文提到的辅警基本培训，不论是在美国还是在英国，参加专业培训的能力以及使用受过训练的能力，变化都很大。在美国，尽管使用全职宣誓辅警的警察机构，比如可能培训辅警使用特种巡逻步枪或者不那么致命的猎枪，但是在其他不像纽约州那样使用辅警的州，既不会为辅警开设这两种培训课程，也不会授权让辅警使用这两种类型的装备。佛罗里达州的奥兰治县县治安官办公室允许后备警察参加任何专业部门的工作，只要后备警察已经被该部门的指挥系统审查过，而且后备警察已经接受了所要求的培训。在奥兰治县县治安官办公室的后备警察，参加摩托车队（摩托车巡逻）、骑警队（骑马巡逻）、要人警
P104 卫、航空飞行（直升机和固定翼飞行器驾驶员以及飞行观察员）以及做调查员。但是，就像他们的全职同事一样，在奥兰治县县治安官办公室的后备警察需要完成一个必要的强制培训，而且必须在专业部门的监督下完成一个在职培训（Wolf，2017；Wolf & Beary，2010）。

注释

①切斯特大学和柴郡特别警员队在 2009 年开启合作关系，这提供了一个基础学位，该学位与新警培训结合在一起，新警培训是加入警察局的每一位新警都要参加的培训。该项目被设计为把学员培训成警察，并且允许学员接受正式的、可转认的、高等教育学分。该项目被设计为培训大约 15 名学员，每年六次；而且成功完成该项目的学员还可以完成一个第三年的学习，以便获得一个荣誉学位（University of Chester，2009）。

②四级资质在英国大概等同于美国的副学士学位。英国学位通常将重点放在整个课程的主要专业领域，这与美国教育系统不同。美国教育系统通常要求学生在开始学习的头两年里，更偏重文科，学习内容更广泛。

③五级资质在美国大致相当于一个为期两年的大学资质。在英国教育系统使用的“等级”以及“毕业证书”与美国教育学位不是直接对等的。

④六级资质在英国被作为荣誉授予完成学士学位的人。这个学士学位可以不是优等，也可以是优等。

⑤佛罗里达州可以作为一个例子。该州使用州学院和技术学校来为已经在该州内接受过培训的多数警察提供培训。警察机构提供资助，所以在整个警察院校期间，警察机构要支付学费并使用学员。时薪要少于支付给被认证的警察的薪水，但是这使学员在参加需要支付学费的院校培训时，可以较少操心经济问题。

参考文献

Bureau of Justice Statistics（2009）（司法统计局）. State and local law enforcement training academies（“州和地方执法培训学院”），2006，NCJ 222987. Washington，DC：US“Department of Justice，Office of Justice Programs，Bureau of Justice Statistics（华盛顿特区：美国“司法部、司法项目办公室、司法统计局”）. 2014 年 12 月 24 日检索网址 www. bjs. gov/content/pub/pdf/sllета06. pdf.

City of Dallas，Oregon（n. d.）（达拉斯城，俄勒冈州〈日期不详〉）. Reserve officer program（“后备警察项目”）. 2017 年 6 月 5 日检索网址 www. ci. dallas. or. us/139/Reserve-Officer-Program.

College of Policing（n. d. -a）（警务大学〈日期不详 -a〉）. Initial police learning（“新警入职培训”）. 2014 年 12 月 24 日检索网址 www. college. olice. uk/what-we-do/Learning/Curriculum/Initial-learning/pages/initial-learning. aspx.

College of Policing（n. d. -b）（警务大学〈日期不详 -b〉）. National Policing Curriculum（“国家警务课程”）. 2016 年 7 月 13 日检索网址 www. college. police. uk/what-we-do/learning/curriculum/pages/default. aspx.

College of Policing（2016）（警务大学）. *Developing and delivering an education frame work for policing：The College of Policing response to the consultation*（《制定并发布警务教育标准体系：警务大学回应咨询》）. Coventry，UK：college of policing（考文垂，英国：警务大学）. 2017 年 3 月 19 日检索网址 www. college. policeearning/Policing-Education-QualificationPages/Responding-to-Recommendations. aspx.

College of the Desert（n. d.）（德瑟特学院〈日期不详〉）. Reserve police officer training（“后备警察培训”）. 2017 年 6 月 5 日检索网址 www. collegeofthedesert. edu/students/ap/psa/pages/bpot. aspx.

P105

Colorado Peace Officers Standards and Training（n. d.）（科罗拉多州治安官标准和培训〈日期不详〉）. Colorado POST-approved basic academies（“科罗拉多州治安官标准和培训认证基础学院”）. 2017 年 9 月 3 日检索网址 www. coloradopost. gov/academy/basic-academy.

Dallas Police Department Reserves（n. d.）（达拉斯警察局后备警察〈日期不详〉）. Becoming a Dallas Police Reserve officer（“成为一名达拉斯警察局后备警察”）. 2017 年 7 月 2 日检索网址 www. dpdreserves. org/a55cd1/recruitiNgnsf/Content/BORS-62NESG？OpenDocument.

Discover Policing（n. d.）（警务发现者〈日期不详〉）. Training/academy life（“培训/院校生活”）. 2014 年 12 月 24 日检索网址 http：//discoverpolicing. org/what_does_takel？fa=training_academy_life.

Georgia Public Safety Training Center（n. d.）（佐治亚州公共安全培训中心〈日期不详〉）. Basic law enforcement training program（“基础执法培训项目”）. 2017 年 9 月 3 日检索网址 www. gpstc. org/training-divisions/basic-training-division/basic-police-officer-training.

Hallman, T. , & Martin, N. （2015, April 20）（霍尔曼和马丁〈2015 年 4 月 20 日〉）. Reserve officers have higher training standards in Texas than Oklahoma（“后备警察的培训标准在得克萨斯州比俄克拉荷马州更高”）. *The Dallas Morning News*（《达拉斯晨报》）. 2017 年 9 月 3 日检索网址 www. dallasnews. com/news/news/2015/04/20/reserve-officers-have-higher-training-standards-in-texas-than-oklahoma.

Home Affairs Committee（2016）（内务委员会）. *College of Policing*：*Three years on*：*Fourth report of session* 2016-2017（《警务大学：三年过去了：2016—2017 学年第四份报告》）. London：House of Commons, Home Affairs Committee（伦敦：下议院，内务部委员会）. 2017 年 1 月 11 日检索网址 www. publications. parliamentuk/pa/cm201617/cmselect/cmhaff/23/23. pdf.

Kelly, R. W. , Grasso, G. A. , Esposito, J. J. , Giannelli, R. J. , & Maroulis, A. J. （2008）（科利、格拉索、埃斯庖斯托、詹奈利和玛洛里斯）. *Auxiliary police program overview* 2008（《回顾 2008 年协警项目》）. New York：New York City Police Department Auxiliary（纽约：纽约市警察局协警）.

Lewis, B. （2017, March 29）（刘易斯〈2017 年 3 月 29 日〉）. Speech to

the Police Education Qualification Frame work conference（“在警务教育资格评定标准体系会议上发表的演说”）. 2017 年 4 月 23 日检索网址 www. gov. uk/government/speeches/speech－to－the－police－education－qualification－framework－conference.

Louisiana Commission on Law Enforcement and Administration of Criminal Justice（n. d.）（路易斯安那州刑事司法执法和管理委员会〈日期不详〉）. Peace Officer Standards and Training Council（POST）（“治安官员标准和培训委员会”）. 2017 年 9 月 3 日检索网址 www. cole. state. la. us/programs/post. asp.

Marion County，Oregon（n. d.）（马里恩县，俄勒冈州〈日期不详〉）. Enforcement reserve deputy programme（“执行后备警察助理项目”）. 2017 年 6 月 5 日检索网址 www. co. marionorus/soljOinTheteam/pages/reservedeputies. aspx.

Mroz，R. （2001）（穆洛兹）. Cops on bikes（“警察骑自行车”）. *Police：The Law Enforcement Magazine*（《警察：执法杂志》），25（12），41—45. 2017 年 6 月 5 日检索网址 www. policemag. com/channel/vehicles/articles/2001/12/cops－on－bikes. aspx.

New York City Auxiliary Police（2012）（纽约市协警局）. Auxiliary operations order（“协警维持秩序”）. New York：New York City Auxiliary Police（纽约：纽约市协警局）. 2017 年 6 月 5 日检索网址 www. nycapbacom/files/2012/01/aps_operations_order1. pdf.

New York City Police Department（n. d.）（纽约市警察局〈日期不详〉）. NYPD New York's finest：Who are the volunteer auxiliary police（“纽约市警察局纽约的最佳：谁是志愿性质协警”）. 2014 年 12 月 22 日检索网址 www. nyc. gov/nypd/??－police. shtml.

Pepper，I. K. （2014）（帕珀）. Do part－time volunteer police officers aspire to be regular police officers?（“兼职辅警渴望成为正规警察吗?”）*Police Journal：Theory，Practice and Principles*（《警察学报：理论、实践与原则》），87（2），105—113.

Police Scotland（n. d.）（维护苏格兰治安〈日期不详〉）. Police officers：Training（“警察：培训”）. 2017 年 4 月 26 日检索网址 www. scotland. police. uk/recruitment/police－officers/training.

South Carolina Criminal Justice Academy（2012）（南卡罗来纳州刑事司法学

P106

院）. South Carolina reserve officer training program：Administrative guide（“南卡罗来纳州后备警察培训项目：管理指南”）. Columbia，SC：South Carolina Criminal Justice Academy（哥伦比亚，南卡罗来纳州：南卡罗来纳州刑事司法学院）. 2017年6月5日检索网址 www. sccja. sc. gov/Other% 20Files/SC% 20Reserve% 20Officer%20Training%20Program%20Administrative%20Guide%202015. pdf.

State of Rhode Island Municipal Police Training Academy（n. d.）（罗得岛州市警察局培训学院〈日期不详〉）. Interested in becoming a police officer in Rhode Island?（“有兴趣成为一名罗德岛警察吗?”）2017年9月3日检索网址 http：//rimpa. ri. gov/basicrecruitment/requirements. phf.

University of Chester（2009，March 24）（切斯特大学〈2009年3月24日〉）. Foundation degree trains Cheshire's new police officers（“基础课程培训切斯特郡新警察”）. 2017年9月2日检索网址 http：//chester. ac. uk/news/2009/03/19.

Utah Department of Public Safety（n. d.）（犹他州公共安全部〈日期不详〉）. Peace officer standards and training：POST information（“治安官标准和培训：治安官标准和培训信息”）. 2017年9月3日检索网址 https：//post. utah. gov/prospective-officers/post-info.

Utah Valley University（n. d.）（犹他州峡谷大学〈日期不详〉）. Cost of the academy（“上大学的花费”）. 2017年9月3日检索网址 www. uvu. edu/criminaljustice/policeacademy/cost. html.

Valencia College（n. d.）（瓦伦西亚学院〈日期不详〉）. Criminal justice：Basic law enforcement academy（“刑事司法：执法基础学院”）. 2017年9月3日检索网址 https：//valenciacollege. edu/public-safety/criminal-justice-institute/basic_law. cfm.

Wolf，R.（2017）（沃尔夫）. Civic volunteerism in Orange County（Florida）：Sworn police reserves in a metropolitan sheriff's office（“奥兰治县（佛罗里达州）公民志愿精神：宣誓后备警察在大都会县治安官办公室”）. In J. Albrecht（Ed.）（阿尔布雷希特主编），*Police reserves and volunteers：Enhancing organizational effectiveness and public trust*（《警察后备人员和志愿者：提升组织效率和公信力》），pp. 88—92. Boca Raton，FL：CRC Press（博卡-拉顿，佛罗里达州：CRC出版社）.

Wolf, R., & Beary, K. (2010)(沃尔夫和比瑞). The Orange County Sheriff's Office Reserve Unit: A strong, cohesive unit able to handle multiple functions(“奥兰治县县治安官办公室后备警察部门：一个强大有凝聚力的队伍能够履行多项职责”). *Deputy and Court Officer*(《助理和法院官员》), 2 (2), 26—30.

P107
第七章　美国、英国辅警比较

显而易见，学界对美国辅警执法的研究不太重视。仅仅在过去几年里，才有少数研究人员开始关注这一领域，而美国警察机构在使用和管理辅警方面存在众多不同方式这一事实，更是为调查和研究设置了障碍。尽管如此，（美国）全国县治安官协会外联委员会以及后备执法工作队已经把辅警执法研究工作列为重点，并且已经与科研院所的研究人员开展协作来搜集信息，即美国所有县治安官部门使用后备警察、协警以及县治安官特别助理的做法（Wolf，Holmes & Jones，2016；Dobrin & Wolf，2016；Pepper & Wolf，2015）。国际警察局长协会通过旗下的警察管理委员会，也已经开始强调辅警的重要性（Wolf，Albrecht & Dobrin，2015）。

尽管在英国研究辅警的学者比在美国的多，但是英国对特别警员的研究仍然十分不足。然而，还是有少数学者开始关注这一重要领域，尽管这一领域在学界很不受重视（Gill & Mawby，1990；Pepper，2014；Britton，2016；Jones & Wolf，2017；Reay，2012）。

为了将美国和英国的辅警进行比较，本书作者在 2013 年与（美国）全国县治安官协会合作，编写、修改调查问卷并在美国分发该问卷，开展全国调查。在英国也开展了类似的全国调查。全国县治安官协会不是美国一个代表警察局的组织，因而该问卷调查只是面向美国与县治安官办公室有关联的后备警察和协警，收集他们的反馈。全美县治安官办公室的职责不尽相同，有些地方的县治安官办公室仅仅负责管理监狱或社区矫正。但是，在美国大多数地方，县治安官办公室是全职警察机构，其县治安官是一名经选举产生的行政长官。英国的全国调查开展于 2016 年，地点是英格兰和威尔士，委托机构是英国全国警察局长委员会的
P108 事务部，该事务部下设机构是公民参与警务以及英国国家公民参与警务“实践共同体”。不论是在美国还是在英国，上述两个关于辅警的全国调查都是曾经做过

的调查中规模最大的（Wolf et al.，2016）。

样本和数据

（美国）全国县治安官协会的调查问卷发给了3080名县治安官。这些县治安官来自美国全部50个州，截至2013年3月18日，他们都是全国县治安官协会的会员。每一名收到调查问卷的县治安官，都被要求将问卷发给其所在机构的所有后备警察、协警、志愿者或者特别助理。在第一次发出调查问卷要求后一个月，即4月18日，一条提醒不要忘记问卷调查的信息又被发往所有的（美国）全国县治安官协会的县治安官会员们。到2013年5月18日，有1719份答卷被提交。本研究的局限之一与调查采用的方法有关。每名县治安官按照指令将调查问卷发给其所在机构内的志愿性质的执法官员，从而导致不可能统计调查问卷回收率。因为与每一位最初通过E-mail接受要求的县治安官相对应的很可能是多个答卷（Wolf et al.，2016）。

尽管美国全部50个州的县治安官是初始研究人群的组成部分，但是还是有许多州在最后没有提交答卷。这种情况可以用美国县治安官职能各异来解释。美国东北地区县治安官的职能、职责和职权与美国南部或西部的县治安官完全不同。美国东北部各州明显缺席最后的抽样。这可以表明：在这些州里不存在使用执法志愿者的情况，或者即便有执法志愿者，但他们承担的责任最少。来自加利福尼亚州、佛罗里达州、俄亥俄州以及华盛顿州的问卷调查的答卷人在整个样本里占了39%（人数=668）；这些州与美国许多州一样，不但有活跃的县治安官办公室，而且更有可能存在活跃的志愿者项目（Wolf et al.，2016）。

英国的调查问卷起初是为特别警员设计的，但是最终被发给了特别警员和支持警察的志愿者们。出于现实比较的需要，仅仅采用了来自特别警员的答卷。与美国警务不同，所有英格兰和威尔士的警察局都接受统一领导；所以，即便在培训、制服以及职能方面两地的特别警员可能存在不同，但是他们的权力都是一样的，因而避免了上述某些使情况复杂的问题。

与在美国分发调查问卷的方法一样，调查问卷被分发给英格兰和威尔士的警察局里的每一位高级警官，目的是让他们向所有的特别警员（以及支持警察的志愿者们）下发调查问卷。调查问卷被用e-mail方式发送给每一位高级警官并附有要求：每一位高级警官要把问卷下发给合适的志愿者们，然后答卷人提交答卷的电子版。尽管所有警察局都提交了答卷，但是提交答卷的数量不一样。在比较 P109

大的警察局中，有十个警察局反馈的答卷数量大约占了总量的50%。回收的答卷一共有1908份，在英国所有特别警员中，占比不到12%，虽然不是所有问卷调查答卷人都填写了完整的答卷。尽管这种情况所占百分比不大，但是这次在特别警员（和支持警察的志愿者）中所做的问卷调查是曾经做过的调查中规模最大的，而且问卷调查的研究结果为进一步研究打下了坚实的基础（Britton，2016）。

调查工具

在两个国家开展问卷调查的初衷是尽可能让两个问卷版本相同。然而，英国版本在下发的时候被延误了［最初计划在2013年与（美国）全国县治安官协会同一个时间下发调查问卷］，原因是审查过程被延长了，事实上问卷里的问题被换掉/被增加/被忽略。所以，对问卷调查的方方面面进行完整的对比是不可能做到了。但是，对大部分方面加以类比还是可以的。本章下文将对此加以讨论。

在美国开展的问卷调查，其设计和数据收集都是由作者通过在线调查工具实现的，而且作者还咨询了（美国）全国县治安官协会，并且使用Qualtrics ©这一在线调查工具收集调查答卷。美国的调查问卷一共有43道问题，收集个人基本人口信息以及对在机构内使用志愿者的看法。英国的调查问卷有29道问题，且由（英国）全国警察局长委员会在2016年1月用E-mail的方式散发，答卷人提交答卷的电子版。与美国调查问卷版本一样，英国调查问卷收集详细的人口信息、使用志愿者的方法以及志愿者对与警察同事沟通的看法。

结果

人口统计样本

美国

在警察这样的以男性为主导的领域，美国问卷调查的答卷人大多数是男性（92%，人数=1311；见表7.1）。答卷人报告的年龄大多在45岁至64岁（50.3%，人数=712）。大约有78%的答卷人报告目前是已婚（人数=1099），19%是单身和从未结婚或者离婚（人数=263）。至于人种/族裔，89%的答卷人自报是白人（人数=1255），接下来单一最大的族裔是西班牙裔（5%，人数=70）。答卷人报告他们在执法志愿者工作之外，很多时候是全职雇员（67%，人数=952），答卷人选择了问卷中列出的所有可能的职业选项（采用美国劳工部36种不同的工作类别）。答卷人报告的最常见的工作类别是经理或者专业岗位

P110

(27%，人数=325)，消防员或者公共安全岗位（12%，人数=149）。接下来是教育岗位（4.6%，人数=55），以及计算机或数学专业人员（3.7%，人数=45）。

美国答卷人报告的作为志愿执法官员的平均时长为11.05年（人数=1423）。正如在本书前面部分解释的，许多美国辅警来自全职雇员，而且处于准备退休状态，或者正在寻找警务工作外的新的职业。28%的美国答卷人样本表明，答卷人做过全职执法官员。那些做过全职岗位的人都有丰富的经验；那些报告做过全职工作的人员在岗位上的平均工作时长为13年。

表7.1 美国样本的人口统计信息

变量	选项	人数（人）	百分比（%）
性别			
	男	1311	92.0
	女	107	8.0
		1418	100
年龄			
	18岁至24岁	52	3.7
	25岁至34岁	153	10.8
	35岁至44岁	291	20.6
	45岁至54岁	361	25.5
	55岁至64岁	351	24.8
	65岁及以上	205	14.5
		1413	100.0
婚姻状况			
	单身，从未结婚	130	9.2
	已婚	1099	77.7
	离婚	133	9.4
	分居	13	0.9
	丧偶	18	1.3
	同居	22	1.6
		1415	100.0
人种/族裔			
	白人/欧洲、北美、澳大利亚白种人	1255	88.6
	非洲裔美国人	21	1.5
	西班牙裔美国人	70	4.9
	亚裔美国人	20	1.4
	美国土著	20	1.4
	太平洋岛民	6	0.4

续表

变量	选项	人数（人）	百分比（%）
	其他	24	1.7
		1416	100.0
执法机构之外现做职业			
	经理/商业和金融类	325	27.0
	经营企业/金融	63	5
	农民和农场经理	14	1.2
	计算机或数学专业人员	45	3.7
	法律	36	3.0
	教育	55	4.6
	卫生	23	1.9
	消防员/公共安全	149	12.3
	其他职业	497	41.2
		1207	100.0
执法机构之外就业状况			
	全职	952	67.0
	兼职	89	6.3
	无业	22	1.5
	退休	364	18.6
	学生	47	3.2
	其他	47	3.3
		1421	100.0

注：百分比已四舍五入，总和可能不是100。

英格兰和威尔士

英国问卷调查的答卷人同样是男性居多（79.8%，人数=1509；见表7.2），甚至要比所有全职警察的男性人数高，但是百分比不如美国问卷调查统计的多。一半以上的答卷人年龄在34岁或34岁以下（61%，人数=1116），不到1%的答卷人年龄在65岁或65岁以上（人数=18）。在英国的答卷人中，仅有89%多一点的人（人数=1709）自报是英国白人或爱尔兰白人（在美国答卷人中，有同样百分比的答卷人报告自己的人种/族裔是白人），接下来答卷人中单一最大族裔是“来自其他白人背景”（3.6%，人数=69）。

表 7.2 英国样本的人口统计信息

变量	选项	人数（人）	百分比（%）
性别			
	男	1509	79.8
	女	381	20.1
		1890	100.0
年龄			
	18 岁至 24 岁	525	28.7
	25 岁至 34 岁	591	32.4
	35 岁至 44 岁	373	20.4
	45 岁至 64 岁	318	17.4
	65 岁及以上	18	1.0
		1825	100.0
人种/族裔			
	英国白人	1694	88.8
	爱尔兰白人	15	0.8
	其他白人背景	69	3.6
	白人和黑人混血加勒比裔	11	0.6
	白人和黑人混血非洲裔	3	0.2
	白人和亚洲人混血	8	0.4
	其他混血族裔	6	0.3
	亚洲印度裔	23	1.2
	亚洲巴基斯坦裔	13	0.7
	亚洲孟加拉国裔	4	0.2
	任何其他亚洲背景	6	0.3
	黑人加勒比裔	7	0.4
	黑人非洲裔	9	0.5
	其他黑人背景	2	0.1
	华裔	9	0.5
	其他族裔	2	0.1
	无记录族裔	26	0.9
		1908	100.0

注：百分比已四舍五入，总和可能不是 100。

执法职责和服务动机

美国

因为在整个美国，在兼职或志愿执法官员可以行使的职权方面，各州差距很大，所以美国问卷对答卷人的逮捕权进行了调查。大约有一半的答卷人（46%，人数701；见表7.3）说他们不论上班还是下班都拥有完全的逮捕权，而33%的答卷人说他们只在上班期间才有逮捕权（人数=503）。这说明79%（人数=1204）的答卷人在上班期间有逮捕权。美国问卷调查有12%的答卷人说他们作为辅警根本没有逮捕执法权（人数=183）。与英国问卷调查明显不同的是，大多数美国答卷人（90%，人数=1403）说他们有用枪支武装自己的执法权；69%的人（人数=1074）说他们不论在上班还是下班期间都有这一职权，而且21%的人（人数=329）被授权由其所在的执法机构为其配枪，但仅限在上班期间。

问卷调查还要求在县治安官机构的美国答卷人描述他们当志愿执法官员的动机是什么。73%——最大的反馈数据——的答卷人说提供服务是“为我的社区作贡献”的一个途径（人数=982）。69%的答卷人说他们把这种志愿服务的角色看作
P113 “提升自己的一个方法”（人数=938），65%的答卷人说他们服务是因为“对执法和警务工作总体上感兴趣”（人数=878），62%的答卷人说他们觉得他们有“从日常生活中积累的技能/知识，能够提高警察机构的工作”（人数=834）。36%的答卷人说他们以前是正规警察，希望通过当辅警运用从工作中积累的知识（人数=485），30%的答卷人以前是正规警察，希望与自己的同事保持联系（人数=412）。

表7.3　美国：你当辅警的动机是什么

回答	选择人数（人）	百分比（%）
我希望为我的社区作贡献	982	73
我将当辅警视为提升自己的一个方法	938	69
我对执法和警务工作总体上感兴趣	878	65
我有从日常生活中积累的技能/知识，能够提高警察机构的工作	834	62
我希望在我的业余时间做点志愿工作/兼职工作	815	60
我希望加入正规警察局，当辅警让我能够深入了解这个警察局	756	56
我的雇主鼓励我/支持我	538	40
我以前是一名正规警察，希望我的知识和/或专长能够发挥作用	485	36
我以前是一名正规警察，希望与我的同事保持联系	412	30

注：回答这个问题的人数=1353。答卷人可以多选。

美国问卷调查的答卷人说，他们在执法岗位上志愿服务的时间是平均每周9.8个小时（标准差=8.39，人数=1409）。在答卷人履行志愿执法职能的时候，大约有30%的答卷人报告他们独立工作（人数=474）或者与他人一起工作，但不是每次都是同一人（41%，人数=641）。这与美国执法全职岗位的情况一样。

答卷人还被要求描述作为执法官员他们承担什么类型的职责，表 7.4 列出了他们的回答。在所列的选项之外，开放式选项还包括调查、搜查、选举安保、提取儿童指纹、要人保卫，以及其他工作。

表 7.4 美国辅警的职能和执法职责

回答	选择人数（人）	百分比（%）
常规巡逻（步巡）	378	27
常规巡逻（车巡）	1028	74
紧急状态应对（例如，潜水队、特殊反应队等）	431	31
大型活动警务（例如，人群控制、交通管制）	1131	82
现场或设施安保	559	40
执法勤务（例如，设卡查酒驾、查获卖淫嫖娼人员、特殊勤务）	546	39

注：回答这个问题的人数=1353。答卷人可以多选。

英格兰和威尔士

所有在英格兰和威尔士的特别警员都有相同的搜查权力，但是培训的水平和次数、制服以及装备就像一些警务活动一样各不相同。表 7.5 是填完英国全国调查问卷并将之发送回来的特别警员填写的在平常从事得最多的工作。在英格兰和威尔士开展的问卷调查与美国的版本有很多不同，问卷调查的委托机构关注的一个领域与使用特别警员的环境有关，在这个环境中，管理者倾向于使用特别警员维护公共秩序、社区和大型活动治安秩序。调查结果显示，有相当数量的特别警员愿意积极参与其他警务活动。然而，应该指出的是，“希望参与”并不等于“有能力参与”，还应该指出的是，在一些警务活动中，大量当时正在提供服务的特别警员愿意接受适当的培训。

在参与警务活动类型这个问题上，答卷人可以做多项选择。但是调查结果说明，英国的特别警员基本上要履行的职责有：邻里警务（49.7%，人数=948）、紧急状态应对警务（47.1%，人数=898），以及大型特别活动安保（48.7%，人数=929）。但是，按照参与程度多少的顺序，特别警员同样参与维持公共秩序（18.7%，人数=356）、维护道路治安（14.5%，人数=276）、精神健康问题（12.4%，人数=236），以及犯罪侦查（12.3%，人数=234）。

关于特别警员愿意参与的工作类型，最多数量的答卷人选择专业勤务队（64.4%，人数=1228），这个类型的警务工作需要警犬队、海上巡逻队、骑警巡

P115

逻队以及类似的专业队参加。其他英国特别警员愿意更多参与的工作包括情报（48.7%，人数=929）、犯罪侦查（46.6%，人数=889）、维持公共秩序（44.2%，人数=843）、网络犯罪侦查（36.6%，人数=698）、在学校与年轻人一起工作（36.4%，人数=694）、保卫儿童（33.3%，人数=635），以及诈骗和其他经济犯罪侦查（32.9%，人数=627）。

表 7.5　英国辅警的职能和执法职责

警务活动类型	目前正在做（%）	希望未来去做（%）
邻里警务	49.7	7.5
紧急状态应对警务	47.1	11.4
大型活动安保	48.7	12.3
在学校与年轻人一起工作	5.3	36.4
犯罪侦查	12.3	46.6
管理	4.5	6.8
帮助处理公众打来的电话	3.6	17.5
维护道路治安	14.5	47.2
专业勤务队	7.5	64.4
情报	6.2	48.7
公共秩序警务	18.7	44.2
刑事司法，在法院支持案件审理以及为受害人提供帮助	3.4	32.4
网络犯罪侦查	1.2	36.6
诈骗和其他经济犯罪侦查	0.7	32.9
保护儿童	6.2	33.3
精神健康问题	12.4	23.8
管理危险罪犯	4.1	27.9

注：回答这个问题的人数=1908。答卷人可以多选。

英国答卷人还被要求说明他们成为辅警以及在他们当地警察局工作的动机是什么。关于动机这个问题，英格兰和威尔士的调查问卷与美国版本的不同；答卷人被要求说明他们成为一名特别警员时希望有什么收获。调查问卷提供了可选的收获（见表 7.6），而且利他主义的程度在提供的选项里也是显而易见的。选项“我对在警察部门工作感兴趣，而且希望对其有更多了解并且/或者习得技能和经验，为将来申请一个有偿警务岗位打下基础”被选百分比最高（41%，人数=

782）。其次是“我希望为我当地社区做点事，在让我当地社区更加安全这件事上，希望我能发挥重要作用”（19.8%，人数=368）。再次是“我希望做点事让我的业余时间活跃起来”（12.6%，人数=241）和“我希望在我业余时间做点更有价值的事情”（7.7%，人数=147）。

表 7.6 英国：回顾当初你决定成为一名辅警的时候，你最希望从这一经历收获什么

回答	人数（人）	百分比（%）
我希望结识新朋友	55	2.9
我希望做点事让我的业余时间活跃起来	241	12.8
我对在警察部门工作感兴趣，而且希望对其有更多了解并且/或者习得技能和经验，为将来申请一个有偿警务岗位打下基础	782	41.0
我认为这对未来（非警务）的雇主来说是件好事	22	1.2
我希望为我当地社区做点事，在让我当地社区更加安全这件事上，希望我能发挥重要作用	368	19.3
我对警察工作感兴趣而且希望对其有更多了解并与其有直接关系	171	9.0
我希望完善我所在地区维护治安的途径	27	1.4
我希望在我当地社区有更高的见警率	20	1.0
我希望在我业余时间做点更有价值的事情	147	7.7
我希望为我当地社区发声，而且/或者让当地社区参与进来，从而使警方能更好地听取我们的呼声并且更好地工作来解决我们关切的问题	8	0.4

注：回答这个问题的人数=1908。答卷人可以多选。

报酬

正如在本书前文讨论过的，志愿者即便没有因为提供服务获得报酬，志愿者提供服务也不是没有费用的。对于使用志愿者的机构来说，还是有金钱上的开销的；这个开销可以是培训方面的、供应方面的、制服方面的、监管方面的、交通方面的或者类似方面的。不过，一些机构的确决定向志愿者支付报酬，其范围可以从什么都没有到很少的报酬或者为服务支付少量薪水（Brudney，1999）。在美国问卷调查中，80%的答卷人（人数=1213）说他们没有因为提供服务获得任何薪水、有过任何报销或者获得任何报酬，10%的答卷人（人数=151）强调他们能报销一些餐费或者旅行费用，2%的答卷人（人数=35）说他们可以报销赔偿责任保险费或者专业培训费。然而，8%的答卷人（人数=125）说他们得到的报酬要低于全职、宣誓警员的报酬，但是高于国家最低周工资。尽管这些最后的反馈可能不是志愿者的反馈，但这正说明全美在使用后备警察、协警以及特别助理方面存在的复杂性。

美国许多司法区域另一个有趣的特点是，警察机构在为大型活动、商业或者为特定用途提供——由请求者承担经济成本的——额外的特定警察保护时，要具有合法职权。这一类工作往往被称为“下班”工作，因为通常做这些类型工作的全职警察都不是以上班身份在工作。政府机构授权政府服务“外包”，以保留公务员的服务，警察就属于这种情况。警察工会和集体谈判的兴起，可能也会影
P117 响到为警察提供额外补偿，而这种补偿无须直接由公共支出（Brunet，2008）。“下班警察能够提供更大范围的服务，这些服务不论在公共还是私人领域都很受重视，如指挥交通、提供安保、维持秩序以及遏制犯罪”（Brunet，2008，P. 162）。然而，在辅警工作方面特别有趣的是，全美许多警察机构还允许他们的辅警履行有报酬的下班警察职责。这进一步模糊了志愿者与有偿全职警察人员之间的界限，但是对那些有更多下班工作但又不能都由全职警察来做的领域来说，这明显有益。它还为需要在一年的不同时段、由警察提供不同层次服务的领域，创造了一个现成的后备有偿工作人员（尽管不用政府出资）。在本书最后一章探讨辅警未来时，将对下班工作问题有更多讨论。

英格兰和威尔士的问卷调查没有问报酬问题；特别警员没有因提供服务获得任何报酬，不过可能有补偿，覆盖了交通费用、餐费和制服津贴。如果特别警员在正常工作时间以外工作或者不在正常工作的地方工作，他们可以报销住宿费。前往和离开工作地实际发生的交通费能够报销，不论是乘坐公共交通工具还是私人运输工具，均按里程给津贴。与美国任何地方都不同的是，如果特别警员被要求在正常工作时间履行警察职责，他们还有权获得补贴，补贴数额与他们收入的实际损失一致（Home Office，2014）。

给特别警员报酬这个问题，政府已经争论了好几年。1967 年，一个工作组考虑给特别警员发奖金或者津贴，但是这个想法未获得多少支持，所以就不了了之了（Robertson，1993）。然后 1987 年，在一个关于特别警员的会议上，与会者讨论奖金这个想法，但是获得的支持仍然很少（Robertson，1993）。1990 年，这个问题被重新审视，当年时任英国内政大臣宣布在伦敦大都市警察局和两个地方警察局试点奖金方案。然而，最后只有都赛特警察局成为方案试点单位。原以为支付奖金可以推进招聘工作，激励特别警员奉献更多的时间，降低政府费用。结

果表明，支付奖金没有推进招聘工作（Robertson，1993）。尽管对这样的方案有怀疑（Wright，1989），《特别警员（修订）条例》获得通过并允许给特别警员支付奖金。一份成文于 1993 年的后续报告得出的结论是：一个奖金方案在一个警察局范围内试点，这证明该方案不受欢迎，而且，的确，其他同是奖金方案试点单位的警察局，甚至在该试点工作结束之前就已经退出了（Robertson，1993）。 P118

思考和局限

本章概述的调查研究，是力图获得个体看法的研究：在美国，自我认定是后备警察、协警、特别助理或者类似人员，而且附属于县治安官办公室或县治安官部的个体；或者在英国，自我认定是特别警员的个体。本次问卷调查研究是一个基础，在这个基础之上构建关于美国和英国使用志愿性质执法官员的未来研究。虽然在美国有几个后备警察和协警协会，但是没有一个协会声明它们能够与许多担任这一职务的人中的即便是人数很大的少数族裔进行沟通或者保持联系。结果是研究人员要依赖美国全国县治安官协会的大量网络工作，该协会有能力联系一部分志愿执法官员，因为这些志愿执法官员附属于美国全国县治安官机构；英国的全国警察局长委员会也是同样的情况。调查结果分析使研究人员有机会去了解美英两国境内志愿担任这些职位的个体类型。

起初，问卷编写者们试图让英国的调查基本原样照搬在美国采用的调查问卷。然而，英国调查的情况是，调查一经提出，在修改内容或者在对调查的最初分析方面，研究者们都没有参与度。在问卷被分发出去的两年前，有一个对原始版本的实验研究，该版本中某些调查问题与美国调查问卷中的一样。然而，到最终版本获得通过的时候，调查问卷已经被修改了而且被分发出去了，而研究者们没有参与其中。尽管如此，回收的调查问卷有足够的数据来提供有用的信息。

因为两个问卷调查都依赖自我报告的数据，局限性包括归因（把积极的措施归因于自己的机构）以及夸张（表现出比实际可能更有意义的结果）。作为探索性研究，本研究的可推广性有限。因为答卷人是自我认定并且/或者被其所在机构的领导要求填写问卷，所以调查报告不可能有美国的或者英国的问卷回收率。

在文献资料中，对美国和英国辅警工作的比较研究，最近的研究非常有限，而这一点应在此处被提及。沃尔夫、帕珀和多布林（Wolf，Pepper and Dobrin，2017）采用探索性研究去比较美国和英国辅警的自信以及他们各自所接受的履职培训。虽然该研究依赖数量很少的答卷人（41 人来自美国一个警务机构，32 人 P119

来自英国一个提供单一警务服务的机构）的回复，但是该研究表明，问卷调查答卷人对他们所接受的履职培训的看法十分相似，尽管也存在一些不同。在三个用来描述警务场景的短文中，美国警务志愿者对所接受的履职培训比英国志愿者稍微有信心一些。在采访被害人、讯问嫌疑人以及完成所需的案头工作方面，英国答卷人对自己所接受的履职培训的信心明显不如他们的美国同行（Wolf et al.，2017）。一个由帕珀和沃尔夫（Pepper and Wolf，2015）所做的有关研究，调查问卷回收率同样不高，但是值得注意。与本书所写的当前问卷调查相似，他们发现95%的美国志愿者答卷人是男性，而且33%的答卷人处在55岁至64岁。与此不同的是，英国样本中的答卷人84%是男性，且52%的答卷人年龄在25岁至34岁。他们还发现，在英国和美国，志愿者报告他们做辅警每月提供服务的平均时间大约是28小时。与当前问卷调查类似，他们报告说，答卷人做辅警的动机不同，这与他们自己国家的志愿精神有关。在美国，答卷人更有可能给出的回答是：他们过去就是正规全职警察，以及当志愿者是一种回报他们所在机构或社区的方式，或者是与他们的前同事保持联系的一种方法（Pepper & Wolf，2015）。

可以预料的是，这里报告的初始研究，以及对将来要在美国、英格兰和威尔士开展的研究的后续分析，都将为能够开展的和将要开展的进一步的探索和比较提供基础。尤其是在英国，警察和犯罪总监的职能已经可预见地给警察服务的组织和管理带来变革，英国43个警察局无一例外；而且，警察和犯罪总监的职能可能导致警务中的志愿精神产生一些有趣的变革。另外，2012年英国警务学院的建立，随之给整个英国警务组织带来雄心勃勃的变革和蒸蒸日上的效率。第八章将讨论全世界使用辅警的一些不同方式，第九章将讨论一些问题，这些问题可能会影响英国和美国使用辅警的方式。

参考文献

Britton, I. （2016）（布里顿）. *National survey of special constables and police support volunteers: Initial findings report*（《对特别警员和支援警察志愿者的全国性调查：初步调查报告》）. Northampton, UK: University of Northampton, Institute for Public Safety, Crime and Justice（北安普顿，英国：北安普顿大学，公共安全、犯罪和司法研究所）.

P120 Brudney, J. L. （1999）（布鲁德尼）. The effective use of volunteers: Best practices for the public sector（"有效使用志愿者：公共部门的最佳实践"）. *Law*

Enforcement and Contemporary Problems（《执法与现实问题》），62（4），219—256.

Brunet，J. R.（2008）（布鲁内特）. Blurring the line between public and private sectors：The case of police officers′ off-duty employment（“模糊公共部门和私营部门之间的界限：以警察八小时之外的工作为例”）. *Public Personnel Management*（《公共人力资源管理》），37（2），161—174.

Dobrin，A.，& Wolf，R.（2016）（多布林和沃尔夫）. What is known and not known about volunteer policing in the United States（“我们知道的以及我们不知道的美国辅警管理”）. *International Journal of Police Science and Management*（《警察科学与管理国际期刊》），18（3），220—227.

Gill，M. L.，& Mawby，R. I.（1990）（吉尔和莫比）. *A special constable*：*A study of the police reserve*（《特别警员：关于警方后备人员的研究》）. Aldershot，UK：Avebury Publishing（奥尔德肖特，英国：阿维伯里出版社）.

Home Office（2014，April）（英国内政部〈2014 年 4 月〉）. Home Office guidance on special constable expense and allowance rates. London：Home Office（“英国内政部指南：特别警员费用及津贴率”）. 2017 年 8 月 27 日检索网址 www. gov. uk/government/uploads/system/uploads/attachment - data/file/304488/GuidanceSpecialConstableExpenseAllowanceRates. pdf.

Jones，C.，& Wolf，R.（2017）（乔恩思和沃尔夫）. “Special” kind of policing：Volunteer policing in England and Wales（“‘特殊’类型的警务：英格兰和威尔士的辅警”）. In J. Albrecht（Ed.）（阿尔布雷希特主编），*Police reserves and volunteers Enhancing organizational effectiveness and public trust*（《警察后备人员和志愿者：提升组织效率和公信力》），pp. 205—212. Boca Raton. FL：CRC Press（博卡-拉顿，佛罗里达州：CRC 出版社）.

Pepper，I. K.（2014）（帕珀）. Do part-time volunteer police officers aspire to be regular police officers?（“兼职辅警渴望成为正规警察吗?”）*Police Journal*：*Theory*，*Practice and Principles*（《警察学报：理论、实践与原则》），87（2），105—113.

Pepper，I. K.，& Wolf，R.（2015）（帕珀和沃尔夫）. Volunteering to serve：An international comparison of volunteer police officers in a UK north east police force and a US Florida sheriff's office（“志愿提供服务：将英国东北部一家警察局和美

国佛罗里达州的一个县治安官办公室的辅警进行国际对比”). *The Police Journal*: *Theory*, *Practice and Principles* (《警察学报：理论、实践与原则》), 88 (3), 209—219.

Reay, W. T. (2012) (雷亚). *The specials*: *How they served London*: *The story of the Metropolitan Special Constabulary* (《特别警员：他们怎样服务伦敦：大都会特别警员队的故事》). London: Ulan Press (伦敦：尤伦出版社).

Robertson, N. (1993) (罗伯森). Dorset Police Special Constabulary report on the pilot bounty scheme (1st October 1991-30th September 1993) (“都塞特警察局特别警员队关于领航悬赏计划的报告〈1991 年 10 月 1 日—1993 年 9 月 30 日〉”). Unpublished report (未发表报告). Dorset Police Special Constabulary, Winfrith Newburgh, UK (都塞特警察局特别警员队，温弗里什纽堡，英国).

Wolf, R., Albrecht, J., & Dobrin, A. (2015) (沃尔夫、阿尔布雷希特和多布林). Reserve policing in the United States: Citizens volunteering for public service (“美国后备警察管理：公民志愿参与公共服务”). *The Police Chief* (《警察局长》), 82 (10), 38—47.

Wolf, R., Holmes, S. T., & Jones, C. (2016) (沃尔夫、赫尔摩斯和乔恩思). Utilization and satisfaction of volunteer law enforcement officers in the office of the American sheriff: An exploratory nationwide study (“美国县治安官办公室志愿性质执法官员的使用及其满意度：一项全国性研究”). *Police Practice and Research*: *An International Journal* (《警察实践与研究：国际期刊》), 17 (5), 448—462.

Wolf, R., Pepper, I. K., & Dobrin, A. (2017) (沃尔夫、帕珀和多布林). An exploratory international comparison of professional confidence in volunteer policing (“辅警职业自信心的国际比较研究”). *The Police Journal*: *Theory*, *Practice and Principles* (《警察学报：理论、实践与原则》), 90 (2), 91—106.

Wright, P. (1989) (怀特). Letter to the Deputy Under-Secretary of State on special constables, 4th September 1989 (“致副国务卿的一封关于特别警员的信，1989 年 9 月 4 日”). Sheffield: South Yorkshire Police Headquarters (设菲尔德：南约克郡警察总部).

P121

第八章　全球辅警

本书前文讨论以及关注的问题主要是美国各地辅警部门的相似性和差异性，并与英国的情况进行对比。但是，全世界的政府和警务机构已经采用了各具特色但又相似的做事方式，特别是在辅警方面。本章将考察全世界的辅警，当然不是介绍全世界所有的辅警。正如前文所述，即便是对“志愿者”的定义，不同的组织之间各不相同，辅警的情况也是如此。如果人们没有获得报酬，那么他们就是志愿者吗？如果他们被要求以无偿的身份为政府提供几年服务该怎么界定，他们是志愿者吗？如果人们因为提供服务获得少量报酬或者薪水，他们是志愿者吗？尽管某些人可能会质疑本章所述的组织是志愿性质的还是非志愿性质的，我们的用意是，在这一研究不足的警务领域，简要描述全球一些不同情况。

本章开头以英国和美国辅警为例，这为比较相似和差异提供了基础，随后是来自全世界其他地方的案例研究。

英国特别警员

英国在英格兰和威尔士的每一个警察局中，都使用志愿者做兼职警察。苏格兰警方和英国交通警察总队也用特别警员以志愿者身份服务（见图 8.1）。正如本书前文所述，特别警员，或者“特勤”，以被认证的警察身份提供服务，这与他们的全职同事一样。特别警员被赋予与全职警察一样的权力去执法，包括逮捕权。尽管许多特别警员以志愿者的身份提供服务，但是一些警察局给特别警员支付年薪以抵消费用。特别警员可以报销差旅费，警察局给他们配发制服。

P122

在英国当一名特别警员的最低要求是，申请者必须是一名欧洲经济区的公民（或者具有不受限制留在英国的权利）以及年龄至少是 18 岁。在录取过程中，申请者必须通过一项体能测试，而且必须愿意为警察局每月至少奉献 16 个小时。特别警员还可能在人际交往技能，在团队中工作的能力、领导潜力以及主动性方面接受评估。警察局通常还使用初警招募（PIR，the Police Initial Recruitment）考试来筛选候选人，判定申请者清楚准确写作的能力、解答数学问题的能力以及逻辑推理能力。

图 8.1　一位英国交通警察总队的特别警员在英格兰的一座火车站巡逻

目前，特别警员的着装通常模仿其全职同事的式样，而且警察局给全职警察配发什么样的装备，就给特别警员配发什么样的装备，包括警棍、手铐、致残喷雾器、无线电通信装置以及防刺背心。不同的警察局在相同的装备上有不同变化，而特别警员还被授权购买额外装备挂到他们自己的多功能腰带上。

特别警员经常与另一个特别警员或者一名正规全职警察以团队形式一起工作，但是，在成功完成培训后，特别警员可以单独工作。所有警务工作都可以用到特别警员，从犯罪预防和特别大型活动，到处置道路交通事故以及处理入室盗
P123 窃、打架斗殴以及刑事损害。但是，特别警员通常不参与更为专业的警务工作，包括交警工作、刑事侦查工作、搜查队工作或者枪械队工作。

特别警员的制服与正规全职警察几乎相同，但是有一些细小的差别。在英格兰和威尔士，一些特别警员穿戴的警衔与正规警察的相似，但是也有各种变化，即便是在警察局之间也是这样。在苏格兰，特别警员没有警衔也没有职级。在特别警员的肩章上常常有“SC”字样，表明他们的辅警身份以及职位。

招募特别警员的名目有很多。在 2004 年，零售店被要求资助他们的职员申请特别警员岗位并在当地警察局接受培训，然后，在工作时间内履行一些特别警员的巡逻职责。这一做法的思路是在商户邻近地区安插更多的耳目，并且用额外

的激励措施让一些人提供服务。这个方案，称为雇主支持警务（ESP，Employer Supported Policing）方案，鼓励商户支持雇员申请特别警员队里的一个岗位。参与此方案的商户，让职员带薪离岗去参加初次培训，然后每两周有一天参加警务工作。所以，这个方案中的特别警员履行警务职责时是有偿的，但是支付者是给他们发薪水的商户，而不是警方（Metropolitan Police，n. d.）。另一个招聘特别警员的例子发生在2003年。当年，警方招聘经过认证的、有资质的会计进入大都会警察局犯罪专家组内的一个侦查部门工作（Seth，2006）。最近，专家团队被集合在一起处理海上和河流治安问题以及网络犯罪问题，并且用他们自己的马匹在乡村地区开展骑马巡逻。

伦敦城的特别警员队

伦敦城特别警员队的历史是多姿多彩的，而且可以追溯至十六世纪伊丽莎白一世女王在任时期。当时伦敦勋爵市长组织由自由民组成的几伙人，接受培训后平息骚乱。一部1673年通过的法案规定在需要的时候委派临时警察，1831年和1835年通过的特别警员法案官方认定特别警员有权维持和平并保护人民和财产。1911年，伦敦城成立了后备警察队，1935年更名为伦敦城特别警员队（City of London Police，2011）。伦敦辅警的制服不断演变，他们的装备亦是如此。1994年，伦敦城的特别警员首次配备手铐；在此之前，他们得自己购买手铐。到1995年，特别警员配备了可伸展警棍、手铐、防御喷雾器以及防弹衣。

当今时代，伦敦城特别警员配发的制服和装备价值超过1000英镑，特别警员初始培训课堂教学时间超过280个小时，自学时间达400个小时。特别警员为正规警察提供很多帮助，特别警员被用在仪式活动上、示范展示上以及在针对恐怖分子的行动上。但是，特别警员还执行更为常规的警务工作，通过在团队中提供志愿服务以及经警察同意后有资格开展独立巡逻，去处理打给警方的求助电话、公共场所醉酒以及交通控制（City of London Police，2011）。除了警号连着“SC”字样，伦敦城特别警员穿着的制服与正规警员的完全相同（见图8.2），而且伦敦城特别警员必须每年最少履职200个小时。他们没有薪水，但是可以报销自掏腰包的上下班通勤费，还有一份餐补（City of London Police，2017）。

P124

图 8.2　来自世界各地的许多辅警部门开展沟通交流，互相学习运作辅警巡逻职责的方法；此照片中的两位人物分别是奥兰治县县治安官办公室后备部门的中士杰·洛萨瑞奥和来自伦敦城特别警员队的指挥官杨·米勒；此照片拍摄于一次参观交流活动

奥兰治县（佛罗里达州）县治安官办公室的后备警察

佛罗里达州奥兰治县面积大概有 2600 平方千米，居民人口（不包括游客）接近 120 万人。奥兰治县是奥兰多城、沃尔特·迪斯尼世界、水族馆以及环球影城的发源地，还是旅游胜地和目的地。奥兰治县还号称美国第二大会议中心，并
P125 拥有美国最大的一所大学。奥兰治县县治安官办公室大约有 2000 名有偿雇员，其中有超过 1400 名宣誓执法官员，这使奥兰治县县治安官办公室成为全美第十二大县治安官办公室以及美国东南州中第三大县治安官办公室。奥兰治县县治安官办公室负责未正式成为奥兰治县一部分的地区的所有执法和刑事侦查工作。

在佛罗里达州，志愿性质的执法官员由法规授权拥有逮捕权并携带枪支。奥兰治县县治安官办公室后备助理（见图 8.3）必须参加严格的警察院校培训以及佛罗里达州要求的培训，而且要么作为“协助”助理提供服务（超过 300 个小时的院校培训）——在一名获得全面认证的志愿助理或者全职助理的控制之下履行执法职责，要么作为获得全面认证的志愿助理（必须接受与佛罗里达州全职执法官员一样的颁发资格证明的学院大约 800 个小时的培训）——拥有全部与全职执法官员一样的法定职权和职责。除了必须参加的州级院校培训，奥兰治县县治安官办公室要求全部志愿助理成功完成一个在职培训项目。这个培训包括一个为

期六周的迎新情况介绍，接下来是一个相当于十四周的实战培训和评估项目，指导人员是获得州级认证的实战培训教官。

图 8.3 奥兰治县县治安官办公室的后备助理履行巡逻职责，而且在特殊任务和大型群众集会方面提供帮助；在中部佛罗里达州这样的游客目的地，这极其重要

申请志愿助理岗位的人必须完成与全职岗位的录取者一样的体能测试、心理测试、背景审查、身体检查以及面试。全面认证岗位的申请者与全职岗位的申请者一样，必须满足教育/经历要求，尽管申请协警岗位者不必满足这个要求。后备部门的职员与奥兰治县县治安官办公室人力资源处协作，组成一个本机构的聘用委员会，为所有新招聘至本部门的人员提供指导。全部新后备助理被分派给一个经验丰富的后备警察，该后备警察作为指导者在培训期间指导新来的后备助理。尽管后备部门中许多新后备人员在接受了院校培训后直接参加后备部门工作，但是令后备部门受益良多的人员还有那些从执法岗位上退休或者（体面）辞职的全职职员。许多这样的人员接受过上千个小时的培训，同时有多年经验，而且尽管他们可能在找新的工作或者已经退休了，但是他们本着志愿精神，发现自己有许多东西可以继续回报给自己的社区。 P126

奥兰治县县治安官办公室给志愿助理配发与全职助理一样的装备。这些装备包括无线电通信装置、手枪、泰瑟枪、致残喷雾器、多功能腰带、防弹背心、个人安全设备、电子控制装置以及奥兰治县县治安官办公室配发的笔记本电脑。后备助理还可以被授权携带附加武器（如步枪和猎枪），或者配备附加装备（如雷达装置、特种装备等），如果是按要求而且如果后备助理接受过必要的培训。后备部门内全部后备人员的制服与配发给奥兰治县县治安官办公室内全职助理的制服是一样的。后备部门还有十辆有警用标记的汽车，这些汽车仅供后备部门使用，即后备部门在发挥部门职能、执行特别任务、巡逻以及其他经批准的职能的时候可以使用这些汽车，但是这些汽车看上去与全职职员使用的车辆一样。这些巡逻汽车被配发给工作量最高的志愿助理使用，可以被志愿助理开回家，但是后备部门其他任何人都可以使用。

后备部门的组织架构基本上模仿全职机构的架构，在权力的大小和职责的多寡上都是这样。后备部门由一名助理主任领导，有两名少校、四名上尉，分管勤务、管理、培训和特殊任务。后备部门还有两个培训排（每个排由一名中尉领导）、三个勤务排（每个排由一名中尉领导），以及六个勤务小队，这六个勤务小队大约有十名后备人员（每个小队由一名中士领导）。

目前将近有 80 名男人和女人在奥兰治县县治安官办公室内做县治安官助理提供志愿服务。政策要求每一位后备部门成员每月志愿工作的时间必须达到 16 个小时，这包括每月 4 个小时的培训会议。后备部门基本上支持奥兰治县县治安官办公室的目标，特别关注着装巡逻，而且后备人员经常被召唤补充进入道路巡逻小队，因为道路巡逻小队人员短缺，或者特殊任务需要补充人力。但是，后备部门成员可以合法地加入其他不需要着装的工作或者特殊任务，只要他们已经接
P127
受过附加的适当培训。这包括骑马巡逻、海上巡逻、特警队（作为随队医生）、自行车巡逻、旅游导向警务（TOP，tourism-oriented policing）、要人保卫、背景调查、少年犯逮捕和教导（JAM，juvenile arrest and monitor）部门、问题导向警务（POP，problem-oriented policing）、追逃部门、刑事侦查、交通执法、培训部门，以及其他。

作为一个重要的县级县治安官办公室，奥兰治县县治安官办公室后备部门与社区的执法联系非常紧密。对于来自奥兰治县内部其他执法机构要求提供帮助的需求，奥兰治县县治安官办公室的后备部门向来都会满足，而且在救灾工作中也发挥了关键作用，比如在佛罗里达州西南部遭受安德鲁飓风重创之后，在佛罗里达州中部遭受查理飓风、弗朗西斯飓风、珍妮飓风以及厄玛飓风重创之后，后备部门还很荣幸地主办了就后备警察和志愿者问题召开的（美国）国家会议和国际会议，欢迎来自世界各地的警察后备部门直接学习奥兰治县志愿警务（Wolf，2014；Wolf & Beary，2010）。

纽约市警察局的协警

纽约市的面积有1214平方千米，人口超过800万人。纽约市警察局协警的职能极其有限，其特殊作用是警方的身着制服的“眼睛和耳朵”。纽约市警察局协警没有执法权或者警察权，更多的是作为志愿安保力量，身着制服在街区和问题地区开展步行巡逻、机动车巡逻和自行车巡逻，向正规、全职警察报告嫌疑举动。他们还在重要大型活动中提供一些交通引导和帮助工作，以及作为增派的身着制服警员在特殊大型活动、公园、购物地区以及地铁入口和出口执勤。协警部门一般履行步行巡逻职能，两人一组在纽约市的大街小巷工作。如果协警遭遇一个问题，他们奉命用无线电通信装置或者手机向地方分局报告遇到的状况，从而正规警察可以作出应对。在工作日，协警大多数情况下在晚上巡逻（Greenberg，1984）。纽约市警察局协警人数在4000名以上，但是活跃人员数量可能实际上只有一半（Greenberg，1984；Albrecht，2017）。

纽约市警察局协警岗位的申请者必须至少17岁，能读写英语，通过包括毒品“零容忍”政策的背景审查，是一名美国公民或者是一个在美国获准工作的合法永久居民，在纽约市居住或者居住在周边六个授权区域之一，而且拥有有效的纽约市驾驶证或者身份证。尽管纽约市警察局协警是美国最大的协警项目，它的培训要求却是最少的一个。纽约市警察局协警录取者必须通过一个54个小时的协警基本培训课程（作为对比，纽约市警察局正规警察要参加为期六个月、960个小时的院校培训），这个培训课程训练他们成为治安官员；但是，纽约市警察局没有上班或下班警察身份，他们也没有逮捕权（这与纽约市任何公民无异），除非在紧急时刻得到授权。纽约市警察局协警被视为文职人员，而不是宣誓人员，在任何时候，上班和下班都是如此（Kelly，Grasso，Esposito，Giannelli & Maroulis，2008）。但是，在宣布紧急状态的情况下，他们可以被授予治安官员的身份（Albrecht，2017）。 P128

因为他们的文职身份，他们没有被授权对他们没有现场目击的犯罪嫌疑人实施逮捕，除非他们获得一名正规警察或者警察调度员的许可。协警不能被分派执行有危害或危险的任务，也不能被分派从事单独巡逻或者对无线电呼叫作出第一响应（Albrecht，2017）。纽约市警察局协警在上班期间任何时候都不能随身携带武器，但是被允许携带警用直棍、一部无线电通信装置以及手铐，而且可以因为公民某些不法犯罪行为或者重罪行为扣留该人。在2007年两名辅警遭受致命枪击之后，纽约市委员会下令给所有协警购买防弹背心提供资助。但是这个资助中断了，防弹背心目前供应短缺。

纽约市协警的任务是让公众觉得巡逻警察人数在增加。纽约市协警还被授权开展汽车巡逻、步行巡逻以及自行车巡逻。纽约市警察局协警的汽车与正规警察的相似，但是喷涂了“协警”字样。纽约市警察局协警的制服与纽约市警察局正规警察的非常相似；协警警员和协警中士穿着深蓝色衬衫和裤子；协警中尉及以上级别穿着白色衬衫。但是，协警的警徽与正规警察的完全不同。

协警队伍采用的警衔与全职职员的相似。纽约市协警从协警警员起步，可以被晋升为协警中士、协警中尉、协警上尉、协警督察助理、协警督察以及协警副局长。协警督察指挥七个纽约警察区的协警部门，协警上尉指挥每一个警察分局的协警部门（Greenberg，1984）。协警晋升的依据是全职协警协调员的推荐，附加培训也是必需的。

加利福尼亚州后备警察

与纽约市警察局使用协警相比，加利福尼亚州是美国最进步的后备警察机构之一。公民个人可以接受培训，然后以后备警察三个不同类别中的一个类别提供服务。每一个类别不同的培训量，导致辅警从有一点警察职权再到没有警察职权
P129 再到具有与他们的全职同事对等的警察职权。

加利福尼亚州的后备警察按照要求要满足与全职执法官员一样的选拔标准，包括读写能力测评、面试、背景调查以及体检和体能测试。申请者必须至少 18 岁，最少接受过高中教育，而且必须要么是美国公民，要么是一位永久居留的外国人——有资格成为美国公民并已经申请入籍美国。

加利福尼亚州将其后备警察标准分为三种类别：I 级、II 级和 III 级。I 级后备警察，一经完成培训（727 个小时的院校培训加 400 个小时的实战培训），就被授权单独工作并履行与正规、全职警察一样的职责，发挥一样的作用。II 级后备警察，一经完成培训（333 个小时），就从事执法工作，但必须在 I 级后备警察或者全职警察的直接督导下工作。III 级后备警察（144 个小时的培训）可以从事特殊的、受限制的、提供支持的工作，但只能是那些不太可能导致肢体接触逮捕的工作，而且必须同样在 I 级后备警察或者全职警察的直接督导下工作。III 级后备警察可以被用在押解囚犯这种不要求直接督导的工作。III 级后备警察没有被要求完成年度职业培训，而 I 级、II 级后备警察则被要求每两年要完成 24 个小

时的年度职业培训。

加利福尼亚州使用I级、II级后备警察身着制服巡逻，而那些接受适当培训的后备警察还可以在其他领域工作，包括调查、船舶巡逻、骑马队以及搜救队。洛杉矶市警察局（LAPD，the Los Angeles Police Department）后备警察队是一个机构使用接受过加利福尼亚州治安官员标准和培训训练的后备警察的例子。洛杉矶市警察局的后备警察是加利福尼亚州最大后备警察部门之一，有超过650名活跃的后备警察。洛杉矶市警察局给后备警察配发的所有装备和制服都与全职警察的一样，而且后备警察被要求每月最少工作16个小时。洛杉矶市警察局的后备警察没有任何薪水，每年贡献的时间价值估计有700万美元（Garrison，2003；Johnson，Bonner & Hanser，2017）。

以色列国民卫队

以色列国民卫队成立于1974年，既有穿制服的志愿者也有不穿制服的志愿者。这些志愿者帮助以色列警察从事邻里守望工作、步行巡逻和驾驶有标识的汽车巡逻、交通控制、警方海岸保卫巡逻、犯罪预防、设置安全屏障和检查站以及其他工作。国民卫队宣称其是以色列最大的志愿者队伍（Israel Police，n. d. ）。国民卫队是以色列警方的警察和社区机构的组成部分。它的成员受训以提供对任何类型安全状况的最初应对，特别是恐怖分子袭击，直到正规警察部门到达现场（Jewish Telegraphic Agency，1994）。以色列国民卫队的成员接受一名警察署国民卫队指挥官的领导。警察署国民卫队部门接受行政区、分区以及以色列国民卫队指挥官的领导。 P130

国民卫队志愿者在上班时行使警察权，尽管这些警察权可能是有限的，要看志愿者的培训水平。志愿者可以带武器，要看他们所受的培训，而且在上班时能够实施逮捕（World Police，n. d. ）。但是国民卫队志愿者在不上班的时候没有任何警察权。他们在下班后被禁止以执法官员身份行事，而且不能阻止正在进行的犯罪，也不能把自己定位成一名卫队成员去阻止犯罪。

以色列国民卫队为志愿者配发了一件警用背心、手电筒、无线电通信装置、武器、手铐以及其他被分派任务所需的执勤装备。国民卫队志愿者被期望的每月最低工作时间是12个小时，一个轮班的时长通常是2个小时至4个小时（World Police，n. d. ）。国民卫队志愿者还能够接受额外培训以便有更强的服务能力。"雅塔姆"（Yatam）志愿者主要负责交通控制，"马特米德"（Matmid）志愿者履行正规警察的所有职责，包括巡逻、犯罪侦查、预防犯罪。雅塔姆和马特米德国民卫队志愿者都接受高端培训并穿着正规警察的制服（World Police，n. d.）。

在以色列，全职警察与国民卫队密切协作。国民卫队成员收集一线情报并与正规警察分享信息来打击犯罪并与恐怖主义战斗。

爱尔兰共和国辅警后备处

加尔达希奥查纳（Garda Síochána）后备处是志愿性质的、无薪水的爱尔兰警方的后备处。后备加尔达成员穿着与正规警察一样的制服，但是他们的肩章有首字母“GR”，使其与全职警察力量区别开来。后备加尔达没有被授权携带枪支（正规警察也不能携带枪支，除非被分派去执行特殊任务），而且拥有有限的逮捕权。他们被视为警方力量的增强器，被用以提高警察在社区的见警率。后备处成员没有获准身着便装工作。

加尔达希奥查纳后备处申请者必须是爱尔兰公民，或者是欧盟成员国公民，P131 或者是瑞士联邦公民，但必须是爱尔兰的常住居民。加尔达后备处是根据2005年通过的《加尔达希奥查纳法案》建立起来的，在2006年12月开始正常运转。到2014年，在爱尔兰，加尔达后备处成员超过1100人（Garda Síochána，n. d.），但是加尔达后备处成员人数到2016年降低到870人（Lynott，2016）。

加尔达希奥查纳后备处成员必须完成大约四周的培训，给正规警察提供支持，包括履行巡逻职责，有针对性的问题警务（Garda Síochána，n. d.），主要在交通检查站提供帮助，监控闭路电视，步行巡逻，警务站工作以及大型活动警务。后备加尔达还在众多领域接受额外培训，如家暴、警察内部政策、儿童保护以及路侧安全（Raidió Teilifís Éireann，2015）。后备处成员在警察局正规成员的督导下工作（Department of Justice and Equality，2016）。2015年，后备加尔达的权力被扩大了，他们得到允许给司机开罚单、送达交通传票以及扣押车辆。

一个普遍现象是，加尔达后备处成员试图进入警务中的全职岗位，而在后备处的志愿服务可以被候选人当作一个途径，即一个积累有价值的经验、进而向加尔达希奥查纳——爱尔兰的正规警察力量——提出申请的途径（Raidió Teilifís Éireann，2015）。

匈牙利国民卫队

匈牙利国民卫队，或者辅警，成立于1989年。据报道，现在全匈牙利有多达 90000 名辅警（Kardos & Szoke，2017）。国民卫队以它的正式名称而闻名，即（匈牙利）国家国民自卫组织，匈牙利语缩写是 OPSZ。该组织全部由非宣誓志愿者构成，这些志愿者从事各种与警务有关的工作。该组织成员必须是匈牙利公民或者合法居民（Kardos & Szoke，2017）。该组织的目标是作为身着制服的警察工作：打击犯罪、维护公共秩序以及增强公众的安全感。（匈牙利）国家国民自卫组织的成员参与下列部门的工作：邻里巡逻、步行巡逻和驾驶有标识的汽车进行巡逻、交通控制、预防青少年犯罪。（匈牙利）国家国民自卫组织是警方的“眼睛和耳朵”（Selih & Zavrsnik，2012；Civil Self-Defense Organizations of Budapest，n. d.）。

（匈牙利）国家国民自卫组织的成员与任何其他公民相比，没有更多的权力，他们没有任何逮捕权，但是可以而且确实可以将犯罪嫌疑人控制在现场，等候正规警察到达现场并展开侦查。但是除了胡椒喷雾器，他们没有职权携带危险武器（Kardos & Szoke，2017）。除了与正规警察一同从事巡逻工作，匈牙利辅警部门成员还参加一个车辆牌照信息认定部门的工作，这个部门名叫梅特里克斯警察队（Matrix Police）。（匈牙利）国家国民自卫组织成员在巡逻机动车里工作， P132
该车配有一台网络摄像机，能够扫描车辆牌照信息并将之与被盗车辆数据库的信息进行比对。当一辆被盗车辆位置被锁定时，（匈牙利）国家国民自卫组织成员会将机动车信息报告给开展侦查工作的正规警察（Matrix，2015）。

在匈牙利首都布达佩斯，辅警部门被称作布达佩斯国民自卫组织，匈牙利语缩写是 BPSZ。布达佩斯国民自卫组织成员被分派到 73 个地方社区部门中的一个，并驾驶有标识的机动车巡逻，该车看上去很像警车。布达佩斯国民自卫组织以及（匈牙利）国家国民自卫组织的成员均被授权携带警方配发的胡椒喷雾器，而且他们穿着制服或者背心表明自己的身份（Civil Self-Defense Organizations of Budapest，n. d.）。

百慕大后备警察

百慕大后备警员队于 1951 年由百慕大立法机关建立。在百慕大，起初，后备警察配发的是灰色制服，以便把他们与正规警察同事区别开。后备警察最初完全以志愿者身份工作，但是在 1991 年，百慕大立法机关批准了一笔小额津贴，以表彰后备警员队成员对社区的服务。后备警察部门里工作成绩良好的成员现在继续领取这笔津贴，每六个月领取一次（大约 1600 美元/年）。1995 年，后备警员队采用了一套新制服，与正规警察的制服几乎一样，并且更名为百慕大后备警察队（Bermuda Police Service，n. d.）。正规警察在百慕大巡逻时通常没有武器，百慕大后备警察队成员不带手枪（Bermuda Online，n. d.）。

百慕大后备警察队的候选人必须在 19 岁至 50 岁，而且在严密的背景调查之外，候选人必须能够通过对写作、体能和身体健康的系列测试。后备警察的申请标准几乎与百慕大警察局正规警察的一样。后备警察的基础培训课程覆盖的所有内容、领域，与提供给正规警察的培训一样。后备警察部门大约有 80 人，而且辅警们被要求一年中向该部门提供 150 个小时的志愿服务（Clifton，n. d.）。

在百慕大，后备警察从事的工作各种各样，但是都仿照全职警察的工作。这包括交通控制、道路巡逻以及应对求助电话、处理交通事故以及与游客一起工作。百慕大后备警察队还接受问题导向警务培训，与社区的活跃团队一起工作预
P133 防犯罪（Clifton，n. d.）。百慕大后备警察队的成员都是宣誓警察，与全职警察或者说正规警察一样拥有逮捕权。百慕大后备警察队成员配发了制服和装备。

俄罗斯哥萨克人

俄罗斯哥萨克人的历史厚重而多彩，且富有争议。术语“哥萨克”（Cossack）源自突厥语单词“Kazak”，可以被翻译成“自由民”或“探险者”（*History Magazine*，2001）。他们可以把自己的祖先追溯到说突厥语的农民，这些农民向俄罗斯中西部迁徙并在十五世纪联合起来，成为俄国沙皇的武器——忠诚的战士。哥萨克人在俄罗斯六个不同的区域定居，拥有战士的习俗和传统。据说哥萨克儿童从出生开始就被以战士的方式教育着；新生男性婴儿在出生的时候其手要被放在一件武器的上面，而且在其长到三岁的时候就开始骑马。哥萨克人被用于军事目的，包括保卫边境和俄罗斯帝国向西伯利亚扩张（*History Magazine*，2001）。但是，你要是去问不同的人，哥萨克人就有完全不同的形象。在俄罗斯以外的地方，哥萨克人闻名于世，因为他们是严格的俄罗斯东正教基督徒，用暴力维持秩序；在俄罗斯境内，许多人把哥萨克人看作忠诚于国家且拥有丰富且引以为傲遗产的人们（Flintoff，2014）。

自从苏联解体以来，哥萨克人已经建立起武备学院。在武备学院，哥萨克儿童可以学习他们的传统遗产并准备开启军人或警察生涯。在 2010 年的俄罗斯人口普查中，哥萨克人作为他们自己的民族在列，大约有 650000 人宣称自己是哥萨克人（Seddon，2012；Luhn，2014）。俄罗斯总统弗拉基米尔·普京试图培养

哥萨克人的爱国主义服务精神，而且已经开始决定使用哥萨克人组织作为辅警力量（Flintoff，2014）。俄罗斯早在 2012 年就开始试验使用哥萨克人作为辅警，并且在 2014 年的索契冬奥会期间，广泛使用哥萨克人辅警。哥萨克人作为辅警提供服务，就可以免费乘坐公共交通工具，政府免费为他们配发制服（哥萨克人辅警的制服与其政府全职警察同事的不同），而且他们获得的警察权有限（Seddon，2012），包括扣留并检查那些扰乱和平人员的证件（Luhn，2014）。但是，他们的工作不总是与政府机构合拍，在 2012 年，哥萨克人辅警小队被禁止进入莫斯科东南部地区，因为他们频繁在未获官方许可的情况下采取行动（*Moscow Times*，2015）。警方领导们还就哥萨克人的辅警身份行动表示关切，并且承认哥萨克人巡逻辅警经常作出连警察都不被允许做的事情。他们还被贴上了一个现代“道德警察”的标签，因为他们保护俄罗斯的传统价值观（Luhn，2014）。

多伦多协警

在飓风黑泽尔于 1954 年重创多伦多地区之后，政府当局建立起民防组织，包括在 1956 年建立协警，将之作为民防组织的一部分。大都会多伦多警察局也 P134 被建立以来，该局是在合并了当时 13 个市警察局的基础上建立起来的（Fanfair，2016）。1990 年，安大略省的《警察局法案》（PSA，the Police Services Act）确定了安大略省协警的角色。多伦多的协警身着制服，其制服与那些多伦多正规警察的制服稍微有点区别，但是看上去非常相似。多伦多正规警察都有武器，身着深海军蓝衬衫。协警戴的帽子上不是纯红色条纹，而是红黑相间的格子花纹。协警的衬衫是浅蓝色，而且他们手臂袖标上有“协警”（Auxiliary Officer）字样。协警跟随正规警察工作，为犯罪预防项目、特别大型活动、游行、“玩具总动员”[①]以及其他社区工作提供帮助。另外，他们可以被召集在警局周边做安保工作，为社区委员会提供服务，使用多伦多警察局信息系统以及社区警察办公室（Toronto Police Service，n. d. - a；Palamarchuk，2014）。

多伦多警察局协警的职权，与法律赋予任何公民的都一样；但是，《警察局法案》确定：“警察局的协警，如果他或她与一名警察一同工作或者在一名警察的监督下工作，那么他或她就拥有了警察职权，而且警察局局长可以授权协警履行警察职责”。“警察局局长只在特殊情况下可以授权警察局的协警履行警察职责，特殊情况包括警察局的警力不足以应对的紧急情况”（Police Services Act（Ontario），2015）。然而，通常情况下，协警没有配备武器，政策中的例外情况允许多伦多警察局局长授权那些参加过获准培训课程的协警携带武器。协警必须每年重新获得警察使用武力的资格，这包括使用警棍、手铐培训以及防卫战术培训。另外，协警必须持续不断地获得急救和心肺复苏技术资格。

多伦多协警岗位的申请者必须是加拿大公民或者加拿大永久居民并且年龄至少有 18 岁。除其他背景审查的要求之外，候选人必须居住在大多伦多地区，并且最少要在岗位上工作一年。

多伦多警察局报告该局在 2016 年有超过 360 名协警，而且每位协警都配发了制服、装备并且参加了培训。协警不被要求完成一个警察培训项目，或者与同级警察一样获得资质，但是他们被要求要完成一个为期六周的培训项目，包括程
P135 序培训和自我防卫培训。协警被要求每年要完成最少 150 个小时的志愿服务（Toronto Police Service，n. d. –a；n. d. –a），但是，协警要每年平均提供超过 200 个小时的服务。多伦多协警还可以在专业部门工作，如两轮摩托车巡逻部门和海上执法部门（Palamarchuk，2013）。

哈密尔顿警察局协警

同样位于加拿大的安大略省，哈密尔顿警察局协警部门的成员大约有 100 人。哈密尔顿位于安大略湖的西岸，哈密尔顿警察局大约有 800 名全职警察职员。哈密尔顿警察局协警部门实施一个为期七周的培训项目，包括超过 30 个小时的使用武力教学。在完成培训项目之后，协警被要求完成一个试用期，而且要完成正在实施的培训，该培训所有协警每年都必须完成。

协警参加执法工作并提高见警率。他们在下列工作中提供帮助：大型运动会，在指导下开展巡逻和骑行巡逻，公共秩序部门，指挥交通，在社区开展安全宣传，监控闭路电视，参加警方招聘活动，以及为摄影部门和游行团队提供支持。协警部门成员被要求每月提供志愿服务最少 12 个小时，轮班从 4 个小时到 12 个小时不等。

协警的制服与正规全职警察职员的不同，穿着浅蓝色衬衫（而正规警察的衬衫色是深蓝色），臂章上有“协警”字样。像其他安大略省的警察局一样，哈密尔顿的协警没有警察权，而且没有武器。他们的作用就是帮助正规警察履行职责，且以志愿者身份工作。

中国香港辅警队

中国香港辅警队（HKAPF，the Hong Kong Auxiliary Police Force）成立于第一次世界大战之初的1914年。最初设置辅警是为了把辅警作为干部以代替当时正在服现役的正规警察。中国香港辅警队被称为特别后备警队。到1915年2月中旬，特别后备警队全部人员已经发展壮大到250人，成员有葡萄牙人、中国人、英国人和印度人。培训时间长达几个月，培训内容有枪法课以及演习基本指导。最初，特别后备队的成员没有配发制服，直到一位著名的中国居民捐钱给特别后备队从而使辅警有了全套制服（Volunteer Special Constabulary，1998；Lam，1997）。

P136

但是，到1915年9月，正规警察队伍人数减少了，而且此趋势一直持续下来。香港总督将特别后备队所有成员的身份变成特别警员，依法要求这些志愿者汇报工作，而且将逮捕权授权给他们。“他们与正规警察的区别仅表现在一个方面，即薪酬和养老金，这是他们根本没有资格得到的”（Lam，1997，p. 4）。1917年9月，这个机构又被重新命名为香港警察后备队，直到1918年9月被解散。

1927年，为了应对香港地区人口暴涨——大多数是来自中国内地的避难者，香港警察后备队又恢复了。从1914年到1919年的所有警察后备队成员都被重新登记。但是，警察后备队并不是每日做巡逻工作或者做警察工作。相反，后备警察队提供一份待命人员名单，如1938年11月所需的待命名单，当时290名警察后备队员被召集上岗应对日本入侵中国给香港地区带来的风险。

1941年，警察总监召集3000名中国人登记进入特别警员队。1941年9月，《警察（军人身份）条例》要求所有正规警察、警察后备队成员以及特别警员：“如果战争爆发，‘作为民兵履行战斗职责’，他们将还在总监的指挥之下，但是将‘致力于对企图侵略或者以其他方式进行类似战争行动的任何敌人的武装力量采取军事行动’”（Lam，1997，p. 11）。在香港地区被日本侵略期间，警察后备队员履行警察和军队的职责，但在日军占领期间被取消。香港警察后备队在此期间遭受了巨大的伤亡，原因是英勇的行动、误杀或误伤以及敌人的处决。

1946年5月，警察后备队由中国军队再次建立起来并受中国官员的指挥。1949年，特别警员队被再次建立起来，而且除了中国志愿者，允许来自所有族裔的人加入。1951年，根据《强制服役条例》，香港地区所有的男性市民在18岁及以上者，都被要求要么在香港皇家志愿防卫队——基本服务团提供服务，要么在特别警员队提供服务。到1955年，特别警员和后备警察从事全部警务工作，主要是从事救济工作，而且他们还被要求每月只工作 8 个小时。这两支队伍在 1957 年被合并到一起，并被重新命名为香港辅警队，其组织形式与正规警察队伍相似，而且需应征入伍的要求被取消。1965 年，这支队伍有了第一批女性辅警，而 1969 年，香港警务处和香港辅警队都被冠以所谓“皇家”名号。香港辅警队的人数从 1973 年 1 月的 3761 名增长到同年 11 月的 7000 名。到 1979 年，香港辅警队的人数减少到 4714 人；但是他们中大约有 20%的人每天都上班来帮助
P137 全职警察日复一日履行职责。

香港辅警队的角色随时间而变，但是一直关注的是大型公共集会期间的人群管理以及勤务预案。另外，香港辅警队的任务是保护关键点、为指挥和控制中心配置人员、为民兵防卫站配置人员、保护领事馆舍以及在自然或人为危机时刻作为随时待命的后备力量。在 2013 年 6 月，香港辅警队的队员大约有 3850 名（Information Services Department，2017）。现在，香港警务处正规警察和香港辅警队队员在制服方面的区别仅仅是，辅警制服双肩肩章上有“A”字母。辅警新人必须完成一个有 320 个课时的基础培训，然后必须完成每年 208 个小时的连续年度培训。除了年级时间要求，为了合法晋升，香港辅警队队员必须参加晋升培训学习，时间从 76 个小时到 226 个小时不等。香港辅警不是志愿者，他们因为自己提供的服务获得薪酬。香港辅警每 24 小时只需工作 8 个小时（Volunteer Special Constabulary，1998）。辅警的薪酬从新人的 620 港币/天（大约 80 美元/48 英镑）到警察署高级中士的 1436 港币（185 美元/110 英镑），他们是时薪最高的雇员。督察、高级督察、总督察及以上级别，作为领薪雇员，日薪最高为 1940 港币（250 美元/148 英镑）（Information Services Department，2017）。

P138

新加坡志愿特别警员队

新加坡的志愿特别警员队（VSC，Volunteer Special Constabulary）作为新加坡警察志愿后备队（SPVR，the Singapore Police Volunteer Reserve），最初建立于 1938 年，以应对政治纷争和劳资纠纷。该部门当时大约有 30 名警察后备人员，而且其任务是维护公共秩序并帮助警察队伍在示威、游行和罢工期间守护警戒线。在接下来的若干年里，新加坡警察志愿后备队不断成长，但是在 1942 年，后备队被解散，因为当时新加坡被日本占领了。1946 年 10 月，新加坡警察志愿后备队得以恢复，其队员中有 100 名到 150 名是前队员，且该队被重新命名为特别警员队。特别警员队负责岗哨工作，保卫商业区，开展机动巡逻。特别警员队

队员被视为全职雇员，每天工作 8 个小时，薪水是每月 45 新加坡元，或者说大约相当于每月 36 美元/21 英镑（Singapore Police Force，n. d.；Volunteer Special Constabulary，1998；Chia Yeong Jia，n. d.）。1946 年，特别警员队被分成两个部门，各自有不同的职责：在职部门（也就是众所周知的增派警员队），由全职有偿人员组成；后备部门（也就是众所周知的志愿特别警员队），由兼职、志愿性质、无偿的人员组成。新加坡志愿特别警员队接受枪支培训，而且负责每周开展一次 4 个小时的巡逻（Volunteer Special Constabulary，1998；Chia Yeong Jia，n. d.）。

1950 年 12 月，因玛丽亚·赫托抚养权归属纠纷引发的种族和宗教暴动爆发。在此暴动中，在一周的动乱期间，8 人被杀，超过 130 人受伤。志愿特别警员队在暴动发生期间，提供了超过 11500 个小时的志愿服务，实施了几例值得注意的逮捕，包括逮捕一个用手榴弹炸一座宾馆的嫌疑人。随着一个个暴动的发生，志愿特别警员队的力量增长到出乎意料的程度，在 1951 年人数达到 2293 名。志愿特别警员队在 1955 再次经受暴动的考验，当年发生的霍克·李公交车暴动导致志愿特别警员队队员安德鲁·特奥死亡（Volunteer Special Constabulary，1998；Chia Yeong Jia，n. d.）。1956 年发生的更多的暴动进一步考验了志愿特别警员队，新加坡社会在 1967 年最终平静下来，同时在这一年，志愿特别警员队被再次重组。

为了解决被认为防卫力量较小的问题，1967 年，国家强制兵役条例出台，要求公民加入民防组织。这要求所有男性新加坡公民加入新加坡武装部队、新加坡警察局或者新加坡民防局。志愿特别警员队与首次新招的超过 2000 名兼职国家兵役警察合并，组成特别警员队（SC，the Special Constabulary）。志愿特别警员队的队员被称为特别警员（志愿者），缩写是 SC（V）［Special Constabulary（Volunteers）］，而那些为国家服役的人员被称为特别警员（国家军人），缩写是 SC（NS）［Special Constabulary（National Servicemen）］。特别警员队（志愿者）的队员受命培训特别警员（国家军人）。 P139

但是，重组导致那些以志愿者身份工作的人和那些“被迫”服役的人之间出现裂痕。特别警员（国家军人）用玩世不恭的态度看待热情洋溢的特别警员（志愿者），而志愿者看不上他们的同事，因为这些人一般不情愿服役。结果，一些特别警员（志愿者）辞职了。1967 年，每晚上班的志愿者平均有 300 人，到 1973 年，仅有 110 人留了下来（Volunteer Special Constabulary，1998，p. 17）。1981 年，特别警员队与志愿特别警员队分开，女性也受聘成为志愿者。1985 年，志愿特别警员队队员被分配与海岸警卫队（其前身就是众所周知的海警）一起工作。

1993年10月，志愿特别警员队加入新加坡警察局的官方整合开始。这个整合包括志愿特别警员队队员在角色和职责方面的转变，把他们同日常服务中与他们职能相当的人更紧密地联系起来。1997年，新加坡学校有了一个特别的安排，即荣誉志愿特别警员项目开始实施。该项目培训来自学校的雇员成为警察，在学校系统学习打击和预防犯罪（Volunteer Special Constabulary，1998；Chia Yeong Jia，n. d.）。

纵观志愿警员的历史，过去，志愿特别警员们身着有“V”字母的制服，这将他们与正规警察区别开。现在，志愿特别警员的制服与正规警察的没有区别（Volunteer Special Constabulary，1998）。目前，志愿特别警员队的工作人员大约有1200名，只要身体条件允许，他们可以一直保持在职状态，普通警员级别可以工作直到50岁，高级警员级别可以到55岁。志愿特别警员，不论衔级，每小时的津贴是3.60新加坡元（大约是2.88美元/1.71英镑）以抵消花费。在新加坡，志愿特别警员队队员从事所有的警务工作，包括在邻里警务中心工作，驾驶机动巡逻车巡逻街巷而且参与监视行动和其他便衣行动（Koo & Tan，2017）。

P140

泰国普吉岛旅游辅警

在泰国，有两种类型的辅警：协助警察志愿者以及移民警察志愿者。普吉岛旅游辅警，经常被用作游客和警察之间的翻译，帮助正规警察与外国观光客沟通。辅警必须自己购买制服，该制服与正规警察的有区别，包括一件绣有辅警标志的白色马球衫、深灰色裤子和棒球帽。辅警必须购买和穿上工作皮带、闪光灯和无线电通信装置，但是他们也可以选择携带胡椒喷雾器、手铐和警棍（Phuket Tourist Police Volunteers，n. d.）。

普吉岛旅游辅警帮助旅行中的游客，促进泰国的旅游产业。他们为游客提供教育信息，还在游客需要警察的时候做翻译；他们还被用在刑事案件有需要的时候，为游客提供与泰国法律有关的信息。他们还被用作警方的“眼睛和耳朵”，但是未被授权采取执法行为，也没有逮捕权。但是，如果泰国的辅警从一名督导他们的泰国官员那里获得许可，那么他们可以制止酒吧打架行为和抓捕小偷（Forgan，2014）。

申请作普吉岛旅游辅警的人必须拥有非移民身份的“B”或者“O”护照，

表明他们可以合法工作或者在泰国经商。另外，申请者必须高中毕业或者具有同等学力，而且能近乎流利地说泰语，并且在其他要求中，要求至少熟练掌握另外一门语言。

马来西亚警察志愿后备队

像许多亚洲国家一样，马来西亚的辅警不是志愿性质的警察。在马来西亚，辅警是有工资的宣誓安保警察，而且他们更像美国的私人安保人员，而不是为警察组织提供志愿服务的人员。马来西亚的辅警被授权携带枪支，但是他们大多是私有化的，且经法规授权拥有某些警察权，包括逮捕权和开展小型侦查工作。

但是，警察志愿后备队（PVR，the Police Volunteer Reserve；马来语：Sukarelawan Polis）是使用志愿者的马来西亚皇家警察局的支援部门。警察志愿后备队的队员与马来西亚的全职警察履行相同的职责、拥有相同的权力，包括携带枪支的权力以及逮捕权。在 2014 年，警察志愿后备队大约有 1200 名队员。马来西亚的警察志愿后备队队员必须是马来西亚全职雇员，年龄在 18 岁至 45 岁；男性队员必须至少有 5 英尺 4 英寸（约为 1.63 米）高，女性队员必须至少 4 英尺 11 英寸（约为 1.50 米）高。尽管警察志愿后备队队员提供的是志愿服务，但是他们能领到少量时薪，而且每年会得到与每年服务达到某一级别相对应的福利待遇（*Borneo Post*，2014；Malaysian Times，2013）。薪水是按小时支付的，但是仅支付每月的前 96 个小时。超过 96 个小时的时间就完全是无偿志愿性质了。

全部警察志愿后备队队员必须接受大约六个月的标准警察培训，而且在他们工作期间，每年必须参加常规地方培训。但是，在他们参加培训的时候，警察志愿后备队队员获得授权领取薪水和津贴，与相应衔级的全职警察获得的薪水和津贴是一样的。警察志愿后备队队员与他们的全职同事执行特别任务并且在居民区开展巡逻工作，特别是在犯罪高发地区。他们还是正规警察的“眼睛和耳朵”，并提供地方信息帮助侦查犯罪。

南非后备警察队

目前，南非辅警历史相对较新，与南非后备警察队（SAPS，the South African Police Service）以及南非共和国的临时宪法有密切联系（1993 年第 200 号法律）。南非后备警察有两种类型：第一种类型是“职能型治安人员”，成功申请到这种类型的人员在警察署以及其他有需要的地方履行治安职能。正如在英国，这些后备警察为社区安全工作，在一名正规警察或者一名最少有三年工作经验的后备警察的督导下发挥作用。第二种类型的后备警察是“支援型专业勤务人员”，他们有特殊技能，可以被南非后备警察队所用，可以穿或不穿制服，而且他们受到培训确保后备警察坚守“适用于其履行职能的相关法律、政策和教育”（South African Police Service，2014）。正如在英格兰和威尔士，后备警察被要求在特殊部门每月至少工作 16 个小时。尽管英国申请者被要求仅仅需要具有英国
P142 合法居住权，但是，南非的申请者必须是生在南非的人。南非后备警察队的前全职队员受到特别鼓励在离开后备警察队时成为后备警察。

像英国的特别警员一样，南非后备警察被认为不仅对他们的社区而且对警务工作同样发挥着重要作用，因此为社区成员涉足邻里警务提供了机会，而社区成员不必为此成为南非后备警察队的全职队员（Civilian Secretariat for Police Service，n. d.）。

南非后备警察队的后备队员在国家总监的指挥下与正规警察一起工作。在南非，在一些情况下，许可公民拥有枪支，其中一个就是根据《武器控制法》（FCA，Firearms Control Act）第 2 条至第 12 条的规定，允许有关政府部门成员携带枪支（Library of Congress，2015）。南非后备警察被允许携带枪支，只要得到适当许可和培训，这与英格兰和威尔士的情况不同，但是与美国境内各州相似。南非后备警察被视为支援正规警察的力量，特别是在预防犯罪方面。一个与英格兰和威尔士明显不同的地方是，在南非，后备警察只有在需要他们服务的时候才上班。在其他所有时间里，他们不被看作在上班，除非后备警察要么在去上班路上，要么在下班途中碰巧遇到事故发生。所以，后备警察只在上班时间里被看作警察。

结论

尽管本章聚焦了全世界一些有趣的准警务部门，这些部门根据本书给出的定义可能或不可能被视为辅警部门，但是全世界还是有许多其他相似的机构应该被列举出来。尽管本书写到了几个美国辅警部门的例子，但是在美国有上千个不同的辅警部门，而且这些例子仅仅是辅警在大大小小的社区所做工作的一小部分介绍。本章写到的伦敦城特别警员队是英国警察局里辅警类型的例子，但是还有由其他警员队所做的众多杰出工作的例子。

全世界可能引起人们兴趣的其他准警务部门的例子有：韩国辅警，（英属）

开曼群岛的皇家警察局后备辅助人员和特别警员，荷兰辅警，巴哈马皇家警察局后备队，百慕大后备警察，以及西澳大利亚辅警部门。

韩国辅警是年龄在 18 岁至 35 岁的、还没有服强制兵役的男性公民。在辅警部门工作是可接受的另一种服兵役的方式，时长为 21 个月。韩国辅警帮助国家警察从事日常警察工作，包括交通控制以及人群控制。荷兰的辅警效仿英国模式建立组织，辅警与荷兰正规警察一起工作。但是，正规警察和警察工会对辅警工作持批评的态度，以及他们历史上相似但有偿的后备警察部门。荷兰的后备警察穿着警察制服，携带手铐、警棍以及防御喷雾器，他们的装备里没有武器，尽管荷兰正规警察是有武器的（Torn & Verbiest，2017）。

巴哈马皇家警察局在 1965 年 6 月首次建立后备警察队，而且现在还在使用这支力量。在巴哈马，大约有 1000 名男性和女性当警察后备人员（Maura，2011）。（英属）开曼群岛的皇家警察局使用志愿特别警员，他们有全职警察的权力，穿着与全职警察一样的制服。他们还使用辅助警员，身着与特别警员一样的制服，但是在法院系统工作。西澳大利亚把辅助人员用在提供保护服务、托管支持以及财产管理方面的工作上。他们在上班时拥有选定的警务权力，而且可以拥有的权力包括制止、搜查和拘留以及携带和使用枪支。但是，西澳大利亚辅警人员不是志愿者；他们提供有偿服务。

注释

①“玩具总动员”是收集捐赠玩具的社区活动。捐赠活动通常在有意义的假日举办，为了那些被收养的儿童或者孤儿，或那些没有经济能力为孩子买玩具的家庭。

参考文献

Albrecht, J. （2017）（阿尔布雷希特）. Abundance of auxiliary police and volunteer personnel in the NYPD（“纽约市警察局协警和志愿性质职员的人数充裕”）. IN J. Albrecht（Ed.）（阿尔布雷希特主编）, *Police reserves and volunteers：Enhancing organizational effectiveness and public trust*（《警察后备人员和志愿者：提升组织的有效性和公信力》）, pp. 51—56. Boca Raton, FL：CRC Press（博卡-拉顿，佛罗里达州：CRC 出版社）.

Bermuda Online（n. d.）（百慕大在线〈日期不详〉）. Welcome to Bermuda

（“欢迎来到百慕大”）. 2015 年 3 月 13 日检索网址 www. bermuda-online. org/abcbda3. htm.

Bermuda Police Service（n. d.）（百慕大警察局〈日期不详〉）. Making Bermuda safer（“让百慕大更安全”）. 2015 年 3 月 13 日检索网址 www. police. bm/content/reserve-history.

Borneo Post（2014, June 25）（《婆罗洲邮报》〈2014 年 6 月 25 日〉）. Interested to join police volunteer reserve?（“有兴趣加入警察局后备警察吗?”）2016 年 9 月 1 日检索网址 www. theborneopost. com/2014/06/25/interested-to-join-police-volunteer-reserve.

P144

Chia Yeong Jia, J.（n. d.）（夏勇嘉〈日期不详〉）. Volunteer Special Constabulary（“志愿特别警员队”）. Singapore Infopedia, National Library of Singapore（新加坡信息媒体，新加坡国家图书馆）. 2014 年 5 月 7 日检索网址 http://eresourcesnlb. gov. sg/infopedia/articles/SIP_11412010-05-07. html? s=volunteer%20special%20constabulary.

City of London Police（2011）（伦敦城警察局）. *City of London Special Constabulary*（《伦敦城特别警员队》）. London: City of London Police（伦敦：伦敦城警察局）.

City of London Police（2017, December 11）（伦敦城警察局〈2017 年 12 月 11 日〉）. Specials（“特别警员”）. 2017 年 9 月 3 日检索网址 www. cityoflondon. policeuk/careers/specials/pages/default. aspx.

Civil Self-Defense Organizations of Budapest（n. d.）（布达佩斯国民自卫组织〈日期不详〉）. Budapest and agglomeration civilian guard（“布达佩斯与国民卫队聚集”）. 2015 年 3 月 13 日检索网址 www. bpsz. hu/? page_id=32.

Civilian Secretariat for Police Service（n. d.）（警察局文职秘书〈日期不详〉）. *South African Reserve Police Service: Policy framework and guidelines: Establishment and functioning*（《南非后备警察队伍：政策框架与指南:》）. Pretoria: Civilian Secretariat for Police Service（比勒陀利亚：警察局文职秘书）. 2017 年 1 月 20 日检索网址 www. policesecretariatgov za/downloads/policies/reservists_policy. pdf.

Clifton, K.（n. d.）（克利夫顿〈日期不详〉）. Hugh Lewis: Commandant Bermuda Reserve Police Club runner（“休·刘易斯：百慕大后备警察队指挥官警

察俱乐部老板”）. 2015 年 3 月 13 日检索网址 http：//portal. clubrunner. cal2044/Stories/hugh-lewis-commandant-bermuda-reserve-police.

Department of Justice and Equality (2016, February 20)(〈爱尔兰共和国〉正义与公平部〈2016 年 2 月 20 日〉). Garda Siochana Reserve：Minister outlines Garda commissioner's proposal（“加尔达西奥查纳后备警察：部长概要介绍了加尔达总监的提议”）. 2016 年 8 月 25 日检索网址 http：//justice. ie/en/JELR/Pages/PR07000880.

Fanfair, R.（2016, October 28)(范费尔〈2016 年 10 月 28 日〉). Auxiliary celebrates 60 years（“协警 60 年庆”）. Toronto Police Service News (多伦多警察局新闻). 2018 年 1 月 12 日检索网址 http：//tpsnews. ca/stories/2016/10/auxiliary-celebrates-60-years.

Flintoff, C.（2014, February 22)(弗林托夫〈2014 年 2 月 22 日〉). Russia's Cossacks ride back from history as “patriots”（“俄罗斯哥萨克人历来都是‘爱国者’”）. National Public Radio (国家公共广播电台). 2016 年 8 月 24 日检索网址 www. nprorg/2014/02/22/280964932/back-from-history-russias-cossacks-ride-as-patriots.

Forgan, D.（2014, July 4)(福根〈2014 年 7 月 4 日〉). A night out with the foreign tourist police in Thailand's seediest city（“在泰国最肮脏的城市晚上与外国旅游警察出去玩”）. Vice. com. 2016 年 8 月 31 日检索网址 www. vice. com/en_uk/read/a-night-out-with-the-foreign-tourist-police-in-thailands-seediest-city-704.

Garda Siochana (n. d.)(加尔达西奥查纳〈日期不详〉). Garda Reserve（“加尔达后备警察”）. 2015 年 3 月 11 日检索网址 http：//garda. ie/Controller. aspx？Page165&Lang=1.

Garrison, J.（2003, October 23)(加里森〈2003 年 10 月 23 日〉). LAPD has protection in reserve（“洛杉矶警察局有后备警察来保护”）. *The Los Angeles Times*（《洛杉矶时报》）. 2015 年 2 月 9 日检索网址 http：//articles. latimes. com/2003/oct/23/local/me-reserves23.

Gill, M. L., & Mawby, R. I.（1990)(吉尔和莫比). *A special constable：A study of the police reserve*(《特别警员；关于警方后备人员的研究》). Aldershot, UK：Avebury Publishing (奥尔德肖特，英国：阿维伯里出版社).

Greenberg, M. A. （1984）（格林伯格）. *Auxiliary police：The citizen's approach to public safety*（《协警：公民为公共安全做贡献的方法》）. Westport, CT：Greenwood Press（韦斯特波特，康涅狄格州：格林伍德出版社）.

Greenberg, M. A. （2005）（格林伯格）. *Citizens defending America：From colonial times to the age of terrorism*（《保卫美国的公民：从殖民地时代到恐怖主义年代》）. Pittsburgh：University of Pittsburgh Press（匹兹堡：匹兹堡大学出版社）.

History Magazine（2001）（《历史杂志》）. The Cossacks（"哥萨克人"）. *History Magazine*（October/November）（《历史杂志》〈十月/十一月〉）. 2018 年 1 月 12 日 www. history-magazine. com/cossacks. html.

Information Services Department, Hong Kong Special Administrative Region government（2017, July）（信息服务部，香港特别行政区政府〈2017 年 7 月〉）. The police（"警察"）. 2018 年 1 月 12 日检索网址 www. gov. hk/en/about/abouthk/factsheets/docs/police. pdf.

Israel Police（n. d.）（以色列警察〈日期不详〉）. Structure（"组织结构"）. 2015 年 3 月 10 日检索网址 www. police. gov. il/english_contentPage. aspx? pid=4&menuid=5.

Jewish Telegraphic Agency（1994, November 30）（犹太电报局〈1994 年 11
P145 月 30 日〉）. Behind the headlines：Olim join Israeli Civil Guard to help bridge culture gaps（"头条新闻后面的故事：奥利姆加入以色列国民卫队帮助弥合文化差异"）. 2015 年 3 月 10 日检索网址 www. jta. org/1994/11/30/archive/behind-the-headlines-olim-join-israeli-civil-guard-to-help-bridge-culture-gaps.

Johnson, M. S. , Bonner, M. , & Hanser, R. D. （2017）（约翰逊、邦奈尔和汉塞尔）. "Doing more with less"：The professional model of the Los Angeles Police Department（"'少花钱多办事'：洛杉矶警察局的职业模式"）. In J. Albrecht（Ed.）（阿尔布雷希特主编）, *Police reserves and volunteers：Enhancing organizational effectiveness and public trust*（《警察后备人员和志愿者：提升组织的有效性和公信力》）, pp. 101—112. Boca Raton, FL：CRC Press（博卡-拉顿，佛罗里达州：CRC 出版社）.

Kardos, P. , & Szoke, B. （2017）（卡尔多斯和索克）. Auxiliary police in Hungary（"匈牙利协警"）. In J. Albrecht（阿尔布雷希特主编）, *Police reserves and volunteers：Enhancing organizational effectiveness and public trust*（《警察后备

人员和志愿者：提升组织的有效性和公信力》），pp 137—142. Boca Raton，FL：CRC Press（博卡-拉顿，佛罗里达州：CRC 出版社）.

Kelly，R. W.，Grasso，G. A.，Esposito，J. J.，Giannelli，R. J.，& Maroulis，A. J.（2008）（科利、格拉索、埃斯庖斯托、詹奈利和玛洛里斯）. *Auxiliary police program overview* 2008（《回顾 2008 年协警项目》）. New York：New York City Police Department Auxiliary（纽约：纽约市警察局协警）.

Koo，W.，& Tan，D.（2017）（库和谭）. Effectively using police volunteers in the "little red dot" Singapore（"在'小红点'新加坡高效使用辅警"）. In J. Albrecht（阿尔布雷希特主编），*Police reserves and volunteers：Enhancing organizational effectiveness and public trust*（《警察后备人员和志愿者：提升组织的有效性和公信力》），pp. 181—194. Boca Raton，FL：CRC Press（博卡-拉顿，佛罗里达州：CRC 出版社）.

Lam，C. B.（1997）（拉姆）. *Looking back with pride and glory*（《带着自豪和荣耀回首往昔》）. Hong Kong：Hong Kong Auxiliary Police Force（香港：香港辅警队）.

Library of Congress（2015，July 30）（国会图书馆〈2015 年 7 月 30 日〉）. Firearms-control legislation and policy：South Africa（"控枪法案与政策：南非"）. 2017 年 1 月 22 日检索网址 www. loc. gov/law/help/firearms-control/southafrica. php#ft29.

Luhn，A.（2014，February 21）（卢恩〈2014 年 2 月 21 日〉）. The Sochi soldiers：Morality police or outdated vigilantes？A look at the Cossacks patrolling the games-and whipping Pussy Riot activists（"索契士兵；是道德警察还是过时的义务警员？审视哥萨克人在赛事举行期间开展巡逻勤务——并且鞭打俄罗斯女子朋克乐队〈造反猫咪乐队〉积极分子"）. *The Independent*（《独立报》）. 2016 年 8 月 24 日检索网址 www. tndependent. co. uk/news/world/europe/the-sochi-soldiers-morality-police-or-outdated-vigilantes-a-look-at-the-cossacks-patrolling-the-9145387. html.

Lynott，L.（2016，July 23）（吕诺特〈2016 年 7 月 23 日〉）. Garda reserve numbers drop 26 per cent in two years，figures show（"在两年间加尔达后备人数下降了 26%，数据显示"）. *Irish Mirror*（《爱尔兰镜报》）. 2016 年 8 月 25 日检索网址 www. irishmirrorie/news/irish-news/crime/garda-reserve-numbers-drop-

26-8477875.

Malaysian Times（2013, January 10)（马来西亚时报〈2013年1月10日〉）. Volunteers hand-in-hand with police officers（“志愿者与警察携手并肩”）. 2016年9月1日检索网址 www. themalaysiantimes. commyvolunteers-hand-in-hand-with-police-officers.

Matrix（n. d.）（梅特里克斯〈日期不详〉）. What is the Matrix police ANPR system?（“梅特里克斯警察队的车牌自动识别系统是什么”）2015年3月13日检索网址 www. anpr. hu/matrix-police.

Maura, M.（2011, August 10)（莫拉〈2011年8月10日〉）. Ranks of Police Reserves to be increased（“后备警察的衔级将被增加”）. Bahamasnational. com. 2017年9月3日检索网址 http://bahamasnational. com/? q=node/977.

Metropolitan Police（n. d.）（大都会警察〈日期不详〉）. Employer supported policing（ESP）（“雇主支持警务”）. 2017年9月3日检索网址 www. met. poolice. uk/esp.

Moscow Times（2015, December 1)（《莫斯科时报》〈2015年12月1日〉）. Cossack volunteers to guard Moscow's Arbat Street（“哥萨克志愿者们保卫莫斯科的阿尔巴特街”）. 2016年8月24日检索网址 https://themoscowtimes. com/news/cossack-volunteers-to-guard-moscows-arbat-street-51012.

Palamarchuk, A.（2013, November 14)（帕拉马楚克〈2013年11月14日〉）. Veteran auxiliary police officer Hayward has served for 56 years（“资深协警海沃德已经服役56年了”）. Inside Toronto. com（在 Toronto. com 网站里）. 2016年8月25日检索网址 www. insidetoronto. com/news-story/4207800-veteran-auxiliary-police-officerhayward-has-served-for-56-years.

Palamarchuk, A.（2014, December 1)（帕拉马楚克〈2014年12月1日〉）. Kennedy Road BOA members donate cash and toys to Toronto police holiday toy drive（“肯尼迪路银行成员捐献现金和玩具给多伦多警察局假日玩具总动员活动”）. Inside Toronto. com（在 Toronto. com 网站里）. 2016年8月25日检索网址 www. insidetoronto. com/news-story/5164631-kennedy-road-bia-members-donate-cash-and-toys-to-toronto-police-holiday-toy-drive.

Phuket Tourist Police Volunteers（n. d.）（普吉岛旅游辅警〈日期不详〉）. Join our team（“加入我们团队”）. 检索网址 www. huket-tourist-police-volunteers. com/join. html.

Police Services Act (Ontario) (2015) (警察局法案〈安大略〉). Section 52 (1): Auxiliary members of municipal police force (“第52 (1): 市警察局协警成员”). 2017年9月3日检索网址 www. ontario. ca/laws/statute/90p15#BK75.

RaidióTeilifís Éireann (2015, February 20) (爱尔兰广播电视总台〈2015年2月20日〉). Garda Reserves to receive greater powers (“加尔达应该获得更大的权力”). 2016年8月31日检索网址 www. rte. ie/news/2015/0219/681492-garda-reserve.

Seddon, M. (2012, November 27) (赛登〈2012年11月27日〉). Russia's Cossacks start patrolling Moscow streets (“俄罗斯的哥萨克人开始巡逻莫斯科的街巷”). *The Washington Times* (《华盛顿时报》). 2016年8月24日检索网址 www. washingtontimescom/news/2012/nov/27/kremlin-tests-cossacks-as-an-auxiliary-police-forc.

Selih, A. , & Zavrsnik, A. (2012) (塞利赫和扎夫尔斯尼科). Crime and transition in central and eastern Europe (“中东部欧洲的犯罪与转型”). New York: Springer (纽约: 斯普林格).

Seth, R. (2006) (赛斯). *The specials* (《特别警员》). Trowbridge, UK: Cromwell Press (特洛布里奇, 英国: 克伦威尔出版社).

Singapore Police Force (n. d.) (新加坡警察局〈日期不详〉). A member of the home team (“内部团队的成员”). 2014年5月7日检索网址 www. spf. gov. sg/about/org/vsc. html#vsc.

South African Police Service (2014) (南非警察局). How to become a reservist (“怎样成为一名后备警察”). 2017年1月20日检索网址 www. saps. gov. za/services/reservist. php.

Torn, P. , & Verbiest, R. (2017) (措恩和维尔比斯特). Reserve Police Force in the Netherlands: From a “reserve” to a “volunteer” police force (“荷兰后备警察队伍: 从‘后备’到‘志愿’警察队伍”). In J. Albrecht (阿尔布雷希特主编), *Police reserves and volunteers: Enhancing organizational effectiveness and public trust* (《警察后备人员和志愿者: 提升组织的有效性和公信力》), pp. 171—180. Boca Raton, FL: CRC Press (博卡-拉顿, 佛罗里达州: CRC出版社).

Toronto Police Service（n. d. －a）（多伦多警察局〈日期不详 －a〉）. Frequently asked questions（“总是被问问题”）. 2016 年 8 月 25 日检索网址 www. torontopolice. onca/careers/auxfaq. php.

Toronto Police Service（n. d. –b）（多伦多警察局〈日期不详 –b〉）. Toronto Police Auxiliary（“多伦多警察局协警”）. 2016 年 8 月 25 日检索网址 www. torontopolice. on. ca/community/auxiliary. php.

Volunteer Special Constabulary（1998）（志愿特别警员队）. *Service to the nation*：*50 years of the Volunteer Special Constabulary*（《为国家服务：志愿特别警员队的 50 年历史》）. Singapore：Volunteer Special Constabulary（新加坡：志愿特别警员队）.

Wolf，R. （2014）（沃尔夫）. The Orange County（Florida）Sheriff's Office Reserve Unit（“奥兰治县（佛罗里达州）县治安官办公室后备警察部门”）. *Special Impact*（《特殊影响》）（16），12—13.

Wolf，R.，& Beary，K. （2010）（沃尔夫和比瑞）. The Orange County Sheriff's Office Reserve Unit：A strong，cohesive unit able to handle multiple functions（“奥兰治县县治安官办公室后备警察部门：一个强大有凝聚力的队伍能够履行多项职责”）. *Deputy and Court Officer*（《助理和法院官员》），2（2），26—30.

World Police（n. d. ）（世界警察〈日期不详〉）. Israel Police and auxiliary（“以色列警察和协警”）. 2015 年 3 月 10 日检索网址 http：//world－police. com/？page_id＝142.

第九章　辅警的未来发展 P147

本书对美国和英国的辅警，尤其是英国英格兰和威尔士的辅警进行了梳理和探讨。在整个过程中，我们尽力明确了三地之间辅警的异同以及美国各司法管辖区域之间各种各样的辅警类别，而且对全球使用辅警的许多不同方法给出了我们的看法。然而，美国辅警项目如此巨大的差异，使得将美国与任何其他地方——不论是将美国境内的辅警还是在一州之内的辅警进行对比都几乎是不可能的。正如本书前文指出的，在一个州被叫作协警，在另一个州可能被称为参与巡逻的公民；一个州在辅警权力和职权方面的授权就完全不适用于其他州的辅警。美国使用辅警方式的这种多样性，已经成为一个既令人自豪又令人担忧的事情。

本书阐述了警务和志愿服务的原则，并展示了它们取得的一波又一波的进步。在很多更需要志愿服务的时期，如战争时期和自然灾害发生时期，以及在近年来网络犯罪增长以及极端主义和恐怖主义危险加剧时期，志愿服务越来越多。在二十一世纪第一个十年的后半期，全球经济困境[①]已经导致预算紧缩和服务业萎缩，在公共部门尤其如此。这反过来又在不同方面给美国和英国警务部门造成了越来越大的压力，而且辅警的未来可能要依赖于对这些政治和经济威胁的反应。

美国辅警的未来

地方控制和国家控制

使用辅警的警察局局长和县治安官，常常急于表示他们已经用其社区支持的方式塑造了其辅警项目。一些地区以及警察机构现在正在鼓励有警察职权的辅警，而另一些则在担心，给辅警提供警察培训和职权会导致潜在的安全、雇用以及管控方面的问题。高度工会化的州对辅警的反应，往往类似于一个罢工工人对越过警戒线之人的蔑视。在这些州，辅警可能有非常少的职权或者培训；实际 P148

上，一些警察局不使用后备警察或者协警，因为他们的工会合同特别禁止使用有警察权的辅警（Bartels，2013）。

2015 年 4 月，俄克拉荷马州塔尔萨的罗伯特 · 贝茨所处的状况（本书前文有述），同样引发人们对全美辅警未来的担忧。不仅贝茨先生在误用枪支——当时他以为是泰瑟枪——案中因过失杀人罪名成立被判入狱四年，而且塔尔萨的县治安官也被刑事起诉并因为该事故辞职。大陪审团以轻罪指控县治安官史丹利 · 格兰兹，指控包括格兰兹非法截留要求发布有关塔尔萨后备警察助理项目内部调查的电子邮件。在约一年后，格兰兹承认故意违法以及毫不犹豫地拒绝履行公务，[②]因为他没有向新闻界提交一份成文于 2009 年的关于贝茨徇私舞弊的调查报告（Killman，2016）。在这个案子中，塔尔萨县治安官办公室，像过去讲到的其他例子中的县治安官办公室一样，饱受批评：塔尔萨的后备警察部门或者辅警部门都是“金钱换权力”[③]的部门，允许政治支持者们履行执法职能。在塔尔萨此次事故中，县治安官被指控允许贝茨继续做辅警，即便他没有完成要求的培训，因为贝茨是格兰兹的朋友，而且贝茨曾向县治安官办公室捐款（Krehbiel-Burton & Pérez-Peña，2015）。

塔尔萨事故理所当然已经引起美国许多执法机构反思他们有关辅警操作的政策和程序规定，而且已经引起一些警察领导重新思考他们涉足辅警的程度，或者重新思考从中全身而退的可能性。该事故还导致美国执法机构认证委员会（CALEA，Commission on Accreditation for Law Enforcement Agencies）——一个非官方的私人认证组织——要求已经获得认证的执法机构改变自己对有关宣誓警察类型辅警的惯常做法。从 2017 年 4 月 1 日以来，执法机构认证委员会不再为有若干“级别”宣誓后备警察的警察机构实施认证；全部后备警察必须接受与全职警察职员一样的培训。执法机构认证委员会对经过他们认证的执法机构提出这一要求，即便与执法机构所在州的法律规定相悖，就像在加利福尼亚州和佛罗里达州发生的那样（Commission on Accreditation for Law Enforcement Agencies，2017）。美国执法机构没有被要求都要获得认证，而且许多执法机构和研究人员已经在质疑：认证过程昂贵的例行程序，是否切实帮助其避免诉讼或者增强其社区信任度（Hougland &Wolf，2016）。从长远来看，这将怎样影响辅警还有待观察。一些现在具有执法机构认证委员会认证的警察机构和县治安官机构，已经威胁要离开执法机构认证委员会，因为现有的诸多要求（包括参加认证带来的财政压力）。但是另一些执法机构则觉得参加认证将提升辅警的职业精神，而且认证

P149

的导向是正确的。但是，我们应该注意到，美国大多数使用辅警的执法机构不会在意执法机构认证委员会的认证要求，[④]而且很可能会无视那些要求（Hougland &Wolf，2016）。

但是，如果获得认证的执法机构采纳了这些要求，那么执法机构认证委员会的限制要求，会给那些依靠由未获得完全认证的执法辅警们奉献志愿时间以及提供社区联系的执法机构带来相当大的困难。这方面的一个例子就是佛罗里达州高速公路巡逻协警队（FHPA，Florida Highway Patrol Auxiliary）。佛罗里达州高速公路巡逻队（FHP，Florida Highway Patrol）是一个获得执法机构认证委员会认证的机构，而执法机构认证委员会针对获得协助认证的辅警新出台的重大限制规定，可能使佛罗里达州高速公路巡逻队不能继续运作其志愿者项目。佛罗里达州高速公路巡逻协警队已经报告其队员人数呈螺旋式下降，从二十世纪七十年代的最高点大约1000名队员，到现在的人数不足300名协警。舍费尔（Sheffer，2017）报告说这种人数的降低部分原因可能是佛罗里达州对辅警培训要求不断提高。[⑤]

美国全国县治安官协会外联委员会后备执法专门小组也回应了塔尔萨事故。该委员会一直致力于为那些使用后备助理的县治安官的部门和官员们提出标准化建议。现实造成的障碍存在一个大家都熟知的问题：全美对待辅警身份宣誓警察的方式有太多不同，以至于无法制定一项在所有司法管辖区域、在所有州以及对所有当选的县治安官都适用的单一政策建议。国际警察局长协会还曾试图寻找一个处理辅警问题的方法。通过其期刊《警察局长》上的各种论文，国际警察局长协会讨论后备警察的领导、组织、培训以及职能；但是大家的基本看法是一致的：现在完善这些方面的做法太多了。至少有一篇论文已经建议：现在需要标准化，至少应根据辅警的职能确定他们的称谓（Wolf，Albrecht & Dobrin，2015）。该篇论文的建议是，因为美国各地做法不同，也因为培训的作用和水平参差不齐，最好确定辅警常见的级别分类（Albrecht，2017）：

P150

级别1——警察机构事务辅警（未配枪）/无逮捕或执法职权：包括那些接受的警察培训非常少或者没有接受过警察培训的人，他们是穿着制服或者不穿制服的人员，而且他们帮助警察机构履行管理职责、处理公共关系事件、从事小型交通管制工作或者履行其他非执法职能的人。

级别2——社区巡逻（未配枪）/无逮捕或执法职权：这包括那些接受一定

程度的培训且所受培训被记录在案的人员，他们是穿着制服或者不穿制服的人员，他们开展巡逻活动并且是警务机构的“眼睛和耳朵”。这一级别的人员不会履行任何执法职能，也没有获得任何职权。

级别3——警察巡逻（未配枪）/某些执法权：这包括那些接受过部分或中等程度培训且所受培训被记录在案的人员，他们是穿着制服或者不穿制服的人员，他们开展巡逻活动并且是警务机构的“眼睛和耳朵”，但要从事某种类型的执法工作或拥有某种类型的执法职权。这可以包括有能力发布停车罚单、有能力撰写简单警察报告以及从事类似工作。

级别4——宣誓辅警（配枪）/大多数执法权：这包括那些接受过相当程度的培训且所受培训被记录在案的人员，他们是穿着制服或不穿制服的人员，从事或者有能力从事执法工作。他们的执法职权或者职责可能是有限的。例如，这有可能包括那些没有职权独自开展工作或者没有职权在下班后实施警察行为的人。

级别5——宣誓辅警（配枪）/全部执法权：这包括那些穿着制服或不穿制服的人员，他们以相当于全职、职业执法官员的身份工作。这些人与全职执法人员一样，拥有的职权或者承担的责任均不受限，而且遵照相同的法规工作，接受相同的培训。

（Wolf et al.，2015，p. 47）

确立一个全国体系，如上文所述的这个体系，将会使地方警察和县治安官办公室对其希望辅警能够去做的事情可以保持地方控制，而且将会为讨论那些在各种“级别”上提供服务的人员的职权时，创造一个全国通用的术语。如果美国向全国标准化方向发展，这一体系将会考虑到由州法律授权的工作职能所需的具体培训要求。

选拔

在美国做辅警的先决条件各种各样，常常与所需培训的级别一样多。警务全职岗位也是同样的情况。众多州要求全职警察完成高中教育，尽管奥古斯特·沃尔默早在1916年就指出，如果警察接受过更高的教育，[⑥]就很少有警察机构会对

P151

教育提出要求。尽管有研究表明，在关键决策技能、积极态度、更少专断行为以及更容易接受他人种族的方面，大学学位起到了积极作用（Carter & Sapp，1990；Weiner，1976；Dalley，1975），但是还是有研究表明接受过大学教育的警察对警务工作的满意度更少，而且对他们的角色可能会更加愤世嫉俗（Hudzik，1978；Regoli，1976；Lefkowitz，1974）。最后，有研究指出，说到专业性和工作满足感，接受过大学教育的警察与那些所受教育相比较少的人没什么区别（Miller & Fry，1976）。

即使考虑到这个事实，美国招聘警察的要求几乎在近100年没有增加过，[7]但在把接受过更高教育的人招进警察部门方面已经有了重大进展。希拉尔和丹斯莱（Hilal & Densley，2013）发现，他们在明尼苏达州[8]和亚利桑那州研究的964名警察中，有48%的警察至少具有四年制学位。在他们所研究的警察中，有54%的警察回复说自从他们开启职业生涯前后获得过大学学分。包莱恩等人（Paoline et al.，2015）发现，他们开展研究所用的七个警察机构[9]，没有一个要求四年制学位的，但是在他们研究的2109名警察中，有45%的警察具有学士学位或者更高学位，而且这些学位大多数在警察开启警务生涯的时候就已经获得了。

对那些向往获得或者已经获得执法机构认证委员会认证的美国机构来说，那些拥有至少部分执法职权的辅警，被要求具备像他们的全职同事一样的最低教育标准。[10]但是，大多数州（或大多数机构）对辅警没有任何教育标准要求。为了成为更有竞争力的岗位申请者或者为了增加晋升机会，全职警察可以主动获得大学学位（Hilal & Densley，2013），而辅警可能不关注这些事。从事警务工作的辅警来自所有公共和私人职业，包括技工、律师、部长、教师、学校管理者、商户、消防员、会计和航空公司飞行员，因而辅警们具备所有层级的正规教育，而且许多辅警具备研究生学位。当然，在选择辅警时，要求遵照像全职岗位申请者一样的最低教育标准，这是在保持全美后备警察部门和协警部门的专业精神方面迈出的积极一步。

但是，对某些人口的高等教育要求有没有负面影响呢？如果一个机构打算挑选人员做前文所述的级别3的辅警，高中教育要求能够将社区——特别是社会经济更低的司法管辖区域中的一个重要部分排除在外吗？美国同等雇用机会委员会（US Equal Employment Opportunity Commission，2016）建议，警务机构与教育研究机构建立合作关系，以便提供实习机会以及为将要获得大学学位的潜在少数族裔申请者提供一个入职通道。这些合作关系还可以帮助处理少数族裔人员可能

P152

存在的那种对警方由来已久的负面看法（US Equal Employment Opportunity Commission，2016）。[11]如果把已然增加的教育要求应用于辅警，想要知道这一要求会产生何种结果，这是不可能的事情。我们对美国辅警人口统计方面所知甚少（Dobrin & Wolf，2016）。实际上，最近对美国县治安官办公室辅警的研究表明，在辅警中少数族裔的人数甚至比在正规警察中的人数还要少。在该研究中，调查问卷答卷人几乎全是男性（92%），而且几乎全是白人（89%），而全美县治安官助理中大约有80%是白人（Wolf，Holmes & Jones，2016）。

培训

美国警务处在严密的审查之下。这种审查似乎时起时落，但是，在我们即将迎来2020年的时候，警方（可以包括任何与政府组织的警务有关的人员，包括志愿后备警察和协警项目，甚至是邻里守望计划）看起来从来没有处在如此高精度的显微镜之下。[12]在美国接近18000个执法机构中，几乎有一半的执法机构的警察不超过十名，而且许多州对初警培训或年度再培训没有特别要求。而那些对这些培训有要求的州，要求变化则很大。警察机构之间有很大差异，不仅表现在所需培训的数量上，而且表现在聘用前要求方面：背景审查、最低标准以及对全职、有偿警察来说也许最重要的是——薪水。[13]我们一直在国家层面讨论培训要求的改革问题，但不是没有争议。尽管令美国人自豪的一点可能有时是政府的分权制度，然而正是这个分权制度给正规警察全国培训标准的制定造成了冲突。这种例子可以在“使用武力指导原则”中找到。“使用武力指导原则”是由警察高级官员研究论坛（PERF，Police Executive Research Forum）——一个位于华盛顿特区的非营利性组织——制定出来的，希望创造有关警察使用武力的全国标准。“使用武力指导原则”试图影响美国警方应对暴力的方式。该原则被运用在警方
P153 职员培训中，但是遇到来自全美警察领导相当大的抵触（O'Linn，2016）。对专业化来说，培训像警察使用武力一样重要。而如果警察领导不能就培训形成适当的导向意见，那么我们有理由相信，对辅警所需培训达成全美一致是十分渺茫的。

培训还有一个费用问题。提供附加强制培训的大量开销，是许多所受资助不多的警察机构考虑标准化警察培训时，争论的一个矛盾问题，也是辅警部门关注的问题。正如本书前文提到的，志愿者可以无偿工作，但是这并不意味着他们来工作不会给警察机构产生花销。用仅仅几周的培训让有意愿的志愿者参加学习，

使他们能够自愿以警察身份工作，这可能很吸引人，然而，别的机构可能要求在月复一月的院校培训之后，还要求一年或更长时间的在职培训。但是新人们不可能明白的是，可能的最高级别的培训将会切实引导组织更加专业，使组织赢得更多社区信任——或许更为重要的是——降低辅警将来被诉的可能性，这对那些行为不当的执法辅警来说尤为重要。[14]

使用前全职职员做辅警

英国和美国辅警一个主要区别是，一些美国警察机构随时会使用前全职警察。这种情况发生在全职警察退休或者变换职业的时候，而且警察机构使用警察个人的“职业知识”——不然“职业知识”可能会被警察忘记。这种情况不仅仅限于身着制服的巡逻警察。许多警察机构已经允许延续警察职业当后备警察的前全职警察继续工作。前全职警察做实战培训教官、院校教官、侦探和调查员或者驻校警察。正如在第七章讨论过的，一个对全美县治安官办公室开展的问卷调查表明，28%的辅警填写问卷说他们具有以前做全职执法警察的经验。这些辅警报告说，以前做助理或者警察时积累了全职工作经验，在之前的岗位上平均工作时间是 12. 7 年（Wolf et al. , 2016）。问卷调查样本范围有限，原因在于自我选择偏差，但还是对警察机构怎样使用富有前工作经验的警察提出了一些见解。在美国，警察机构使用前警察受地理位置所限。正如前文所讨论的，在美国南部和西部，这是很普遍的现象，但是在美国东部和北部则不太可能出现（由于与警察工会的矛盾，此点在上文有述）。

通过考察 2001 年 9 月 11 日之后纽约市警察局发生的事情，我们可以从中看到有可能使用前全职职员的例子。纽约市警察局协警项目，本书在前文几处描述过该项目，是一个由志愿者做警方的“眼睛和耳朵”、为警方提供巨大支持的项目——然而，他们没有任何执法职权。在 9 · 11 事件那天，与美国其他地方的执法机构不同，纽约市警察局没有正式措施让退休人员和前全职警察做富有警务经验或具备警察职权的“随时后备”市民。2001 年纽约市遭遇恐怖袭击后，纽约市警察局被那些已退休的前警察打来的电话淹没了，因为他们希望帮助纽约市恢复常态。不幸的是，这些美好意愿未能实现，因为没有协调这一努力的举措、方法，也没有预案可用（Mormino，2001；Tobin，2017）。2005 年，纽约市启动一个退休人员动员计划（RMP，Retiree Mobilization Plan）。该计划将纽约市警察局“活跃的退休警察”列出一个名单，作为危急时刻动员人员的资料。尽管这不是

P154

一个后备警察项目（退休人员没有执法职权），但是这一做法彰显了前警察对其警察机构的价值（Reuss，2005），而且这使身怀特殊技能的退休人员随时准备在危机事件期间自愿提供服务。[15]尽管在美国有一些城市已经开始实施短期项目，再次雇用退休警察[16]到全职警察岗位上工作，但是，尤其是在美国东北部，只有少量执法机构注意到持续培训的潜在好处以及宣誓后备警察项目的志愿性质。

现在，人们寄希望于联邦政府制定法律让美国辅警至少在某些方面能够有统一标准。在全美就一名警察从一州到另一州后是否可以或者是否应该合法持枪这个问题争论多年之后，联邦政府采取行动制定了《执法官员安全法》（LEOSA，the Law Enforcement Officers Safety Act）。这部联邦法律允许，不论是现在有资质的执法官员还是有资质的退休执法官员，在美国任何地方都可以隐秘携带枪支（一些情况例外），无视并取代所有州的法律。[17]联邦干预还有可能对规范警察机构使用前全职警察或退休警察做后备人员的能力有所帮助，减少警察机构在全职警察离开某一岗位时发生的“人才流失”情况，而退休警察在岗位上形成的良好信誉本来可以被好好利用。

关于辅警项目以及参与者的年度数据

目前，美国司法部的司法统计局收集全美所有警察机构和县治安官机构的数
P155 据。这些数据是司法统计局要求这些机构上报才收集起来的，并且通过执法管理和行政统计（LEMAS，Law Enforcement Management and Administrative Statistics）调查，司法统计局每隔几年就会对这些数据加以整理。执法管理和行政统计汇编来自所有雇用100名或者更多宣誓警察的地方执法机构的数据，并且汇编来自全国有代表性的更小规模的执法机构样本的数据。执法管理和行政统计仅仅收集每个参与调查的机构内无偿提供服务的后备警察和协警的人数。而人口统计学数据，如受教育层次、性别和种族以及非宣誓辅警人数的数据，没有被收集或者被报告。美国联邦调查局的统一犯罪报告系统，同样收集警察机构内全职有偿警察的数据，但是不收集兼职警察或者辅警的任何数据。另外，有辅警项目的美国州内，几乎有一半的州报告说它们不保留兼职警察或者辅警的任何数据或者收集这些人的任何信息资料（Dobrin & Wolf，2016）。辅警项目可能对地方社区和政府预算产生经济影响，但受目前可用数据的限制，不可能估算该经济影响的州级和全国范围的成本。

对美国辅警的未来发展来说，迫切需要将数据收集和报告的方法在国家层面

正式化，包括参与者的人口统计信息以及已完成培训的级别。通过同时搜集辅警参与他们项目的程度来增加有用的数据。之前提到的明确辅警职责范围的“级别”体系，还将会对数据价值有所帮助。收集那些使分析辅警使用情况成为可能的数据也很重要。正如本书讨论过的，辅警在传统巡逻职责之外被用在各种岗位上。辅警在多大程度上被用在犯罪侦查、送达逮捕令、在专业部门工作（如海上巡逻队、骑警队、警犬队、搜救队、潜水队等）、酒驾检查点、学校和年轻人项目以及其他非巡逻活动上，就此问题搜集的信息数据将会使警察机构确定此类项目在其司法管辖区域中的实用性。

英国辅警的未来

大多数人作出恰当的决定——遵守法律和秩序，而且在早期声明中，如罗伯特·比尔爵士的 1829 年“执法原则”，包含一个依赖原则——“警察履行职责的权力”有赖于公众对警察的存在、行动、行为的认可，有赖于警察获得并保持公众对其尊重的能力（Peel，1829）。“满意决定警务”已经是英格兰和威尔士重要的且长期存在的警务原则，因此公众对警方提供服务的信心在维持法律和秩序方面是很重要的因素。另外，公众在向警方提供信息方面表现出的协作精神和心甘情愿，是犯罪行为经常被侦破的原因。 P156

杰克逊、布拉德福德、霍夫和默里（Jackson，Bradford，Hough & Murray，2012）对警察合法性和公正性开展了详尽的讨论，警察合法性和公正性与警方/公众之间的信任有关。公众信任警方很重要，这是英格兰和威尔士刑事司法系统的一个重要组成部分，而且从 1981 年以来，通过英格兰和威尔士犯罪调查（以前称为英国犯罪调查），警方对公众开展持续不断的问卷调查。在该调查中，对警方信任的问题是一个例行题目。尽管该问题没有特别提到特别警员而是简单提到警察，但是，有足够的证据表明，公众对辅警这个类别只有一点点认识或者没有任何认识。

英国警务的现状

美国地方警察机构遇到的公众负面评价问题，英国最近没有遇到。[18]在英格兰和威尔士，公众反对警方开枪这个问题很少出现，因为武装警察在英格兰和威尔士不常见。对大多数人来说，他们对犯罪和警务的看法来自媒体，因而媒体的价值取向和政治节操左右着对所发生事情的“解释”（Reiner，2002）。2017 年 7

月，政府统计表明，尽管警察人数减少了，但是对地方警察的信任度从 2005—2006 年的 63%上升到 2016—2017 年的 78%（Flatley，2017）。但是，新闻舆论喜欢描绘一幅更为暗淡的画面，它们关注的是警察人数的降低以及警察开枪导致的事故增多。例如，新闻报道显示英格兰和威尔士目前仅仅有超过 123000 名全职警察，从 2010 年以来减少了 20500 名（Hargreaves，Husband & Linehan，2017）。同样的情况是，特别警员的人数从 2008 年的 14544 名到 2017 年 3 月下降至 13503 名（Hargreaves et al.，2017）。在同一时间段，专业武装警察的人数也从 2010 年的 6796 名到 2016 年下降至 5639 名（Mason & Walker，2017；Bletchly，2017）。但是，在 2017 年 8 月，有新闻报道说，接受枪支培训的警察随着涉枪事件的增加而增加（Jones & Rodger，2017）。2017 年 3 月的一则报道说："在截止到 2017 年 3 月 31 日的年度里，警方在十起事件中有开枪行为，比上一年的七起有所增加"（Home Office，2017）。

上述广为人知的数据显示了警察人力资本的显著下降，并且使正规全职警察的水平处于自 1985 年以来的最低点。新闻报道同样关注了警务人数降低对全职
P157 警察的影响。一则报道指出，自 2012 年以来，47%的警察因为压力、焦虑以及抑郁而请假，这加剧了全职警察人数的减少（Sutherland，2017）；该报道还指出，自 2011 年以来，警方经费减少了 20%，而女王陛下警察监察局（HMIC，Her Majesty's Inspectorate of Constabulary）已经报告说侦探和其他调查员出现的严重短缺现在属于"国家危机"（Grierson，2017）。

观察小组已经提出警告：如果达到 2011 年时规模的骚乱今天在伦敦再次出现，那么警方将会仓促应对。英国内政大臣安伯·吕德已经意识到，过度为警方提供资源的做法不可能继续下去，尤其是考虑到 2017 年在伦敦和曼彻斯特发生的恐怖袭击。警方需要大量的财力和人力资源去应对混乱，迫使警方动用预算储备（Grierson，2017）。不幸的是，关于警察队伍实力和警方经费的统计最终是一个政治问题——根据媒体的报道，这个问题使时任英国首相特蕾莎·梅在 2017 年 6 月处于守势，当时人们在谈论削减警务和武装警察的人数（Mason & Walker，2017）。

正规警务的未来发展在英国是不明朗的。媒体不断充实话题，呼吁增加更多的武装警察、更多的穿着制服巡逻的警察、更多的调查员以及更好的预算。尽管在英格兰和威尔士，只有不到二十分之一的警察有配枪（英国的组成部分北爱尔兰，倒有一支武装警察部队）。而且尽管近期发生这样的事件，一项于 2017 年在

大都会警察中开展的研究发现，只有26%的警察人员觉得他们应当例行携带枪支（Rathi，2017；Walker，2017）。但是，几乎有一半（43.6%）的伦敦警察对相同调查的回答是：他们认为应该有更多的用枪专才（这表明受过用枪培训的、有能力应对高风险危机事件的警察人数应该增加），而且12%的调查问卷答卷人说他们从来不想带枪上班（Walker，2017）。

给警察配枪在英格兰和威尔士是有争议的，这个问题最近再次出现，在大都会警察局成员中这是最常见的问题。大都会警察局的成员在这个国家一个又大又多样的地区——包括伦敦大都会地区（但是不包括伦敦城）维护法律和秩序。[19]在英格兰和威尔士携带枪支并使用枪支与美国警务风格表现十分不同。例如，2017年3月31日，在英格兰和威尔士有6278名经授权可以带枪的警察（AFOs，authorized firearms officers）。但是，这些警察大多数并不是日常部署的时刻备勤的武装人员，而是在一辆武装防暴车里听候召唤参加突发事件处置的武装人员（Hargreaves et al.，2017）。这部分人员仅仅相当于所有全职警察的五分之一。据说，武装警察不是常规可调动人员，而是仅可用在特殊、高危地区，如机场、海港以及大型群众集会场所。他们仅可被用在需要被使用的地方。仅仅在极端环境中，才会拿出类似武器，而且在更少的情境下，才会开枪。来自2017年3月的警方数据显示，在前一年，共发生15705起需要武装警察处置的事件，在其中84%的事件中警方出动了武装防暴车。在全部事件处置中，仅有十起导致警察开枪（Home Office，2017）。 P158

在英国，经授权可以带枪的警员在未来枪支培训以及增加人数方面的问题将怎样发展还有待观察，而且这要看许多因素，包括公众的认知、警方的经费以及英国警察局的领导力。这些问题将怎样影响特别警员履行警务职责的方式，同样有待观察。如果为应对国家关切的问题，英国正规警察局向武装更多的警察方向发展的话（而且根据前期问卷调查，这一点也无法被保证），那么这会不会影响目前的状况，因为现在没有特别警员可以受训去做经授权可以带枪的警察？

通过非常有限的方式，英国警察局已经看到了在非传统岗位使用特别警员的好处，[20]但是，这会继续扩大吗？特别警员通常在需要的时候被派去帮助正规警察（例如，在骚乱平息之后，或者像奥运会这样的大型活动），但是，特别警员的大多数职责都是“围绕着相当单调乏味的工作，用清晰可见的人数充斥辖区，由此让公众产生安全感”（Duerden，2017）。当然，个别警察局也的确允许它们的特别警员接受特殊专业培训，一如本书前文所述。

在英国近代史上，“辅警”被允许带枪的历史中可以找到的最近的例子，是在英格兰地区发生的獾灭除案。在英格兰地区，一些专家坚持认为牛结核病（bTB，bovine tuberculosis）是由獾传染给牛的，灭除（杀死动物）是最快、最有效的减少危险的方法。尽管关于牛结核病与獾之间关系的研究遭到质疑（Carrington，2016），但是已经持有猎枪的英国地方农夫被登记在册，得到五年射击獾的许可，这是政府项目的一部分（Department for Environment，Food and Rural Affairs，2016）。已经有报告说，从 2013 年灭除行动开始以来，已经有超过 14000 只獾被杀死。尽管这些志愿者本身没有接受任何警方或政府的培训，但是这是在英国能找到的仅有的例子：本地人，普通人，而不是警察，获得此种授权去使用枪支（Department for Environment，Food and Rural Affairs，2016；Carrington，2016）。

特别警员的看法以及对特别警员的看法

P159 对特别警员的培训在英国基本上是标准化的，尽管英国对辅警的使用不是标准化的。正规英国警察（与美国一些机构的同行相似）可能把特别警员视为缺少培训的人员、业余爱好者以及不太专业的人员。尽管英国特别警员组织的规划要依赖标准化，但是对特别警员怎样使用、怎样培训或者怎样授权他们参加执法工作，警察局之间仍然存在差异。一个例子就是，某些警察局不允许特别警员受训驾驶警用汽车或者从事警用汽车驾驶工作。但是，另一些警察局没有类似的限制，而且在这些警察局，特别警员不仅被授权可以驾驶警用汽车，而且可以在高危、紧急情况下驾驶警用汽车。

一名英国警察，用警员艾莉·布劳格斯这个笔名写作，写出一本关于她在 2007 年做正规警察的经历，书名是《随叫随到女警日记》。她还向记者讲述了特别警员以及英国正规警察对特别警员缺乏尊重的情况。“他们（特别警员）中大多数每周只工作一天。”警员布劳格斯说。“不是所有警察都像他们那样。是的，事实如此。例如，特别警员不能一路跟着案子直到法庭审判，因此他们对调查没有什么帮助。而且许多特别警员甚至不能正确地陈述，因为他们不知道怎么陈述。如果你不能做陈述，那么你就不能完全明白法律”（Duerden，2010）。

在 2016 年的一项对伦敦特别警员的定性研究中，许多参与者感觉到需要有附加培训（在这次研究中，重点是急救）；他们指出，每年的培训是不够的，而且每三个月或六个月培训一次，将会使特别警员在处置紧急情况时有更好的准备。在此研究中，特别警员同样感觉到，现场第二人是全职警察或者志愿性质的特别警员，对特别警员来说都是身体和情感支持的来源（Chandan & Meakin，2016）。其他研究已经表明，英国特别警员对他们在一个警务现场处置问题的职业能力很有信心，但是对访谈和管理性质的警察文书工作不太有信心（Wolf，Pepper & Dobrin，2017）。

北安普顿大学的公共安全、犯罪和司法研究所（IPSCJ，Institute for Public Safety，Crime and Justice），在2014年对北安普顿郡特别警员开展了调查研究。该研究发现，激励特别警员自愿奉献的一个关键因素是：他们渴望在未来成为全职警察。过去，那些想成为正规警察的特别警员发现，通常情况下，当他们向他们选择的警察局提出申请时，他们做辅警的经历不被考虑在内。但是，这种情况在最近几年发生了彻底改变，现实的情况常常是，全职警察岗位申请者必须在培训期间成为特别警员。公共安全、犯罪和司法研究所的研究发现，那些年轻的特别警员更有可能想要升到全职岗位上，而且这一激励因素对特别警员队维持人员来说可能是一个长期存在的问题（Institute for Public Safety，Crime and Justice，2014）。这可能同样倾向于让他们自己产生这样的看法，即特别警员的职业性不如他们的正规、全职警察同事们。尽管特别警员可能个人有技术、有知识、有能力可以运用到自己的岗位工作中，但是许多特别警员觉得，在一个根据可用性分配任务的系统里，这些技术、知识和能力都被浪费了。正如我们在下面关于网络犯罪部分讨论的，有效使用这些技能可以帮助警察局更加有效地使用专业人才（Institute for Public Safety，Crime and Justice，2014）。 P160

一些特别警员注意到了一些令人担忧的问题：缺少适当装备，警察局没有给他们提供执法记录仪（BWCs，Body-Worn Cameras）。从警察局到警察局，给特别警员配发装备要依据警察局优先考虑的东西和可用的经费，因此，尽管一些特别警员将会配发大多数配发给全职警察的装备，但是在别的警察局他们携带不多的装备来保护他们自己或者完成被指派的工作。

同样有报告说，专业人才离开辅警岗位，原因是他们觉得没有得到警察组织的尊重，而且“令人难以置信的是，现在缺少对特别警员的帮助和支持”（BBC，2017）。当然，不是所有的特别警员都同意当前存在对其辅警工作不尊重的情况，但是未来的研究需要对提供服务的个人不同的动机、忠诚以及士气加以探究。

网络犯罪

以前由全职调查员和侦探一手把控的网络犯罪侦查领域，现在已经向特别警员开放了。2016 年，时任英国内政大臣的特蕾莎・梅宣布多项变革，允许志愿者在计算机调查或会计调查方面为警察局工作。特蕾莎・梅说："我们希望鼓励那些在特别领域有技术的人员，如那些具备 IT 专业知识或者会计技术的人员，与警察一起工作侦查网络犯罪或金融犯罪，并且帮助警察和警方工作人员在更广泛领域里与犯罪作斗争"（Barrett，2016）。汉普郡警察局和格洛斯特郡警察局是英国最先宣布正在使用受过高级培训的 IT 工作人员的警察局。这两个警察局使用 IT 工作人员支持一个为期 12 个月的飞行员项目，有五名特别警员和五名支援警察的志愿者。[21]如果该飞行员项目成功完成，那么网络特别警员和网络志愿者（CSCV，Cyber Special Constable and Cyber Volunteers）项目有可能成为全英国的

P161 样板，但是该项目遭到警界一些领导人的批评。反对者认为，通过为全职、有偿职员提供培训和资源来打击不断增长的网络犯罪问题，政府将会获得更好的服务。

有关辅警的其他问题

在过去的几年里，美国反对警察的示威活动不断增加，同样增加的还有导致执法警察死亡或受伤的伏击事件。由此产生一种担忧：雇用新警察将会更加困难，而且目前的全职警察有可能决定另谋他路。这同样会对辅警的角色产生影响。那些自愿以警察身份工作的人可能受社会负面压力的影响，很可能这种影响的程度与那些在这些岗位上为服务而获得报酬的人一样。

英国同样正在面临警务工作的压力，尽管他们这些压力源自经济削减而不是袭击事件。根据英国全国警察荣誉榜，从 2010 年到 2017 年 7 月，在 43 个警察局有 42 人死亡，但是只有一名警察是被恐怖分子袭击杀死，有三名是被枪杀（其中两人在同一起事件中牺牲）（National Police Officers' Roll of Honour, n. d.）。自 2010 年以来，只有一名特别警员被列入全国警察荣誉榜，这名特别警员是因为下班撞车而亡。

在伦敦，针对警察的以及在曼彻斯特针对市民的恐怖分子高调袭击事件增多，[22]使警察不是牺牲就是严重受伤（Tacopino，2017；Sheth，Mark & Edwards，2017；Mills，2017）。这对那些做特别警员的人将会产生的潜在影响还有待观察。

考虑到袭击事件，那么这些事件会起到鼓励作用吗，即鼓励更多有公民意识的社区成员进一步接受必要的培训成为特别警员队的一名成员；或者这些事件会起到阻止作用吗，即阻止公民以警察身份提供服务。

尽管本书试图证明辅警能够为社区和警察机构提供的巨大内在价值，但是要证明一名辅警有可能为一个警察机构节省的实际财政价值几乎是不可能的。许多警察机构根据小时工资数字乘以辅警提供服务的小时数，得出一个节省成本的数字。但是，这些计算大多数都是不准确的。比如，在一名辅警花一天时间参加培训时，一个警察机构没有真正节省小时成本。警察机构培训辅警可能产生额外的成本，而培训课程本身并不能为预算节省成本。只有在辅警工作的岗位也可以由一个有偿雇员来填补的时候，节省成本才可能实现。辅警的未来发展将需要包括制定体现节约成本的账务措施，以便警察机构的领导者能够明白辅警具有的真正价值（Dobrin & Wolf，2016）。 P162

下班后和晚间角色

在过去大约二十年的时间里，随着犯罪范围的扩大和犯罪机会的增加，政治（和财政）见证了警察工作在专业方面的显著增长，以及公共/私人空间（如购物中心、飞机场以及娱乐场所）对警察工作的更大需求。然而，为股东带来收益是管理这些设施的基本要求（Bonnet，De Maillard & Roche，2015）。在美国，许多全职正规警察参与“下班”或者“晚间”工作，他们以警察的身份工作，并获得其所在警察局的支持。私人公司、屋主协会、购物中心以及其他场所向警察机构支付费用，让警察机构派一名（或者几名）指定的警察。支付给警察局的费用（或者甚至有时直接支付给警察本人，同时一部分费用支付给警察机构作为管理费）要求全副武装的警察，身负全部警察职权和有关警察权力，为特殊目的在指定区域工作（例如，小心可能的汽车窃贼，起诉商店扒手，在职业运动会上提供安全保障，等等）。全美许多警察局有这些正式项目，在政府提供的正常服务不能满足要求或者意识到有需要的时候，提供额外警察服务，但不是所有警察局都允许这样做。

洛杉矶市警察局、纽约市警察局、奥兰多警察局、坦佩警察局（亚利桑那州）以及奥兰治县县治安官办公室（佛罗里达州）是美国警察机构中允许这些服务的机构，而且它们为这些“下班”警察制定了正式监督方案。尽管这些警察局中一个警察局的警察可以按指派工作，满足组织或者私人公司的特殊需要，而且这些组织或者私人公司要为使用警察支付费用，但是这些警察仍然是警察而且仍然具有全部警察职权。尽管许多美国警察机构允许并监督下班警察的工作，但是一些美国警察机构并没有授权警察这样做。例如，加利福尼亚州的奥兰治县县治安官办公室不允许其警察下班后工作。该机构认为，当一名警察为别的雇主工作，那么保护公众利益和保护单一实体利益之间的界限就变得模糊不清，而且可能会带来伦理挑战，这与大多数不允许警察下班从事这类工作的警察机构在报告中所说的一样（Jenkins，2016）。

对本书有特别意义的事实是，一些美国警察机构对下班警察工作问题做了进一步解决。一些警察机构允许宣誓辅警以下班身份从事有偿工作。这意味着一个
P163 私人实体或者组织可以为附加警察服务向当地警察机构支付一笔费用，而且有的正常做辅警的人可以履行所要求的工作职责，并且更为重要的是，为他的服务获得报酬。这给辅警角色添加了特别维度。一名全职警察可以得到的诸多好处之一是，以下班身份工作赚取额外收入的能力。在警察即将退休的时候，警察能够继续工作赚取额外收入，而且警察继续工作还可以作为替代他们为警察机构提供最短志愿工作的时间，这些可能都非常吸引人。这一现象既有积极的一面，也有消极的一面：警察机构保留勤奋工作的雇员作为辅警，在他们有空的时候，换取从事下班有偿工作的机会；但是，如果没有足够的下班岗位可用，那么正规全职职员可能会把他们机构里的辅警看作“拿走”他们赚取额外收入机会的人。

在英格兰和威尔士的警察局，全职警察在其闲暇时间能够从事有偿雇用工作，由雇用他们的组织支付报酬。作为警察局的成员，他们获得认证的身份意味着他们在任何时候都有全部逮捕权。当然，他们可以仅仅“护卫”私人空间，因此降低利益冲突的风险。特别警员可能同样担任这样的角色，而且，与全职警察一样，雇用机构直接向他们支付报酬。

使用兼职、有偿、“志愿”警察，在全球不是一个新鲜事物。新加坡志愿特别警员队、中国香港辅警队以及马来西亚警察志愿后备队，都是为其从事的特别工作获得报酬的“志愿”警察的例子。一个警察局有能力为其兼职的、训练有素的职员支付报酬，可能是在按计划实施的大型公共集会或者不期而至的自然或人为灾害发生时，具备一支随时可用的后备力量的一个重要因素。

在本书前文，我们确定并讨论了在单个警察局对特别警员进行试用并落实“报酬”或者奖励的情况。实际上，1965 年颁行的《特别警员条例》规定：“特别警员不应就其服务领取任何名目的酬金，本条例另有规定者除外”（Legislation. gov. uk，n. d.，p. 2）。但是，在 2013 年，英国考虑给那些达到某些要求的特别警员每年 1000 英镑的报酬。新闻媒体报道此计划没有受到欢迎，即便是特别警员队的队员，他们的表态获得赞扬：他们担心的是，如果特别警员开始因工作接受报酬，那么这很可能吸引不同类型的人到特别警员岗位（Beckfor Thed，2013）。英国特别警员以及美国后备警察和协警的薪俸、津贴或酬金以后的情况，还有待观察。 P164

新技术以及装备开销

在近代历史上，警察工作仅仅要求某些有限的装备。在美国，这些装备包括一支枪、一副手铐、一套制服以及可以四处开动的车辆。在英国，这些装备包含的东西甚至更少：手铐、警棍和制服。但是，在过去五十年里，在美国和英国，已经有很多昂贵的设备加入警用装备。在美国是一个警用无线电通信装置（一种神奇的现代通信设备）、一个防弹背心，在英国是一个防刺背心，这些都是很昂贵的、但属于必需的防护装备。但是，还有笔记本电脑、急救专用物品［包括美国许多警察机构在用的鼻喷雾剂（NARCAN[23]）以及医用止血纸（QuickClot Combat Gauze[24]）］、特种武器、电控设备（泰瑟枪），以及给执行任务的警察配备的最新装备——执法记录仪。

许多警察机构现在仍处在获取执法记录仪的过程中，而购买和使用执法记录仪的实际成本也不低。不仅一个机构需要选择一个平台并培训警察怎样使用执法记录仪，而且使用执法记录仪还会产生成本，即与存储所需数据、受公共信息要求所需的从数据文件中编辑信息以及为刑事诉讼目的上传数据有关的成本。尽管美国几乎每一个大型警察局已经计划在它们的机构内配发执法记录仪设备，但是在计划使用执法记录仪的警察机构中，仅有 18%的警察机构已经将执法记录仪“完全投入运行”（Maciag，2016），而且许多警察机构已经把辅警排除在其使用执法记录仪的计划之外。警界领导者们需要考虑辅警的作用以及他们参与执法记录仪计划的必要性。英国实际上也是这样的情况。在英国，许多警察局给全职职员配发了执法记录仪，但是不给特别警员配发（West Yorkshire Disclosure Logs，2016），而其他警察局却更具包容性，它们同样有能力给特别警员配发执法记录仪（Compston，2016）。

在英国，为特别警员配发泰瑟枪的时候，引发了争议，而在美国，同样的事情发生在为辅警配发泰瑟枪的时候。在美国，为辅警配发泰瑟枪，很大程度上仅限于在那些辅警拥有执法职权且携枪执法的司法管辖区域内。用一把泰瑟枪武装一名辅警，为辅警在特定情境里作出正确反应提供了另一种工具，这就像他们的全职同事一样。但是，泰瑟枪很贵，而且技术在不断更新。这意味着，即便一个警察机构已经给其全部宣誓职员配发了泰瑟枪，很有可能因这个警察机构需要对泰瑟枪进行升级，进而要重新承担全部成本（同样的情况适用于笔记本电脑、执法记录仪、无线电通信装置以及其他类型的技术）。

P165

英国开始在英格兰和威尔士给那些在2004年经授权成为武装警察的全职警察配发泰瑟枪。起初这些警察使用泰瑟枪极其受限，但是在2007年，携带泰瑟枪的武装警察在很多勤务中被许可使用泰瑟枪，包括在使用武器都不会受到制裁的事件中。与此同时，英国警察局给受到特别培训的警察配发泰瑟枪：非武装警察，但是他们要像他们武装警察同事一样遵守使用限制规定；配发泰瑟枪，仅仅在“他们面对暴力或者暴力威胁严重到他们将需要使用武力保护公众、他们自己或者当事人”（National Police Chiefs' Council，2015）。现如今，每一个警察局局长都可以把泰瑟枪配发给受过特别训练的警察，而且那些警察要为使用武力的大小负责。许多特别警员觉得因为他们面对的危险与他们的正规警员同事一样，所以为工作所需，他们应该被用相同的工具武装起来，“只要他们接受了适当的培训，经过适当的选拔，并且经过适当的部署”（Greenwood，2014）。特别警员遇到的当事人可能与他们全职同事遇到的一样，但是英国全国警察局长委员会对警察局给全职成员开展泰瑟枪培训加以特别限制（National Police Chiefs' Council，2015）。

结论

使用辅警情况在美国和在英国现在均处于波动状态。尽管相当确定的是，在所有国家使用公民警察的现象将继续存在，但是这些辅警所在的各自警务机构使用他们的特殊方式，取决于各种因素。单一被公开的事件可能永远改变辅警；诸多事故，类似发生在塔尔萨的枪击事故，或者在奥兰多县勇敢到达现场应对疯狂枪手的县治安官志愿助理们，能够显著改变公众的看法，从而改变政策、规则和法律。2017年间发生在伦敦和曼彻斯特的事故可能让公众更加支持更好地武装在英国从事巡逻工作的辅警。在治安工作中使用辅警，对提升社区对警察在社会中发挥作用的支持，是相对来说不那么昂贵的途径。但是，使用他们不是免费的；如果警务机构愿意承担额外的负担，即为组织完备的辅警项目提供培训、装备以及时间投资，那么他们可以发现相当可观的投资回报。但是，一个管理不佳的辅警项目有可能导致正规警察及其所服务社区对该项目产生负面评价，而对后备人员的低估，有可能导致成员人数降低以及招聘不力。不管原因是什么，对资源紧张的警务机构来说，成员人数降低同样会有财政影响。

P166

注释

①在七国集团（加拿大、法国、德国、意大利、日本、英国和美国）中，美国和英国在 2017 年第一季度的经济增长最慢。英国经济受到的影响有通货膨胀和消费支出缓慢，加上英国脱欧以及英国政坛的不确定性。美国同样经历了消费支出缓慢，还有许多美国人十分担忧唐纳德·特朗普总统任期将会对国家的长期经济产生的影响，尽管在新政府的第一年经济有积极表现（Nelson，2017）。

②格兰兹对“拒绝履行公务”的抗辩，是因为他没有回应新闻界提出的法律要求：提交一份稍早（2009 年）对罗伯特·贝茨进行调查的报告。对格兰兹的起诉是他告诉他的雇员“坚持不动”，即便媒体要求提交该调查报告（Killman，2016）。

③对辅警项目持批评意见的人认为，管理不当的项目可能成为那些渴望拥有警务职权但是没有满足培训要求之人通过捐助获得利益的途径。比如，县治安官连任基金的大额捐款者，可以获得的好处是做县治安官志愿助理而且获得办公室的随行装备，包括一把枪、徽章、身份卡以及作为警察通常有隐秘携带枪支的合法能力。

④在美国，极少数警察机构选择加入执法机构认证委员会的认证过程。执法机构认证委员会自从 1984 年成立以来，只向 623 个美国州、地方和国家执法机构颁发了认证书，在全美 18000 个警务机构中占比略高于 3%。在过去十年间，这一数字保持不变。这意味着几乎 97%的美国警察管理者选择不参加这个自愿参加的认证过程。这个认证过程要求很高、问题多多、花费昂贵而且很耗时（Hougland & Wolf，2016）。

⑤在 2017 年，佛罗里达州执法局（FDLE，Florida Department of Law Enforcement）宣布它将增加在佛罗里达州担任辅助执法官员所需的小时总数，将院校培训时间从之前要求的 319 个小时增加到新要求的 364 个小时。在本书写作的时候，佛罗里达州执法局在考虑允许一个混合方法，将辅助性质的院校在线自主学习与传统院校课程学习相结合，以便落实这一新出台的培训要求。

⑥奥古斯特·沃尔默是全体警察具备大学学位的直言不讳的拥护者和首位支持者。沃尔默觉得更高的教育将会提升警务的职业性，同样能够提升警方的能力，使警方在打击犯罪的工作中更加聪明（Paoline，Terrill & Rossler，2015）。

P167

⑦在美国只有不超过 1% 的警察机构规定四年制学位的招聘要求（Hilal & Densley，2013）。

⑧明尼苏达州在警察认证方面要求两年制学位。

⑨阿尔伯克基警察局、夏洛特-梅克伦堡警察局、哥伦比亚警察局、韦恩堡警察局、诺克斯维尔警察局聘用警察要求高中教育，而科罗拉多斯普林斯警察局和波特兰警察局则要求两年制大学学位（Paoline，Terrill & Rossler，2015）。

⑩“选拔后备警察的标准与选拔宣誓全职警察的标准一样。这确保宣誓后备警察与全职警察一样经历就业前测试”（CALEA，2017）。

⑪不管对竞争性警务工作的教育要求是什么，在美国，在超过 12000 个地方警察局中工作的少数族裔警察的百分比，在 1987 年至 2013 年几乎增长了两倍，从 1987 年的大约 78000 名警察（大约在工作人员中占 15%）到 2013 年的大约 130000 名警察（大约在工作人员中占 27%）（Reaves，2015）。

⑫ 美国消极的全国性言论将“黑人的命也是命（Black Lives Matter）”运动推向了反对警察的方向，这被指责是伏击警察的起因，也是导致被称为反警察言论增加的原因。政治氛围被称为“YouTube 效应（YouTube effect）”，也就是说警察可能继续做他们的工作，但是很少采取额外动作主动面对可能导致逮捕的问题——因为害怕任何这样的遭遇有可能被拍下来且视频被上传到互联网，进而被公众挑选出来（Davis，2015）。

⑬ 在美国许多地区，尤其是在警察局很可能不大的小镇和乡村地区，支付给全职警察的报酬可能每小时不到 11 美元，比许多快餐店工人的时薪还要少（Johnson，2015）。

⑭ 不幸的是，诉讼在美国警务中是很常见的事。当一家警察局因一名执法警察的行为被起诉的时候，该名警察常常同样被起诉。这给该名警察造成相当大的压力，而且辅警也不能免于这些诉讼，同样会伴随压力。许多反对警察的案件被驳回，依据的是警察从事他的工作时有豁免权，但是事实并非总是如此（Schott，2012）。《华尔街日报》曾报道：自 2010 年以来，警方诉讼开销增长显著；最昂贵的指控是侵犯公民权利以及其他类型的不当行为，其次是因汽车相撞而向警方提出的民事索赔。十个有美国最大警察局的城市在 2014 年支付的和解

金和判决费有 24800 万美元，对比在 2010 年支付的是 16800 万美元，增长了 48%。《华尔街日报》报道说：民事案件中可用视频片段的增加，可能对警察局支付费用的增加有影响，同样因错误定罪而支付错误监禁案件费用的城市也在增加（Elinson & Frosch，2015）。

⑮参与退休人员动员计划的志愿者没有执法职权，但是纽约市警察局给他们配发了某些“制服”，包括退休人员动员计划衬衫、交通管理背心、口哨和手电筒。纽约市警察局提醒退休人员动员计划的成员负责临时区域的工作，方式主要是通过电子邮件和电话。尽管退休人员动员计划的成员没有获得警察培训，但是纽约市警察局的确开展了一些“演习”，退休人员动员计划的成员能够参与其中，了解紧急状态下他们可以起到的作用。响应动员号召的退休人员动员计划的成员，可以依据适用于纽约市警察局协警的同一部法律，获得保险的承保范围有体检、工资损失、丧葬和遗属津贴（Tobin，2017）。 P168

⑯佐治亚州的亚特兰大城就是一个例子。亚特兰大城曾面临警力资源短缺问题。2013 年，亚特兰大城启动一个再次雇用已退休警察最长三年的项目——不用支付养老金、人寿保险以及老年保健医疗费用，这些费用已经为雇员支付了，因为他们是退休人员。该项目被称为“夺回”项目（Beech，2015）。

⑰这部联邦法律同样在辅警身份执法官员中引发关于该法对其岗位适用性的巨大争论。该法最初起草时把大多数兼职人员和辅警排除在外，该法现在的文字表述，允许政府机构的“经法律授权致力于或者监督预防、打击和侦查，或者处置，或者监禁任何违反法律的任何人，并且拥有法定逮捕权”的“雇员”隐秘携带枪支（请阅读最新的《执法官员安全法》用词，以确定当前资格）。许多警察机构考虑，为了符合《工人赔偿法》，让有警察职权的辅警成为“雇员”，这样就可以解释《执法官员安全法》：适用全职职员的规定同样适用于那些志愿执法官员岗位。

⑱尽管公众的负面看法在美国似乎更严重，但是英国警方与其所服务的社区之间也不是没有冲突。2011 年，伦敦大都会警察局号召其他英国警察局帮助平息由马克·杜甘之死引发的大范围骚乱。马克·杜甘是一名被警方杀死的犯罪嫌疑人。一开始只是一个和平游行集会，后来发展为全城范围的骚乱。这场英国自 1995 年布里克斯顿骚乱发生以来最大规模的骚乱，是回应人们对警方的抱怨：警方没有就枪击事件进行沟通，或者正在就事发情况说谎（Lewis，2011）。令人毛骨悚然的是，这起骚乱与 2014 年在密苏里州弗格森发生的迈克尔·布朗枪击

案后在美国出现的事件相似。在伦敦和弗格森事件中，涉事警察被证明没有做错任何事。

⑲应该指出，“大都会警察局”是英国最大的警察局，负责管理非常多样的流动人口，且覆盖多个敏感区域，包括圣詹姆士宫、白金汉宫、议会大厦以及唐宁街十号，还有著名的购物街区和 Soho 的娱乐区。

⑳正如在第五章讨论过的，2015 年，特别警员约翰·鲍尔成为英国首位经认证做警犬管理员的特别警员。警方的这支警犬队能够定位爆炸物。这是在穿制服的警察的非传统工作中使用特别警员的例子。英国同样尝试在其他非传统的调查工作中使用特别警员，包括本章后文要讨论的网络犯罪部门。

P169

㉑一般情况下，支援警察的志愿者没有执法权，但是在网络犯罪部门项目中赋予的调查角色，使警察局局长可以让这些志愿者具备执行某些警察职能的能力，如分发固定的处罚通知书和记录证人证言（Barrett，2016）。

㉒柴郡警察局的侦探警员伊莱恩·麦凯韦尔被杀于曼彻斯特，但她当时不在上班，因而未穿制服。她与其他被害人一样，是加害者的随机选择。

㉓NARCAN 是一种鼻喷雾剂，通过美国食品和药品管理局的批准，可用于对已知或疑似阿片类药物过量的紧急处置。首位处置人员对患者通过鼻子给药，喷雾与因药物过量引发的威胁生命的作用（包括呼吸抑制）发生反作用，但是处置人员仍然必须对患者实施紧急医疗护理。

㉔QuickClot 是一种止血剂，在严重出血伤口（包括枪伤）的紧急护理中，可以激活血小板并增加血液的凝固性。

参考文献

Albrecht，J. （Ed.）（2017）（阿尔布雷希特主编）. *Police reserves and volunteers：Enhancing organizational effectiveness and public trust* （《警察后备人员和志愿者：提升组织效率和公信力》）. Boca Raton，FL：CRC Press（博卡-拉顿，佛罗里达州：CRC 出版社）.

Barrett，D. （2016，January 20）（巴勒特〈2016 年 1 月 20 日〉）. Volunteers to be handed police-style powers in war on cybercrime（“在与网络犯罪斗争中志愿者被赋予警察式权力”）. *The Daily Telegraph*（《每日电讯报》）. 2017 年 7 月 27 日检索网址 www. telegraph. co. uk/news/uknews/crime/12108994.

Bartels，E. C. （2013）（巴特尔斯）. *Volunteer police in the United States*：

Programs, challenges, and legal aspects（《美国辅警：计划、挑战与法律方面》）. New York：Springer（纽约：斯普林格）.

BBC（2017, April 6）（英国广播公司〈2017 年 4 月 6 日〉）. Northamptonshire Police special constable numbers have "halved"（"北安普顿郡警察局特别警员人数'减少了一半'"）. 2017 年 7 月 30 日检索网址 www. bbc. com/news/uk-england-northamptonshire-39503807.

Beckfor Thed, M.（2013, November 23）（贝克福·泰德〈2013 年 11 月 23 日〉）. "Policing on the cheap" row over plan to pay special constables to make up for cutting full-time officers（"'廉价警务'使为弥补裁减全职警察而给特别警员发工资的计划被否决了"）. *Daily Mail*（《每日邮报》）. 2017 年 8 月 6 日检索网址 www. dailymail. co. uk/news/article-2512554.

Beech, B.（2015, August 27）（比奇〈2015 年 8 月 27 日〉）. Atlanta renews recapture program, hires retired officers（"亚特兰大重新启动'夺回'计划，雇用退休警察"）. 2017 年 7 月 25 日检索网址 http：//news. wabeorg/postatlanta-renews-recapture-program-hires-retired-police-officer.

Bletchly, R.（2017, March 28）（布莱奇利〈2017 年 3 月 28 日〉）. After London terror attack -should all police be armed? Arguments for and against（"伦敦恐怖袭击之后——所有警察都应武装起来吗？支持意见和反对意见"）. *Daily Mirror.*（《每日镜报》）2017 年 7 月 26 日检索网址 www. mirror. co. uk/news/uk-news/after-london-terror-attack-should-10087838.

Bonnet, E., De Maillard, J., & Roche, S.（2015）（邦讷特、梅拉德和罗切）. Plural policing of public places in France：Between private and local policing（"法国对公共地区采取加倍治安维护：在私人和地方警务之间"）. *European Journal of Policing Studies*（《欧洲警务研究》）, 2（3）, 285—303.

Carrington, D.（2016, December 16）（卡灵顿〈2016 年 12 月 16 日〉）. Badger cull kills more than 10, 000 animals in three months（"獾捕杀运动在三个月内杀死了超过 10000 只动物"）. *The Guardian*（《卫报》）. 2017 年 9 月 5 日检索网址 www. theguardian. com/environment/2016/dec/16/badger-cull-kills-more-than. 10000-animals-three-months-bovine-tb.

Carter, D. L., & Sapp, A. D.（1990）（卡尔特和萨珀）. The evolution of higher education in law enforcement：Preliminary findings from a national study（"执

P170

法领域高等教育演变：从一次全国性研究得到的初步研究成果”）. *Journal of Criminal Justice Education*（《刑事司法教育》），1（1），59—85.

Chandan, J. S. , & Meakin, R. （2016）（尚丹和梅金）. Do special constables in London feel that they are adequately prepared to meet their first aid responsibilities? A qualitative study（“伦敦特别警员觉得自己做好充分准备承担急救责任了吗?”）. *BMJ Open*（《英国医学期刊网络版》），6（1），doi（数字对象标识符）：10. 1136/bmjopen-2015-010082.

Commission on Accreditation for Law Enforcement Agencies（2017）（执法机构认证委员会）. Reserve officer program in the 6th edition（“后备警察项目第六版”）. 2017 年 7 月 21 日检索网址 www. caleaorg/content/reserve-officer-program-6th-edition.

Compston, T. （2016, September 19）（康普斯顿〈2016 年 9 月 19 日〉）. Weighing up the evidence for body worn video cameras（“为执法记录仪仔细考虑证据问题”）. UK Security Expo 2018（2018 年英国安全博览会）. 2017 年 7 月 30 日检索网址 www. uksecurityexpo. com/security-news/weighing-up-the-evidence-for-body-worn-video-cameras.

Dalley, A. F. （1975）（达莱）. University and non-university graduated policemen: A study of police attitudes（“大学毕业和非大学毕业警察：关于警察态度的研究”）. *Journal of Police Science and Administration*（《警察科学与管理》），3（4），458—468.

Davis, A. C. （2015, October 8）（戴维斯〈2015 年 10 月 8 日〉）. “YouTube effect” has left police officers under siege, law enforcement leaders say（“‘YouTube 效应’已经使警察处于包围之中，执法领导如是说”）. *The Washington Post*（《华盛顿邮报》）. 2017 年 7 月 25 日检索网址 www. washingtonpost. com/news/post-nation/wp/2015/10/08/-left-police-officers-under-siegelaw-enforcement-leaders-youtube-crreosay/? utm_term=. ada9eObd85f9.

Department for Environment, Food and Rural Affairs（2016, December）（环境、食品和农村事务部〈2016 年 12 月〉）. Guidance to Natural England on licensed badger control to prevent the spread of bovine tuberculosis（“为阻止牛结核病传播，英国自然保护局獾控制许可指南”）. London: Department for Environment, Food and Rural Affairs（伦敦：环境、食品和农村事务部）. 2017 年 9 月 5

日检索网址 www. gov. uk/government/publications.

Dobrin, A. , & Wolf, R. （2016）(多布林和沃尔夫). What is known and not known about volunteer policing in the United States (“我们知道的以及我们不知道的美国辅警管理”). *International Journal of Police Science and Management* (《警察科学与管理国际期刊》), 18 (3), 220—227.

Duerden, N. （2010, April 9）(杜尔顿〈2010 年 4 月 9 日〉). Hobby bobbies: On the beat with the special constables (“警察爱好者：与特别警员在辖区工作”). *The Independent* (《独立报》). 2017 年 7 月 30 日检索网址 www. independentuk/news/uk/crime/hobby-bobbies-on-the-beat-with-the-special-constables1938251. html.

Elinson, Z. , Frosch, D. （2015, July 16）(埃林森和弗罗施〈2015 年 7 月 16 日〉). Cost of police-misconduct cases soars in big U. S. cities: Data show rising payouts for police-misconduct settlements and court judgments (“警察不当行为成本在美国大城市激增：数据显示警察不当行为和解和法院判决的支出不断上升”). *The Wall Street Journal* (《华尔街日报》). 2017 年 7 月 29 日检索网址 www. wsj. com/articles/cost-of-police-misconduct-cases-soars-in-big-u-s-cities-1437013834.

Flatley, J. （2017, July 20）(弗拉特莱〈2017 年 7 月 20 日〉). Crime in England and Wales: Annual supplementary tables (“英格兰和威尔士的犯罪问题：年度补充报表”). London: Office for National Statistics (伦敦：国家统计办公室). 2017 年 8 月 13 日检索网址 www. ons. gov. uk/peoplepopulationandcommunity/crimeandjusticeldatasets/crimeinenglandandwalesannualsupplementarytables.

Greenwood, C. （2014, July 21）(格林伍德〈2014 年 7 月 21 日〉). Special constables' chief says officers should be armed with Tasers because they “face the same dangers” as regular police (“特别警员的领导说特别警员应该装备泰瑟枪，因为他们与正规警察一样面对‘同样的危险’ ”). *Daily Mail* (《每日邮报》). 2017 8 月 6 日检索网址 www. dailymail. co. uk/news/article-2700739.

Grierson, J. （2017, March 1）(格里尔森〈2017 年 3 月 1 日〉). Watchdog says police cuts have left forces in “perilous state. ” (“监察机构说警察人数削减使警察局处于‘危险状态’ ”) *The Guardian* (《卫报》). 2017 年 7 月 26 日检索网址 www. theguardian. com/uk-news/2017/mar/02/inspectorate-police-engaging-

P171

dangerous-practices-austerity-cuts-diane-abbott.

Hargreaves, J., Husband, H., & Linehan, C. (2017)（哈格瑞阿维斯、哈兹本德和兰汉）. *Police workforce*, *England and Wales*, *20 July* 2017（《警察队伍，英格兰和威尔士，2017 年 7 月 20 日》）, Statistical Bulletin 10/17（统计公报 10/17）. London: Office for National Statistics（伦敦：全国统计办公室）. 2017 年 8 月 10 日检索网址 www. gov. uk/government/uploads/system/uploads/attachment-data/file/630471/hosb1017-police-workforce. pdf.

Hilal, S. M., & Densley, J. (2013)（希拉尔和丹斯莱）. Higher education and local law enforcement（"高等教育与地方执法"）. *FBI Law Enforcement Bulletin*（《美国联邦调查局执法公报》）, 82 (5), 1-3. 2017 年 7 月 23 日检索网址 https: //eb. fbigov/2013/may/higher-education-and-local-law-enforcement.

Home Office (2017, July 27)（英国内政部〈2017 年 7 月 27 日〉）. Police use of firearms statistics, England and Wale: April 2016-March 2017（"警察使用武器统计，英格兰和威尔士：2016 年 4 月—2017 年 3 月"）. 2017 年 8 月 11 日检索网址 www. gov. uk/government/publications/police-use-of-firearms-statistics-england-and-walesapril-2016-to-march-2017/police-use-of-firearms-statistics-england-and-wales-april-2016-to-march-2017.

Hougland, S., & Wolf, R. (2016)（霍兰德和沃尔夫）. Accreditation in police agencies: Does external quality assurance reduce citizen complaints?（"警察机构认证：外部质量保证降低公民投诉了吗?"）*The Police Journal*: *Theory Practice and Principles*（《警察期刊：理论、实践与原则》）, 90 (1), 40—54.

Hudzik, J. K. (1978)（哈德兹克）. College education for police: Problems in measuring component and extraneous variables（"警察的大学教育：测量分量和外部变量的问题"）. *Journal of Criminal Justice*（《刑事司法》）, 6 (1), 69—81.

Institute for Public Safety, Crime and Justice (2014, December)（公共安全、犯罪与司法研究所〈2014 年 12 月〉）. The Special "experience" in Northamptonshire: A critical review（"北安普顿郡特别警员的'经验'：重要评论"）. Northampton, UK: University of Northampton, Institute for Public Safety, Crime and Justice（北安普顿，英国：北安普顿大学，公共安全、犯罪和司法研究所）. 2017 年 7 月 27 日检索网址 www. empac. org. uk/wp-content/uploads/2016/02/Specials-summary-report-final. pdf.

Jackson, J. , Bradford, B. , Hough, M. , & Murray, K. H. （2012）（杰克逊、布拉德福德、霍夫和默里）. Compliance with the law and policing by consent: Notes on police and legal legitimacy（“遵守法律与民众满意警务：关于警察与立法合法性的说明”）. In A. Crawford & A. Hucklesby（Eds.）（克劳福德和胡克莱斯柏）, *Legitimacy and compliance in criminal justice*（《刑事司法的合法性与合规性》）, pp. 29—49. Abingdon, UK: Routledge（阿宾登，英国：劳特利奇出版公司）.

Jenkins, J. （2016, December 27）（詹金斯〈2016 年 12 月 27 日〉）. Study finds that police officers moonlight regularly to earn extra income（“研究发现警察夜间通常去挣外快了”）. KUAR Public Radio（库尔公共电台）. 2017 年 7 月 30 日检索网址 http：/lualrpublicradio. org/post/study-finds-police-officers-moonlight-regularly-earn-extra-income#stream/0.

Johnson, K. （2015）（约翰逊）. Lack of training, standards means big problems for small police departments USA Today（“对当今美国的小型警察局来说，缺乏培训标准意味着大问题”）. 2017 年 7 月 25 日检索网址 www. usatodaycom/story/news/nation/2015/06/23/small-police-departments-standardstraining/28823849.

Jones, J. , Rodger, J. （2017, August 6）（乔恩思和罗德格〈2017 年 8 月 6 日〉）. How the number of armed West Midlands Police officers is soaring（“西米德兰兹武装警察人数是如何激增的?”）. *Birmingham Mail*（《伯明翰邮报》）. 2017 年 9 与 4 日检索网址 www. birminghammail. co. uk/news/midlands-news/how-numberarmed-west-midlands-13437889.

Killman, C. （2016, July 16）（吉尔曼〈2016 年 7 月 16 日〉）. Former Sheriff Stanley Glanz pleads guilty to one misdemeanor charge and no contest to another（“前县治安官史丹利·葛兰兹对一项轻罪指控认罪，对另一项指控没有异议”）. *The Tulsa World*（《塔尔萨世界》）. 2017 年 7 月 20 日检索网址 www. tulsaworld. com/news/courts/former-sheriff-stanleyglanz-pleads-guilty-to-one-misdemeanor-charge/article_f0648017-282e-571a89bc39296606e25. html.

Krehbiel-Burton, L. , & Pérez-Peña, R. （2015, September 30）（克雷比尔-布尔顿和裴雷兹裴纳〈2015 年 9 月 30 日〉）. Tulsa sheriff to resign over killing by deputy（“塔尔萨县治安官因助理持枪杀人而辞职”）. *The New York Times*（《纽约时报》）. 2017 年 7 月 23 日检索网址 www. nytimes. com/2015/10/01/s/

P172

tulsa-sheriff-indieted-on-misennduecharges-in-killing-by-a-deputy. html.

Lefkowitz, J. (1974)(莱夫科维奇). Job attitudes of police: Over all description and demographic correlates（“警察的职业态度：总体描述与人口统计学”）. *Journal of Vocational Behavior*（《职业行为》）, 5 (2), 221—230.

Legislation. gov. uk (n. d.)(日期不详). The Special Constables Regulations 1965（“特别警员法规 1965 年”）. 2017 年 8 月 12 日检索网址 www. legislation. gov. uk/uksi/1965/536introduction/made.

Lewis, P. (2011, August 7)(刘易斯〈2011 年 8 月 7 日〉). Tottenham riots: A peaceful protest, then suddenly all hell broke loose（“托特纳姆骚乱：一场和平请愿，然后突然彻底失控”）. *The Guardian*（《卫报》）. 2017 年 7 月 26 日检索网址 www. theguardian. com/k/201 1/aug/07/tottenham-riots-peaceful-protest.

Maciag, M. (2016, January 26)(马西亚格〈2016 年 1 月 26 日〉). Survey: Almost all police departments plan to use body cameras（“调查：几乎所有的警察局都在计划使用执法记录仪”）. *Governing* (online)(《治理》〈在线〉). 2017 年 7 月 30 日检索网址 www. governing. com/topics/public-justice-safety/gov-police-body-camera-survey. html.

Mason, R., Walker, P. J. (2017, June 5)(马森和沃克〈2017 年 6 月 5 日〉). Under-fire Theresa May hits back over police cuts（“受到攻击的特蕾莎·梅因警察人数削减而反击”）. *The Guardian*（《卫报》）. 2017 年 7 月 26 日检索网址 www. theguardiancom/uk-news/2017/jun/0. 5/karen-bradley-police-cuts-armed-officers-bbc-today-programme-london-bridge-attack.

Miller, J., & Fry, L. (1976)(米勒和福瑞). Reexamining assumptions about education and professionalism in law enforcement（“重新检查关于执法领域的教育与职业性假设”）. *Journal of Police Science and Administration*（《警察科学与管理》）, 4 (2), 187—198.

Mills, J. (2017, May 25)(米尔斯〈2017 年 5 月 25 日〉). Female police officer killed in Manchester bombing named as Elaine Mclver（“一位名叫伊莱恩·麦金维尔的女警察在曼彻斯特爆炸案中被杀”）. *Metro*（《大都会》）. 2017 年 9 月 3 日检索网址 http://metroco. uk/2017/05/2. 5/female-police-officer-killed-in-manchester-bombing-named-as-elaine-mciver-6661049.

Mormino, B. (2001)(莫尔米诺). Police Reserve Program proposal (“后备警察项目提案”). New York City Police Department(纽约市警察局). 2017 年 7 月 23 日检索网址 www. nycop. com/jan_02/poLiceReserves_Program/body-police _ reserves_program. html.

National Police Chiefs′ Council (2015)(〈英国〉全国警察局长委员会). ACPO questions and answers on Taser, January 2015 (“ACPO 对泰瑟枪的问题和答案, 2015 年 1 月”). 2017 年 8 月 6 日检索网址 www. npcc. police. uk/ThePoliceChiefsBlog/201410TaserBlog. aspx.

National Police Officers′ Roll of Honour (n. d.) (〈英国〉全国警察荣誉榜〈日期不详〉). Indexes (“索引”). 2017 年 7 月 31 日检索网址 www. policerollofhonour. org. uk/national_roll/roll_intro. html.

Nelson, E. (2017, June 1)(纳尔逊〈2017 年 6 月 1 日〉). The US and the UK are now the slowest growing economies in the G7 (“美国和英国现在是七国集团中经济增长最慢的国家”). Quartz. 2017 年 7 月 29 日检索网址 https://qz. com/996097/the-us-and-uk-are-now-the-slowest-growing-economies-in-the-g7.

O′Linn, M. (2016, February 14)(欧林〈2016 年 2 月 14 日〉). Response to PERF's “30 Guiding Principles” document (“回应警察高级官员研究论坛的‘30 项指导原则’”). Law Officer(法律官员). 2017 年 7 月 25 日检索网址 http:/lawofficer. com/exclusive/perfresponse.

Paoline, E. A., III, Terrill, W., & Rossler, M. T. (2015)(包莱恩、特里尔和罗斯勒). Higher education, college degree major, and police occupational attitudes (“高等教育、大学学位与警察职业态度”). *Journal of Criminal Justice Education* (《刑事司法教育》), 26 (1), 49—73.

Peel, Robert, Sir (1829) (罗伯特·比尔爵士). Principles of law enforcement (“执法原则”). Durham Police (达勒姆警察). 2017 年 8 月 12 日检索网址 www. durham. policeuk/aboutUs/documents/Peels _ Principles _ Of _ Law _ Enforcement. pdf.

Rathi, A. (2017, June 4)(拉提〈2017 年 6 月 4 日〉). Even with all these terror attacks, it's still very rare to see police with guns in England (“即便有这么多恐怖袭击, 在英格兰仍然很少看到携带枪支的警察”). Quartz (Quartz 网站).

P173

2017 年 7 月 26 日检索网址 https：//qz. com/998266/ondon-attack-how-the-uk-police-deal-with-a-terrorist-attack-when-most-officers-dont-carry-guns.

Reaves, B. （2015）（雷阿维斯）. Local police departments, 2013：Personnel, policies, and practices, NCJ 248677（“地方警察局，2013 年：职员、政策与实践，NCJ 248677”）. Washington, DC：US Department of Justice, Office of Justice Programs, Bureau of Justice Statistics（华盛顿特区：美国司法部，司法项目办公室，司法统计局）. 2018 年 1 月 10 日检索网址 www. bjs. govlcontent/pub/pdf/pd13ppp. pdf.

Regoli, R. M. （1976）（雷戈利）. The effects of college education on the maintenance of police cynicism（“大学教育在维持警察玩世不恭方面的效果”）. *Journal of Police Science and Administration*（《警察科学与管理》）, 4（3）, 340—345.

Reiner, R. （2002）（雷纳尔）. Media made criminality：The representation of crime in the mass media（“媒体制造的犯罪：大众媒体呈现的犯罪”）. In M. Maguire, R. Morgan, R. Reiner（Eds.）（马圭瑞、摩甘和雷纳尔主编）, *The Oxford Handbook of Criminology*, 3rd Edition［《牛津犯罪学手册》（第三版）］, pp. 302-340. Oxford：Oxford University Press（牛津：牛津大学出版社）.

Reuss, E. （2005, October 25）（雷伊斯〈2005 年 10 月 25 日〉）. NYPD retiree mobilization plan（“纽约市警察局退休人员动员计划”）. New York City Police Department（纽约市警察局）. 2017 年 7 月 25 日检索网址 www. nycop. com/fall2005/RMP-PLAN/body_rmp_plan. html.

Schott, R. G. （2012）（绍特）. Qualified immunity：How it protects law enforcement officers（“有限豁免权：它怎样保护执法警察?”）. *FBI Law Enforcement Bulletin*（《美国联邦调查局执法公报》）, 81（9）, 22-32. 2017 年 7 月 25 日检索网址 https：//leb. fbigov/2012/september/qualified-immunity-how-itprotects-law-enforcement-officers.

Sheffer, S. （2017）（舍费尔）. Florida Highway Patrol Auxiliary（“佛罗里达州高速公路巡逻辅警”）. In J. Albrecht（Ed.）（阿尔布雷希特主编）, *Police reserves and volunteers：Enhancing organizational effectiveness and public trust*（《警察后备人员和志愿者：提升组织效率和公信力》）, pp. 57—66. Boca Raton, FL：CRC Press（博卡-拉顿，佛罗里达州：CRC 出版社）.

Sheth, S. , Mark, M. , & Edwards, J. (2017, July 4)(设斯、马克和爱德华兹〈2017 年 7 月 4 日〉). Police arrest 12 people in London attacks that killed 7 and left 3 attackers dead ("在导致 7 人死亡 3 名袭击者死亡的伦敦恐袭中，警察逮捕了 12 人"). Businessinsider. com. 2017 年 9 月 3 日检索网址 www. businessinsider. com/british-policeinvestigating-london-bridge-incident-after-reports-of-van-hitting-pedestrians2017-6.

Sutherland, J. (2017, July 24)(萨瑟兰〈2017 年 7 月 24 日〉). Time for a Royal Commission? Why we need to talk about policing ("是时候履行皇家使命了？我们谈论警务的原因"). *Policing Insight*(《领悟警务》). 2017 年 7 月 26 日检索网址 https://policinginsight. com/opinion/time-royal-commission-need-talk-policing.

Tacopino, J. (2017, March 22)(塔科皮诺〈2017 年 3 月 22 日〉). Police officer killed in London attack identified as 48-year-old father ("在伦敦恐怖袭击中被杀害的警察被证实是一名 48 岁的父亲"). *The New York Post*(《纽约邮报》). 2017 年 9 月 3 日检索网址 http://nypost. com/2017/03/22/police-officer-killed-in-london-attack-identified-as-48-year-old-father.

Tobin, T. C. (2017)(托宾). NYPD's retiree mobilization plan: Keeping retired officers active ("纽约市警察局的退休人员动员计划：让退休警察充满活力"). In J. Albrecht (Ed.)(阿尔布雷希特主编), *Police reserves and volunteers: Enhancing organizational effectiveness and public trust*(《警察后备人员和志愿者：提升组织效率和公信力》), pp. 241—248. Boca Raton, FL: CRC Press(博卡-拉顿，佛罗里达州：CRC 出版社).

US Equal Employment Opportunity Commission (2016, October)(美国同等雇用机会委员会〈2016 年 10 月〉). Advancing diversity in law enforcement ("提升执法人员的多样性"). 2017 年 7 月 29 日检索网址 www. eeoc. gov/eeoc/interagency/police-diversity-report. cfm.

Walker, P. J. (2017, February 12)(沃克〈2017 年 2 月 12 日〉). Nearly half of Met police officers want more firearms specialists ("大约有一半的大都会警察希望武装特别警员再多些"). *The Guardian*(《卫报》). 2017 年 7 月 26 日检索网址 www. theguardian. com/uk-news/2017/feb/13/half-met-police-officers-firarms-specialists-union-survey.

Weiner, N. L. （1976）（韦纳）. The educated policeman（“受过教育的警察”）. *Journal of Police Science and Administration*（《警察科学与管理》）, 4（4）, 450—457.

West Yorkshire Disclosure Logs（2016）（西约克郡披露日志）. Reference number 1510/16（文献编码 1510/16）. 2017 年 7 月 30 日检索网址 www. westy-
P174 orkshire. police. uk/sites/default/files/files/disclosure-logs/foi_1510_16_body_worn_cameras. pdf.

Wolf, R. , Albrecht, J. , & Dobrin, A. （2015）（沃尔夫、阿尔布雷希特和多布林）. Reserve policing in the United States：Citizens volunteering for public service（“美国后备警察管理：公民志愿参与公共服务”）. *The Police Chief*（《警察局长》）, 82（10）, 38—47.

Wolf, R. , Homes, S. T. , & Jones, C. （2016）（沃尔夫、赫尔摩斯和乔恩思）. Utilization and satisfaction of volunteer law enforcement officers in the office of the American sheriff：An exploratory nationwide study（“美国县治安官办公室志愿性质执法官员的使用及其满意度：一项全国性研究”）. *Police Practice and Research：An International Journal*（《警察实践与研究：国际期刊》）, 17（5）, 448—462.

Wolf, R. , Pepper, I. K. , & Dobrin, A. （2017）（沃尔夫、帕珀和多布林）. An exploratory international comparison of professional confidence in volunteer policing（“辅警职业自信心的国际比较研究”）. *The Police Journal：Theory, Practice and Principles*（《警察学报：理论、实践与原则》）, 90（2）, 91—106.

索　引

（条目后数字系原书页码，检索请查本书边页码）

A

B

C

D

E

F

G

H

I

J

K

L

M

N

O

P

Q

R

S

T

U

V

W

Y

Z

译　后　记

翻译此书源于我国公安机关辅警管理改革实践及其理论研究的需要。

2019 年，译者参与公安辅警胜任力开发研究课题，并赴沈阳、丹东、烟台、厦门、岳阳等地公安机关开展实地调研。在调研座谈中，公安一线领导和辅警表达了了解国外辅警管理实践经验的愿望。

返校后，译者一头扎进图书馆外文资料室，搜集国外辅警管理著作和研究论文；经过比较，选择《辅警志愿服务：美英辅警管理的探索、比较及评估》（*Volunteer Police, Choosing to Serve: Exploring, Comparing, and Assessing Volunteer Policing in the United States and the United Kingdom*）一书。该书由美国中佛罗里达大学刑事司法系罗斯·沃尔夫教授与英国北安普顿大学公共安全、犯罪和司法研究所卡罗尔·伯兰德·乔恩思博士合作撰写，2018 年由 Taylor and Francis 出版集团出版。全书共有九章，涵盖有关基本理论、辅警历史发展与当今职能、辅警的全球考察和美英辅警管理比较、辅警的未来等热点问题。

两位作者在多年关注美英等国家和地区辅警管理实践和学术研究的基础上，立足全球视野，历史与现实相结合，合力撰写了此部代表国外辅警管理研究前沿的力作。译者希望通过翻译本书，为我国公安辅警管理研究提供国外借鉴，丰富公安学基础理论、比较警察管理等领域的教学和研究，同时为深化我国公安机关辅警管理改革、创新辅警管理制度和方法提供有益的国际参考。

全书由刘君玲独立翻译。

我要感谢所有促成本译著出版的人！感谢中国人民公安大学出版社陈学礼副总编、王哲主任的推荐，感谢张欣编辑为本书的编辑和出版工作付出的辛勤劳动，感谢原书作者沃尔夫教授和乔恩思博士撰写英文版序言，感谢北京大学政府管理学院教授萧鸣政博士在百忙当中撰写序言，感谢中国人民公安大学犯罪学学院党委的关心和大力支持，感谢我爱人匡萃冶博士倾情相助！

由于本人水平有限，译文难免存在疏漏不妥之处，敬请读者不吝赐教。

刘君玲

2021 年 11 月于中国人民公安大学